Redefining Disability

Personal/Public Scholarship

VOLUME 12

The titles published in this series are listed at *brill.com/pepu*

Redefining Disability

Edited by

Paul D. C. Bones, Jessica Smartt Gullion and
Danielle Barber

BRILL

LEIDEN | BOSTON

Cover illustration: Artwork and photography by Megan Klenke

All chapters in this book have undergone peer review.

Library of Congress Cataloging-in-Publication Data

Names: Bones, Paul D. C., editor. | Smartt Gullion, Jessica, editor. |
   Barber, Danielle (Sociologist), editor.
Title: Redefining disability / Paul D.C. Bones, Jessica Smartt Gullion and
   Danielle Barber.
Description: Leiden ; Boston : Brill, [2022] | Series: Personal/public
   scholarship, 2542-9671 ; volume 12 | Includes bibliographical
   references.
Identifiers: LCCN 2022002197 (print) | LCCN 2022002198 (ebook) | ISBN
   9789004512689 (paperback) | ISBN 9789004512696 (hardback) | ISBN
   9789004512702 (ebook)
Subjects: LCSH: People with disabilities. | Sociology of disability.
Classification: LCC HV1568 .R395 2022 (print) | LCC HV1568 (ebook) | DDC
   362.4--dc23/eng/20220120
LC record available at https://lccn.loc.gov/2022002197
LC ebook record available at https://lccn.loc.gov/2022002198

ISSN 2542-9671
ISBN 978-90-04-51268-9 (paperback)
ISBN 978-90-04-51269-6 (hardback)
ISBN 978-90-04-51270-2 (e-book)

Advance Praise for
Redefining Disability

"*Redefining Disability* offers a unique and vivid combination of lucid explanations and evocative accounts. Featuring essay, narrative, poetry, and photography, this outstanding collection opens a creative window into the richness of disabled experience and calls out systemic ableism that radically diminishes the lives of disabled folks. This provocative, insightful book is essential reading for anyone committed to the work of inclusivity, diversity, equity, and access."
– Laura L. Ellingson, PhD, Patrick A. Donohoe, S.J. Professor of Communication, Santa Clara University and author of *Embodiment in Qualitative Research*

"*Redefining Disability* brilliantly takes readers on a tour through disabled people's lives. It skillfully talks frankly and directly to readers through a delightful array of short and pithy chapters covering expansive topics such as disability and pets, the COVID-19 pandemic, disclosure in higher ed, and being chronically ill. There are photographs and poems, short essays and longer ones. It's at times emotionally raw and other times fun. To make this book extra-teachable, each chapter ends with discussion questions. A celebration of the act of telling disabled people's stories, *Redefining Disability* is a must-read."
– Laura Mauldin, PhD, NIC, Associate Professor at the University of Connecticut and author of *Made to Hear: Cochlear Implants and Raising Deaf Children*

"*Redefining Disability* is a collection 100% shaped by disabled people, not just through the individual chapters and the perspectives contained in the book, but all the way through editing until completion. The book takes aim at ableism and discrimination against disabled people through critique, with humour, with powerful imagery and art, with indelible writing, and does so from a diverse range of perspectives. But the book, its authors and editors, are also very intentional about accessibility, modeling the values it promotes with a clear and engaging introduction, through plain language and careful explanations and definitions, and with terrific discussion

questions. The result is a book that could be taught in high school, college or university, but also is distinctly non-academic in its appeal. *Redefining Disability* captures and conveys disability culture and community more successfully, accessibly, and compellingly than any other book you could pick up."
– Jay Dolmage, PhD, Professor of English, University of Waterloo and author of *Academic Ableism: Disability and Higher Education* and the founding editor of the *Canadian Journal of Disability Studies*

To everyone in the disabled community
Wherever you are, we are with you

∴

Contents

Preface

In the fall of 2019, Dr. Bones taught a Gender and Sexualities course. One of his students, a wonderful scholar and conscientious individual, asked to speak to him after class. They were examining the sexist and paternalistic frames used to describe Greta Thunberg. The student was a clear fan of Ms. Thunberg, but had a problem. "Do I call her disabled? She has autism, but I don't want to be mean to her," the student said. Dr. Bones smiled and told the student, "I don't personally know if she identifies as disabled, but disability is not a bad word. It's not an insult. It's okay to be disabled, and it's okay to refer to disabled people as disabled."

All too often, non-disabled people struggle with how to understand, describe, and interact with disability. This is not our way of calling out a former student or critiquing them. The fact is, due to ableism, segregation, and cultural fear, we are never really taught how to view disability. We look away from the person in the wheelchair, try not to stare at the person with a limb or facial difference, tell people with depression to cheer up, it's not that bad. As a result, disabled people are often marginalized, excluded, and rendered invisible. We're left out of conversations that directly impact us, conversations about social programs and policies, support plans and accommodations. We hope that this book makes a small stride toward addressing this very real social problem.

Part of the trepidation and unease with which non-disabled persons approach disability is because we, the disabled, have been relegated to passive objects in art, science, and the humanities. Our personhood is questioned, and we remind people of their own frailties, because the reality is that most people will have some sort of disability at some point in their lives.

When disabled people are given attention, it is most often in the form of "inspiration porn," stories that are meant to motivate ableds, narratives of "See? If this person with this horrible disability can accomplish something, you should be able to do it too." Or we see "amazing transformations" in which the disability is "cured." Videos of the color-blind person seeing colors and crying at their beauty, the deaf child who hears her mother's voice for the first time. Though these seem like nice, happy videos, they are ableist, and reduce disabled people to passive objects who exist only for the value they can bring to others. While we will explore the concept in more depth in the introduction, *ableism* may be defined as "a pervasive system of discrimination and exclusion of people with disabilities...privileging temporarily able-bodied people and disadvantaging people with disabilities" (Evans et al., 2017, p. 1).

The only way to fix ableism is to engage with those who have suffered from it the most. When we began soliciting chapters for this book, we hoped that we could find enough disabled authors to fulfill the book contract, but knew that we might need to accept some non-disabled scholars of disability. Fortunately, the tremendous response from the disabled community allowed us to create a volume that is 100% shaped by disabled hands—from authorship, to editing, to completion—which means it truly represents the slogan "nothing about us without us."[1]

While we advertised through traditional academic channels (journals, listservs, and scholarly networks), we decided to focus our energy on the people out there doing the work of disability advocacy every day. In particular, we decided to focus on disability Twitter. Given the geographic constraints and barriers in the physical world (even in the best of times, let alone during a global pandemic), social media and digital spaces are crucial for the disabled community. Disability culture lives, and disabled individuals thrive, in online spaces such as the #DisCo (Disabled Community), #DisabilityTwitter, and #NEISVoid (No End In Sight). We want to extend a special thank you, and acknowledge the everyday discourse and advocacy in this community, and are pleased to bring a slice of that vibrant digital community to print.

We received a number of excellent submissions from parents of disabled children. While they certainly have a right to speak for their experiences, we decided to center disabled voices in this volume. This was an intentional move to allow disabled people to speak for themselves.

Though not featured in many of the articles, this book was very much a product of the global COVID-19 pandemic. The book contract was signed weeks before the U.S. shutdown, so all recruitment and writing were completed when disabled people were shut in, offered up as sacrifices to brunch and "opening the economy," and largely abandoned by the federal, state, and local government. Much of the COVID discourse was that ableds would be okay—COVID caused the most deaths among the elderly and disabled. So in many ways, this book stands as a testament to our combined strength and our unwillingness to accept being silenced or forgotten.

Note

1 The phrase "nothing about us without us" comes from James Charlton's 1998 book of the same title. It has become a rallying cry for disabled activists, as we demand the right to control our lives.

Acknowledgments

We would like to thank everyone at Brill who helped bring this book to fruition. This book was supported in part by the Creative Arts and Humanities Grant from Texas Woman's University. We appreciate the support of our Dean and the TWU Office of Research and Sponsored Programs for championing this project, and honoring our own disabilities and needs. Thanks to Dona Hightower Perkins for assistance with copy editing. We would also like to thank all of the authors who donated their time and energy to making this book possible.

Paul D. C. Bones would like to thank his wonderful wife Bradlin for always supporting him, as well as his fur babies Inara Bacon, Mildred Sausage, and Allan Hamsteak for constantly interrupting his writing. He would also like to thank all of the friends and colleagues he met throughout this process. Thank you for sharing your disabled lives with him.

Jessica Smartt Gullion would like to thank Paul and Danielle for the experience of working together on this project. She hopes it is the first of many collaborations. She would also like to thank Greg, Renn, and Rory for their love and light.

Danielle Barber would like to first thank Dr. Bones and Dr. Gullion for the amazing opportunity to be a part of this book. Danielle would like to acknowledge the disability community, and disability rights movement, without which this book would not be possible. She would also like to thank her parents Angie Johnson and Brian Johnson for their unconditional support.

Notes on Contributors

Jessi Aaron
(she/her) is an Associate Professor of Spanish Linguistics at the University of Florida. Formally trained as a sociolinguist and anthropologist, Jessi grew up in the green beauty of western Oregon. She is also a poet, a mother, and a painter. Jessi was born with arthrogryposis, which affects her ability to use her limbs; she uses a power wheelchair for mobility and freedom.

Anonymous 1
(she/her) is a friendly person. She volunteers and visits with people. Under COVID, she can't do that anymore, so she crochets blankets at home to give to people. She is doing this project because she wants people to know survivors' stories and what happened to them, especially to her and her sister. They were separated and that was very difficult on them. She thinks it's good that we're telling survivors' stories. She thinks it's good to let people hear what happened to everybody in their life. She would like everyone to be much nicer to the disability people. It's not their fault the way they were born. You have to be nice to everybody. It's the way you feel in your heart, to give it back.

Anonymous 2
(she/her) is a human being with rights. She is doing this project because she wants people to know that what they did in the institution was wrong, so that they won't do it again. She would like to see changes made so that people with disabilities are more respected, listened to, and believed.

Anonymous 3
(he/him) is a survivor of physical, mental, and psychological abuse that he experienced during his years in the [deidentified] institution. He had experiences at another kind of institution as well. Staff had different attitudes toward their patients depending on the kind of institution you were in. He is doing this project because he is a former patient of the [deidentified] Regional Centre, which used to be the [deidentified] Hospital [deidentified] in the 1950s. He wants to let people know what former patients had to go through during their

years in this institution. People need to know what everyone had to go through during their time growing up inside of an institution. He wants there to be a better understanding of it. It is important to know that not all institutions are like that; only some are.

Anonymous 4
(she/her) is a woman who lives in Toronto, Canada. She has a better life now than she ever did. She is doing this project because she wants to educate people. She would like to see more direct funding go to individuals who can't work. She would like to have things change, for people to be educated about people with disabilities and their history.

Kara B. Ayers
(she/her) is an Assistant Professor at the University of Cincinnati Center for Excellence in Developmental Disabilities (UCCEDD). She studies parenting with a disability, bioethics, health care inequities, and the role of media in stigma and disability culture. Kara is a proud disabled woman. She aims to infuse the mantra, "Nothing about us, without us," into her work and life.

Danielle Barber
(she/her) is a doctoral candidate in Sociology at Texas Woman's University in Denton, Texas. She is passionate about sociological research surrounding health and illness and disability. She is also a chronic illness warrior and advocate.

Aurora Berger
(she/her) is a queer disabled artist and writer from Strafford, Vermont. She holds an MFA in Visual Arts from Claremont Graduate University and a BA and BFA from Prescott College. She is currently working on a manuscript exploring the intersections of disability and contemporary art. Berger's writing has been previously published by Gambling the Aisle, Drkrm Press, and the National Institute for Learning Outcomes Assessment. Her artwork has been shown nationally and internationally.

Paul D. C. Bones
(he/him) is an Assistant Professor of Sociology at Texas Woman's University in Denton, TX. His primary research areas are disabilities,

ecological predictors of crime, and hate crimes. His publications have appeared in *The Journal of Quantitative Criminology, The Social Science Journal, The Journal for the Scientific Study of Religion, Sociological Spectrum,* and *The Journal of Transformative Learning.* He has also published chapters in *Hate Crimes* (Carolina Academic Press) and *A Legacy of Gloria E. Anzaldúa: "May We Do Work that Matters"* (Texas A&M Press).

E. J. K. Bremner

(she/her) is a small void creature feeding off 2,000-year-old ghost stories. She absolutely cannot be found on social media pretending to be anonymous while complaining about her niche research interests.

Christopher Bryant

(he/him) is an award-winning playwright and arts educator currently living in Melbourne, Australia. His creative and academic work focuses on the intersection of the crip-queer experience and 'history from below': readdressing traditional narratives from the viewpoint of marginalized communities. He's had plays published through Play Lab and Australian Plays, and in 2020 completed his PhD at Monash University.

The Committee for the Sick and Useless

is headed by an anonymous duo. Both authors have been useless for as long as they have been alive, and have spent most of that time writing things down. This manifesto was written in consultation with other committee members who have spent less time writing things down. We owe some inspirational debt to the Manifesto of the Committee to Abolish Outer Space.

Sheelagh Daniels-Mayes

(she/her) is an Indigenous Australian Kamilaroi woman who lost her eyesight as a child following measles. Sheelagh is located with the Indigenous Research Hub and is the Coordinator for the Sydney Indigenous Research Network. Her work focuses on Aboriginal education, Indigenous Studies and methodologies, and is a disability scholar and activist. Dr. Daniels-Mayes is particularly concerned with higher education's responsibilities in achieving equity and social justice for society's marginalized peoples. She uses Critical Race Theory, cultural responsiveness, and Critical Access Studies, alongside

Indigenous methodologies. Sheelagh acknowledges the unceded lands upon which the campuses of the University of Sydney now sit.

Terri Juneau Eklund

(she/her) is a graduate of Collin College, The University of North Texas, and Texas Woman's University. Cancer has been living with her for the better part of a decade, off and on.

Vanessa Ellison

(she/her) is a Sociology Doctoral Candidate at Texas Woman's University. Her research interests include food culture, veganism, sustainability, disability, race and ethnicity, and health in the Black community. She is an activist scholar and an agent of change.

Marie Gagnon

(she/her) is a doctoral candidate who studies stories. She also teaches writing workshops for disabled people through a local nonprofit. When she's not working, you will find her resting her achy body in a hammock deep, deep in the forest.

Elizabeth Glass

(she/her) teaches Humanities at the University of Louisville. She has received an Emerging Artist Award in Nonfiction from the Kentucky Arts Council and a grant from the Kentucky Foundation for Women. Her writing has appeared or is forthcoming in publications such as Redivider, River Teeth's "Beautiful Things" series, and Appalachian Review. She lives in Louisville, Kentucky.

Jasmine (Jaz) Gray

(she/her) is a researcher, advocate, and transformational storyteller from Memphis, TN. She speaks and leads workshops on a range of topics including the power of stories, research ethics, diversity, equity, and inclusion, and divine purpose. Her nonprofit Jaz's Jammies, Inc. has donated over 6,000 pairs of new pajamas to sick and homeless children and created opportunities for over 2,000 donors and volunteers. In addition to a BS from Middle Tennessee State University and an MA from Syracuse University, she is currently pursuing a PhD at the University of North Carolina at Chapel Hill where she is an instructor.

Jessica Smartt Gullion

(she/her) is Associate Dean of Research for the College of Arts and Sciences at Texas Woman's University. She is also an Associate Professor of Sociology and Affiliate Faculty of Multicultural Women's and Gender Studies. She teaches a variety of courses on qualitative research methods and on medical and environmental sociology. Dr. Gullion has published more than 35 peer-reviewed journal articles and book chapters. Her writing has appeared in such journals as the *International Review of Qualitative Research*, the *Journal of Applied Social Science*, and *Qualitative Inquiry*. Her essays and Op-Eds have appeared in a variety of outlets, including *Newsweek*, *The Conversation*, *AlterNet*, and *Inside Higher Ed*, and she is regularly quoted by national media. Her other books include *Doing Ethnography* with Susan Harper (Guilford Press, forthcoming); *Writing Ethnography* (2nd ed., Brill, 2022); *Qualitative Research in Health and Illness* (Oxford University Press, 2022); the award-winning *Researching With: A Decolonizing Approach to Community-Based Action Research* with Abigail Tilton (Brill I Sense, 2020); the award-winning *Diffractive Ethnography: Social Sciences and the Ontological Turn* (Routledge, 2018); *Fracking the Neighborhood: Reluctant Activists and Natural Gas Drilling* (The MIT Press, 2015); and *October Birds: A Novel about Pandemic Influenza, Infection Control, and First Responders* (Sense, 2014).

Nicholas R. Helms

(he/him) is the Assistant Professor of British Literature at Plymouth State University. Nic earned his PhD in Renaissance Literature from the Hudson Strode Program in Renaissance Studies at the University of Alabama. His recent book *Cognition, Mindreading, and Shakespeare's Characters* applies cognitive science to Shakespearean character criticism to argue for (dis)ability and neurodiversity-minded reading and teaching practices. At PSU he teaches British and Global literatures and advocates for more inclusive and accessible teaching practices through PSU's Open CoLab. He also organizes the Intersectionality Talks speaker series.

Nicholas Herd

(he/him) is an actor, performer, and talk show host. He does interviews with the disability channel. He is doing this project so that he can educate students, teachers, police officers, principals, etc. He wants to see the whole world know about people with disabilities and their stories. Stories can help the education system to learn from people with disabilities; from institutional survivors, as well as people with disabilities who were not in institutions. He is doing this project so that people can understand how everyone is different. Some of us are advocates fighting for people with other disabilities. Teaching about disability in schools, and to medical students as well, is important so that they can understand what disability is about and they can learn from people with disabilities. He wants to see people think about how we can shape our world, where everybody can belong and each of us is part of all of us. He wants people to learn how people with disabilities can contribute from many different parts of who they are and how they can express themselves in different ways. Everybody is different and we need to celebrate difference.

Summer M. Jackson
(she/her) is an Assistant Professor of Criminal Justice at California State University, East Bay. Her research and teaching focus on issues related to terrorism, policing, women and crime, deviance, and race and ethnicity. She has published and presented on various aspects of terrorism, policing, and deviance at national and international conferences.

Doreen Kalifer
(she/her) believes in justice and fairness. She believes that people are special in their own way. She likes being part of the DiStory group because she fights for the justice of people not being bullied because they are different. She wants people to have a better understanding of people with disabilities and for people described as 'different' to have better rights, and for more knowledge to be spread out to the universe about these things. She writes poetry about justice and bullying because this has always been a cause for her.

Alison Kelly
(she/her) received her Bachelor of Fine Arts from the University of North Texas with a studio focus in Watercolor, she also enjoys digital and 3D animation and Web Design.

Erin Kuri
(she/her) is a PhD candidate in the School of Social Work and a PhD Diploma student in the Department of Gender Studies and

Feminist Research at McMaster University. She has over a decade of practice experience as an advocate and psychotherapist, specialized in Art Therapy and Trauma, primarily working in the areas of child welfare, gender-based violence, and maternal and infant mental health. Erin draws on interdisciplinary feminisms, ethics, critical disability studies, motherhood studies, and trauma theory to develop collaborative and arts-based approaches to knowledge building. She is the Study Coordinator for the DiStory project. Her SSHRC-funded (Social Sciences and Humanities Research Council) doctoral research explores how young mothers make meaning of the concept of support within the context of service provision. Erin is also a mother, a visual artist, fiber crafter, and lover of tea, cats, and gardens.

Cassandra Lovelock

(she/her) is a disabled survivor researcher currently working toward a PhD in Health Policy at the London School of Economics and Political Science. She is also a researcher at the Tavistock. Her research interests revolve around unpaid care, mental health, disability, and race.

Raymond Luczak

(he/him) is the author and editor of 25 titles, including *Once upon a Twin: Poems* (Gallaudet University Press) and *QDA: A Queer Disability Anthology* (Squares & Rebels). His work has appeared in *Poetry*, *Prairie Schooner*, and elsewhere. He is the editor of the literary journal *Mollyhouse*. An inaugural Zoeglossia Fellow, he lives in Minneapolis, Minnesota.

Megan Marshall

(she/her) is an Assistant Professor of English at Marshall University, where she teaches secondary English education methods, composition pedagogy, young adult literature, professional writing, and other classes focused on popular fiction and lit to screen adaptations. In between teaching and committee work, she tries to write about topics ranging from moral panics on social media to the potential of contemporary adaptations to scrutinize mainstream, normative institutions. When she's not working, she's likely reading for pleasure, attempting to garden, or going on adventures with her family.

R. McGuire
(she/her or they/them) believes in the unknowability of the self. You can find out more about her by knowing less about yourself.

Katherine O'Connell
(she/her) is a queer and disabled sex educator and activist with a Master of Education in Human Sexuality Studies from Widener University. She has been a reproductive justice advocate for more than 10 years, and is a trained abortion and birth doula. She specializes in advocacy and sex education for people with chronic pain and disabilities. Katie lives in northern Virginia with her very anxious and wonderful dog Ella. You can connect with Katie at katieroconnell.com

Corin Parsons
(he/him) is a PhD candidate in Geography at the University of British Columbia and an instructor at Langara College. He studies cats, gender, and domestic space. He tweets as @the_tweedy.

Katherine A. Reed
(she/her) is an undergraduate student at Ohio State University studying psychology and disability studies. Katherine plans to continue her education in psychology and work as a therapist, with a focus in serving the disability community. She has a unique perspective as a disabled person, as Katherine lives with physical disabilities, chronic illnesses, and neurodiversity.

Corey Reutlinger
(he/him) is a doctoral candidate at Arizona State University. His research focuses on conflict-ridden communication in everyday social interactions. He employs applied mathematics to identify people's varying communication strategies, how these choices are reflected in talk, and how this might influence negotiated responses in organizational and interpersonal contexts. His interests extend to critical disability studies and arts-based research methodologies.

Jill Richardson
(she/her) is a PhD candidate in Sociology at University of Wisconsin at Madison. She began suffering daily migraines in 1995, and feels

lucky that—these days—she found effective treatment and only gets migraines some of the time. She researches human conflicts and cooperation for management of polarizing species like wolves, and is happiest when hiking up a mountain.

Ellen Samuels

(she/her) is a queer disabled poet and professor whose verse memoir *Hypermobilities* was published by The Operating System in 2021. Her writing on disability can be found in academic forums like *Disability Studies Quarterly*, *Signs*, GLQ, and *Amerasia*, and in literary journals like the *Colorado Review*, *Copper Nickel*, *Brevity*, *Rogue Agent*, and *Mid-American Review*. She teaches at the University of Wisconsin at Madison. Find her on twitter @ehlastigirl.

Ann Fudge Schormans

(she/her) is an Associate Professor in the School of Social Work at McMaster University (Ontario, Canada). Her many years of social work practice background, combined with ongoing activist work, inform her teaching, scholarship, and research. Working alongside people labelled/with intellectual disabilities, her research both employs and explores the potential and challenges of inclusive, co-researcher methodologies and knowledge production, along with arts-informed methods, to work toward epistemic and social justice.

Cole Sorensen

(he/him) is a mostly-nonspeaking trans autistic person, a public speaker, writer, and consultant. He holds a bachelor's degree in special education from the University of Minnesota Twin Cities. He has worked extensively with both disabled young people and the professionals who support them as a consultant, PCA, and lecturer. His work focuses on promoting autonomy, self-determination, communication access, and dignity of risk for young people with intellectual and developmental disabilities.

Jessica Spears Williams

(she/her) is a graduate student at Texas Woman's University working on her PhD in Sociology, with an emphasis in Medical Sociology. Her areas of interest are medical sociology, gender, and sexuality.

Introduction

Paul D. C. Bones, Jessica Smartt Gullion and Danielle Barber

Defining Disability

In order to redefine disability, one, presumably, needs to define it first. But where to begin? Do we take the historic religious/moral approach (Retief & Letšosa, 2018)? In some cultures, those with mental illnesses were said to have been blessed by the gods, and often became Shamans. We could examine the Old Testament and other ancient religious texts, where God or other powerful beings cursed people with physical impairments (some religions to this day view disability as a curse for one's sins, and argue that disability will go away with enough prayer and faith). Perhaps we should start with the term *disability* itself.

Disability, as a term, has historically been conceptualized as the inverse of ability; the negative side of a false dichotomy (Retief & Letšosa, 2018). Throughout most of human history, disability has been a demarcation of difference, a sign of inferiority, and an inescapable stigma. Sociologist Erving Goffman (1963) went so far as to designate disability as the ultimate stigmatized identity, "spoiling" the entirety of someone's being. As you can probably guess, disabled people were not included in this meaning-making process.

Most contemporary definitions of disability depend on meeting some kind of official criteria or being certified by an authority. Since the passage of the Americans With Disabilities Act (ADA) in 1990, most Americans—as well as many outside of the United States—have relied on it as a guide for how to approach disability. According to the ADA:

> a person with a disability [is] a person who has a physical or mental impairment that substantially limits one or more major life activity. This includes people who have a record of such an impairment, even if they do not currently have a disability. It also includes individuals who do not have a disability but are regarded as having a disability.

DOI:10.1163/9789004512702_001

Other attempts to codify disability include the U.S. Census categories, which prior to 2008 included sensory, physical, mental, self-care, go-outside-home, and employment (U.S. Census Bureau, 2021). In response to feedback that these options did not adequately encompass disability, a new set of categories was proposed: difficulties with hearing, vision, cognitive, ambulatory, self-care, and independent living. You will notice that mental disability was dropped in favor of a more general cognitive category, and that the term *disability* itself was erased. Keep in mind that while these are two official government definitions of disability, neither are universally applied, and other laws or institutions—such as Social Security—may have their own formal requirements to "be" disabled in an official sense and can involve complex, if somewhat arbitrary, quantifications of ability. For this book, we chose to utilize our own definition of disability as a condition, state, or characteristic that, on its own or due to social norms, disrupts routine activity. This includes conditions, states, and characteristics that may abate over time, vary cross-culturally, or are only apparent in specific contexts or situations. Due to the barriers in obtaining a formal diagnosis, which will be discussed later in the book, we consider self-diagnosis[1] (self-dx) as a valid claim to disability.

Vocabulary and Identification

The decision to call oneself disabled, to self-identify,[2] is best understood as ascribing to a group with a rich culture. Throughout this book you will be introduced to the larger disability community and disability culture. However, before beginning we feel it is important to understand the significance of labels and language. Due to the stigma of disability, and the general sense of dis-ease with impairment in general, many alternatives have been proposed such as special needs, diffability, disAbility, differently abled, limited, non-normative abilities, etc. Although attempts to destigmatize the concept of disability tend to come from a place of care, most disabled people shy away from these labels, which tend to infantilize or minimize the impact of disability in the lives of disabled people, such as insistence on the use of person-first language as opposed to identity-first language.

"Understanding words about disability as culturally created metaphors gives us opportunities for figuring out who creates disability, where it is created, who is supported by it, who benefits from it, and how to deconstruct it," Smith (2018, p. 16) writes. The language people use in relation to disabled people has the potential to increase or decrease stigma surrounding disability discourse (Olkin, 2002). For example, Olkin writes that the term "'physically challenged' puts the focus on the limitations of the person rather than on the handicapping environment. 'Special needs' implies that the needs of people with disabilities are outside the norm, as opposed to their civil rights" (p. 135).

Person-first language includes phrases such as person living with a hearing disorder or person who has a mental illness. The idea behind this languaging is a desire for the speaker to be "politically correct," and acknowledge the humanity of a person—to not label them in terms of their disability (as if being disabled makes one less than human). The argument that others "see us as a person first" is always interesting, because there are no other minoritized groups that experience this. For example, we do not talk about "persons with gay" during Pride month or those who struggle against police injustices committed against people who are Black. Smith (2018, p. 13) writes that he, like many other disabled people, avoids person-first language as a way "to highlight their social identity as disabled people. It's a way for them to identify with and gain solidarity from a social group that gives them strength and power in the world. It is also a way for them to point toward the fact that disability is not something that is part of them, is not part of their mind or body, but is something imposed on them by society." At the same time, people do not need to be defined solely by their disability. *I am disabled, but I am not my disability*. There will be times when a disabled person has different needs from ableds. Believe them when they set limits, allow them to have the autonomy to know for themselves what they can and cannot do, and for how they need to go about their lives without judgement. If I tell you that I am mentally ill, I don't need you to reframe that as I am a person with a mental illness.

Of course, some disabled people do use these alternative terms and use person-first language, but anecdotally speaking none of the three editors have ever been aggressively corrected when using identity-first language for ourselves or our community by a fellow disabled person. In this book, or in the DisCo in general, you may come across a derivation of the word "cripple." This is a reclaimed slur that many disabled people use to describe either a cultural identity or a space (loosely defined) created with disabled people in mind. As with other reclaimed slurs, it is for ingroup members only. Instead of making assumptions about what to call a disabled person, simply ask them what they prefer. Everyone is different—some people may prefer identity-first language. Others may not. Use the term that the person uses to describe themselves. And don't correct them on their terms. As with any minoritized population, autonomy and self-determination when we decide how we would like to be perceived, recognized, and described is of the utmost importance. So, if you are ever unsure about what to call us feel free to ask. Or just use our names if you know them.

In addition to disability itself, there are specific conditions, communities, and "types" of disability that have their own terminology. Disabilities can be either visible or invisible (or both, depending on access needs at the time). Many of the symptoms of chronic illnesses follow a relapsing-remitting pattern and are not always easily apparent to others. Some hidden (or less visible) symptoms of chronic illnesses include chronic pain, fatigue, inflammation, bowel and bladder disturbances, and limitations in mobility, just to name a few. Unfortunately, stigma often derives from issues of legitimacy related to the visibility of chronic disease symptoms because the symptoms might not be discernible to others. When symptoms of impairment cannot be seen or are difficult to see, relatives, friends, employers, and colleagues are unlikely to understand the seriousness of the illness and its impact on the life of the person. Even worse, often the individual will not be believed by others, and sometimes are accused of faking or making up their illness to avoid obligations or gain special advantages (Green et al., 2005; Vickers, 2017). We can assure you, as all three of us have invisible disabilities, that the benefits of being disabled (in the minds of ableds) are grossly overstated.

There also are some conditions that present in a similar fashion to disability, but for whatever reason a person may choose not to identify with the word disability. Often invisible, chronic illnesses meet criteria for disability "set forth by the United Nations' definition of disability in that they restrict the ability of a person to perform the activities of daily living in ways that result in economic and social disadvantages" (Jung, 2002, p. 178). Clark argues that the distinction between visible and hidden impairments need not be made because "they both meet the ADA (Americans with Disabilities Act) definition of what constitutes a disability, are both socially experienced, and cannot be understood as a separate category within the lives of disabled people" (2006, p. 313). Likewise, many people with what could be considered mental disabilities prefer to identify as "mentally ill" or "with a mental illness." Part of the reason for this may be due to the increased stigma of being mentally ill, as well as the perceived permanence of a disability, as an illness is often thought to be episodic, whereas a disability is unending.

Additionally, some specific conditions have their own distinct terminology. For example, being Deaf is not the same thing as being deaf, and both are distinct from being hard of hearing (Ladd, 2003). Non-Ddhh people are often referred to as "hearies." Blind people prefer that terminology over "visually impaired," unless someone has a visual impairment, which is not the same thing as being blind. Autistics tend to prefer identity-first language (over person-first language), tend not to capitalize the "a," largely reject the language of severity, abhor the term *Asperger*, may or may not see autism as a spectrum, and will often use the term "autie" as a term of endearment for ingroup members. Autism also falls under the category of neurodivergence or neurodiversity.[3] These are umbrella terms that include conditions where neurological development and/or performance depart from the neurotypical norm. Neurodiverse conditions include autism, ADHD, learning disorders, intellectual disabilities, dyslexia, Tourette, and other conditions that affect cognitive processes (Singer, 1999). The goal of this term is to remove the stigma from conditions that have been seen as "defects" while also highlighting the variety of ways humans think, plan, act, and understand. As you can see, disability labels are complex and can change over time.

At the same time, people do not need to be defined solely by their disability. Many identify as disabled, but do not want to be perceived *as* their disability. Conversely, some feel that their disability is their master status, or the role by which they are primarily perceived and identify (Becker, 2008). These terms may seem arbitrary and in fact will almost certainly change over time. However, self-definition is a key component of autonomy. This is important for strangers, peers, parents, and caregivers to remember; disabled people deserve the right to self-define. Disability and the disabled community have long existed as more than just medical conditions. Disability is a cultural identity, with its own separate subgroups, language, and symbols. To understand disability, you need to engage with it on these terms.

Models of Disability

Because disability is so complex and incorporates so many facets, most people (academics and non) prefer to approach it from a "model" perspective, which breaks these dimensions down.[4] Widely considered out of date by most disabled people and disability scholars, the Medical Model of Disability views disability "as a problem that exists in a person's body. As a consequence, that the individual is thought to require treatment or care to fix the disability, to approximate normal functioning, or perhaps as a last measure, to help the individual adapt and learn to function despite the disability" (Goering, 2015, p. 134). This point of view is problematic, specifically in terms of chronic illness, because most individuals living with chronic illness will never find a cure or even a treatment for their condition (Goering, 2015). The Medical Model came about during the early nineteenth century when social service agencies, health care personnel, educational institutions, and policy makers designated disability as a medical issue to be treated by medical professionals (Evans et al., 2017; Nielsen, 2012). Of course, it wasn't until an alternative model of disability was created, which was the Social Model (Oliver, 2004), that the term *medical model* was coined; before that it was just considered how disabilities were. The Medical Model is widely considered out of date by most disabled people and disability scholars.

In 1983, the (British) Social Model was created, or at least the term was coined, by Mike Oliver. Born out of the Disability Rights Movement, the Social Model was cultivated by disability activists who resisted the common medical approach to disability (Evans et al., 2017; Shakespeare, 2006). The Social Model separates impairment (the medical condition) from disability (social barriers and attitudes about impairment). Tom Shakespeare explains that "the social model is distinguished from the medical or individual model. Whereas the former defines disability as a social creation—a relationship between people with impairment and a disabling society—the latter defines disability in terms of individual deficit" (2006, p. 198). According to the Social Model, most (if not all) of the negative life events faced by disabled people stems from a lack of access, denial of inclusion, and the cultural beliefs that devalue disabled people (Shakespeare, 2006; Olkin, 2002). The Social Model suggests we can change environments in such a way that the disability is no longer limiting.

The Social Model has rightly been critiqued for being overly simplistic and dismissing the impact of impairments themselves. In particular, the Social Model was conceived with only physical impairments in mind, which omits individuals with hidden or less visible impairments. This means that individuals with chronic illnesses are not included in this model, which also excludes persons with learning and psychological disabilities. When discussing the need for the Social Model to evolve, Shakespeare (2006) contended that under the original model, individuals with degenerative conditions and impairments that cause chronic pain and discomfort are not socially created, and therefore left out of the Social Model. However, we would disagree and feel that many chronic illnesses develop because of our environment, which is full of not only pollutants and hazards, but also full of chronic stressors that can create chronic pain, chronic illness, and mental disability (Geronimus, 1992).

Increasingly, research has shown that chronic stress has the potential to influence not only psychological health, but also physiological health by wreaking havoc on the human body in various ways. For example, extensive research has documented that trauma exposure adversely affects most of the human body systems, and over time, exposure to trauma increases the risk for developing chronic disease (Longest & Thoits, 2012). The most common physiological disruptions impacted by trauma exposure pertain to gastrointestinal health, immune system functioning, neuroendocrine functioning, and pain in the musculoskeletal system (Longest & Thoits, 2012). Additionally, just as with physical disabilities, there are ways to accommodate persistent pain, chronic illness, and mental disability, so it seems odd that these conditions are singled out as "not social" in nature. This is why even Shakespeare (2006) himself stated that the Social Model is not an all-encompassing, end-all, be-all theory on disabilities but rather should be used as a tool and perspective to think about disability.

Given the ever-evolving nature of theory, several new models have been theorized with an aim to better combine the lived experiences of disabled people (including hidden disabilities/chronic illness and interpersonal interactions) with social barriers. Two examples of attempts to expand or reform the Social Model are social-relational theory and resistance theory. Social-Relational Theory (Thomas, 2004) combines both the medical and social models, as it contends that disruptions to activities can be caused by social reasons (such

as ableism) or impairments (cerebral palsy). Conversely, Resistance
Theory states that models themselves are often the product of
active resistance on the part of disabled people to push back against
otherizing and reductive understandings of disability and impairment
that center ableds (Gabel & Peters, 2004). This resistance takes place
at the structural, cultural, and individual levels, as the disability rights
struggle itself creates a constantly shifting model of disability. As part
of this process, we see field-specific models and theories of disability,
such as critical disability theory, feminist disability theory, queer
disability theory, etc. Under resistance theory, these smaller identity
movements reflect a recognition of and response to oppression from
different minoritized populations, under the shared label of disabled.

As mentioned earlier, some authors view mental illness as part of
disability, while others see it as a distinct category due to its unique
contexts (diagnosis, stigma, treatment, etc.). The inherent problem
in differentiating between mental illness and mental disability lies in
the subjective array of definitions of disability, as well as in subjective
evaluative criteria for mental illness and impairment. Currently, the
DSM-V does not provide any "simple definition or explanation of
what constitutes psychiatric impairment" (Gold et al., 2008, p. S6).
However, "many DSM diagnoses include a criterion requiring that
the symptoms cause clinically significant distress or impairment in
social, occupational, or other crucial areas of functioning" (Gold et al.,
2008, p. S6). Additionally, ADA, private insurance plans, and the Social
Security disability program all legally define disability differently (Gold
et al., 2008). Many psychiatric care providers are not comfortable
providing disability evaluations, in which case, the person seeking
evaluation is typically referred to a forensic psychiatrist (Gold et
al., 2008). Clinicians who provide psychiatric disability evaluations
use practical scales such as the Global Assessment of Functioning
in attempts to quantify the extent of functional impairment (Gold
et al., 2008). Gold et al. are careful to point out that "the scores
assigned have an element of subjectivity and may vary depending
on the psychiatrist's experience and perspective" (2008, p. S6). Korn
argues that the distinction between physical and mental illness need
not be made because "many 'physical' disabilities have a cognitive
component, and many 'mental' disabilities have direct physical effects"
(2003, p. 585). Part of this issue lies in the mind-body dichotomy
pervasive in Western medicine's conceptualization of diseases.

In response to the way medicalization has historically defined
mental illness as aberrant, Mad Studies arose to re-center the

experiences of persons labeled as mentally ill, mentally disabled, crazy, and/or mad (Menzies, LeFrançois, & Reaume, 2013). Because of the medical trauma that often has accompanied mental health treatment, along with the overall stigma of mental illness in contemporary society, Mad Studies takes a survivor approach to mental disabilities. The goals of Mad Studies include questioning the sanist norms of society, destigmatizing mental illness, raising awareness of mental health trauma at the hands of medical experts, and advocating for more autonomy for mentally ill and mad people.

Although models may not make much sense in terms of the daily phenomenology of disability—in other words, when it comes to feeling disabled in one's own skin—models of disability do serve several key functions. First, a model that is typically created in the academy, and thus subject to peer-review, lends authority to the experiences of disabled people.

Anecdotally speaking, though flawed, the Social Model is often an important starting point for persons who acquire a disability later in life or want to engage more fully with disability culture. Two of the editors of this book were personally (and professionally) impacted by the discovery of an academic source of authority who told us that the added burdens we faced were not our fault, but that of society. Second, models are important because they make meaning of our lives in a world that defines us as "other," and inform non-disabled people who work directly with disabled populations, as well as policy makers. For example, a study by Dirth and Branscombe (2017) showed that not only does awareness of structural discrimination (from a Social Model standpoint) increase support for policies that benefit disabled people, but medical model representation actually decreases support for disability justice policies. Although we tend to approach theory as set in stone, we would encourage readers to remember that if you find a theory or model that mostly works for you, or that has an obvious flaw, you can fix it. As with language, larger theoretical constructions about disability do and should change over time.

Ableism and Contempt

To this point, we have stuck to official definitions of disability, and centered the meaning-making of disabled people. But what does disability signify to the larger, non-disabled society? Although disability is the one minoritized group that anyone can be a part of, and according to the World Bank (2021), 15% of the world's population (approximately 1 billion people) is disabled (compared to 26% of the U.S. population—61 million, according to 2021 U.S. Census Bureau figures), disability remains primarily controlled by the non-disabled. Disability is a topic we love to talk about, but rarely mention. Think of your three favorite insults. Chances are at least one is an ableist slur. Scroll through social media and you will see references to intellectual disability (stupid, dumb, retarded, low IQ, etc.) and mental illness (crazy, mad, insane, unhinged, etc.). This is particularly true when it comes to politicians we dislike. Likewise, we employ ableist frames when dealing with violence, particularly mass-casualty events. Mental illness is the primary narrative of mass shooters. Following a mass shooting event, policy experts, politicians, and armchair sociologists argue that the shooter must be/have been mentally ill. Rather than address the gun problem itself, they shift the focus to mental health (although there has not been a big push to increase mental health services in the U.S.). Some people who are violent are also mentally ill. Some aren't. But rarely do we ever actually investigate to see if the person in question has been diagnosed with a mental illness. This comes at the expense of millions of mentally ill people who are not violent, who don't pick up guns and shoot people. Similarly, we use ableist terms to describe racism, sexism, homophobia as resulting from "stupidity." This not only minimizes the role of structural and cultural factors in shaping violent and hateful behaviors, it comes at the expense of stigmatizing an already demonized population. As Linton (1998, p. 128) describes it, these are "[f]igures of speech [that] further objectify and alienate people with disabilities and perpetuate inaccurate information about disabled people's experience."

Disability is often seen as a fate worse than death. Again, one can see this narrative with a simple scroll through social media. When disabling events like a car crash happen, ordinary people flock to news story comment sections or tweets to express how terrible disability is, and how they "couldn't live like that" (without having any idea what life is like for disabled people). We see stories on the news of disabled people accomplishing ordinary things, as ableds ohhh and ahhh over how brave we must be to simply exist, insisting "they couldn't do it." In a global pandemic, one that not only has been far more deadly for disabled people but creates disability, we've seen eugenics under the form of "rationed care." In California, as COVID-19 spiked, health care professionals and emergency drivers were tasked with conserving supplies such as oxygen, making decisions based on "quality of life" (Parrish, 2020). What group do you think is most likely to be viewed as having none? Disabled people. In the UK, 60% of all COVID deaths were of disabled people (BBC News, 2021), and there was discussion of rationing care for intellectually disabled persons because of a perceived low quality of life (Tapper, 2021). To clarify, intellectual disability has zero effect on the survivability of the virus or the chances of acquiring long COVID symptoms. It should not be part of any rationed care calculus. And rationed care is a concept that should itself not exist.

Even the anti-vaccination movement so prominent in the West is based on the idea that disability is worse than death. Despite firm scientific consensus on the benefits of vaccination against deadly diseases, and the utter lack of any evidence that vaccines cause autism, millions of parents are willing to risk the lives of their children to "protect" them from disability (Hussain, Ali, Ahmed, & Hussain, 2018). Parents of autistic children have also been known to embrace deadly "cures," such as injecting or ingesting bleach (Zadrozny, 2019). Yes, you read that correctly. In hopes of curing their disabled children, parents are willing to poison them with a known toxin, based on shoddy medical advice from Facebook. If that isn't a damning indictment of the pervasiveness of ableism, we don't know what is.

Ableism and the denigration of disability also appear in seemingly trivial situations. One of the people who worked on this book has obsessive-compulsive disorder. They said:

> OCD is not what most people think. It's not always about wanting to have a clean house or to be super organized (although that can be a way that people cope with their obsessions). Often OCD involves an irrational thought that gets stuck in your mind, and ritualistic behavior to try to release the anxiety that thought brings. My most recent obsessive thought is, what if I drive my car into a tree? I then think about all the possibilities of how that could happen. I don't want to drive my car into a tree—I have no wish to harm myself or my car (or even a tree). But every time I drive I think about it. This leads me to have someone else drive so that I don't have the option. Or I stay home, instead of leaving the house to do something I want to do. When I take a shower, I have to knock on the shower wall

three times. I don't know why. But if I don't do it, I will be anxious all day, and the anxiety will only be released when I go home, climb in the shower, and knock three times. These are some of the ways OCD manifests for me.

When someone says they are "feeling OCD" because they cleaned their pantry or organized their clothes by color, people who actually do have OCD can find that insulting, and their experience dismissed. Same with when Target released a holiday shirt about OCD—Obsessive Christmas Disorder. OCD is a terrible disease that gets in the way of living life, and using the term otherwise erases that experience. This makes it more difficult for people who do have OCD to get needed accommodations or treatment. The same is true for ADHD, anxiety, depression, and any number of other potentially debilitating conditions that are often presented as quirky personality traits. If "everyone is a little autistic," then that suggests that autism is not a serious condition, and requires little in terms of accommodation. The co-opting of disability minimizes its impacts, and harms actually disabled people.

The most telling part about the widespread use of ableist language is how ableds react when called out on its usage. Often, there is a resistance to accept responsibility, change behavior, or even recognize that their words are ableist. There are no formal studies we are aware of, but anecdotally speaking, one of the most common reactions to being called out for ableist language is to insist that one would "never call a handicapped person that" or that "they didn't mean disabled people" when using words rooted in disability stigma. These answers are always puzzling, because the person in question is literally calling someone disabled as an insult, so whether they would call a disabled person disabled as an insult is immaterial. Furthermore, a politician or celebrity probably will not hear anyone call them "crazy," but a disabled friend, acquaintance, or family member will.

In many ways, this noncommittal, unintentional ableism may be the truest face of disability prejudice and antipathy. It's not an angry hatred; it's a forgetful one. It's prioritizing abled norms because someone "didn't think about" disability. It's insisting that, at the height of a deadly pandemic, sports bars be opened because at-risk people can just "stay home." It's designing school buildings where the only accessible entrance is down a dangerous loading ramp, right next to the dumpsters. It's putting "must be able to lift 20 lbs" on a job listing for a speech writer. It's canceling disability benefits if a disabled person gets married or has more than $2,000 in assets. It's assuming disabled people are faking, because we're lazy and just want to get paid for staying home when it's legal to pay disabled workers a sub-minimum wage. It's deciding that accessible parking is discriminatory to non-disabled people (Volker, Levingston, & Seslja, 2021). It's not caring if we live or die, so long as we're not an inconvenience.

Redefining Disability

Ableism, just like any prejudice or system of oppression, is a learned behavior. That is why we have to change how we think about disability and how we define it. Based on the previous discourse, there are two different sources of what it means to be disabled: the abled community, who see disability as something shameful to be avoided at all costs, and the disabled community, who view disability as a rich cultural identity. The problem is that when it comes to the larger narrative of disability and impairment, too much of disability discourse and the way society defines disability has been left in abled hands. Quite frankly, we deserve better.

We need to stop viewing disabled people as passive objects and see us as active subjects. Disability labels can no longer be slurs. Instead, we need society to see the culture that has formed around impairments. We have to push back against the idea that being disabled is a fate worse than death, when in reality it is a life event similar to many others. Non-disabled people have to understand that for many of us, our disability is a source of pride, not a mark of shame. So how do we do this? To begin, we must center the voices of disabled people.

This book is part of a larger social movement to empower disabled people by demanding that our stories be told. We have to use our words—our experiences—to push back against deficit-based narratives of what it means to be disabled. This requires destroying the myth that disability is a monolith. There is so much diversity in the disabled community. Our members have different racial identities, genders, sexual orientations, class backgrounds, regional differences, educational experiences, personal interests, and everything that makes a person distinct from their peers.

These intersections matter because there is an endless possibility of disabled experiences, and persons who can share their lives. There is also a tendency to reduce disability to one narrative or genre: tragedy. Yes, sometimes our impairments cause us pain and sometimes we have bad days, but isn't this true for everyone? Disabled people experience the exact same ups and downs in life as everyone else. We hope that by sharing stories from an array of authors on an assortment of topics that readers will realize just how expansive the disability community is. In selecting chapters for this book, we included academic works, personal narrative, and artistic pieces because disability touches every part of our lives, but we still live.

We also hope to bring more truth and authenticity to the definition of disability than one typically finds in popular media. Disability should not be a plot device to get quick sympathy for an uninteresting character. It shouldn't be used as a convenient origin story for a villain. Above all else, disability should never be used to make non-disableds in the audience marvel at our mere continued existence. These definitions of disability all exploit our experiences for the benefit of people who are not us. Disability is never just one thing, and as you'll see in the readings, disabled people are the most dynamic of characters.

Society has also given too much authority to non-disabled "experts" on disability. Having spent endless hours in various diversity and inclusion events, or disability-related training, run by (and for) non-disabled persons in academia, we know how rare it is for these roles to actually engage with the disabled people they purport to serve. Instead of addressing how institutions can accommodate disability and facilitate the success of students, employees, or members, many of these helpful programs provide new tools for exclusion. This provider versus client assumption is rooted in the idea that disabled people are served by institutions, not that we are in fact often experts in our fields of employment. Consequently, the lack of disability representation in education and high-profile occupations means that many disabled students internalize the idea that they do not belong; that everything should be more difficult for them than their peers, and that they have to "prove" their worth time and time again. This too stems from the definition of disability as a marker of difference. In reality, no two people are alike, and what works for one may not work for another. However, because we cast disability in a different light, we forget that disabled needs are not special...they are human.

Disability inclusion in school, the workforce, and in everyday life too often depends on a non-disabled person deciding what we can and cannot do. Traditional views of disability as incompatible with success allow expressions of professional preference to masquerade as evidence-based facts. We hope the stories in this book demonstrate how disabled people can excel, if we are properly accommodated, allowing us to reclaim our bodily authority. This means viewing disability not as something that must be cured or overcome on the part of the individual, but as a condition (or conditions) that many institutions could accommodate, but choose not to. More than that though, we want disabled people to be viewed as the resource that we are. To exist in a system of unequal access and ableism creates ingenuity. Although deeply unfair, it makes us adaptable in ways that non-disabled people may not be.

Finally, we hope to redefine disability as a social construct that can change over time. All three editors of this volume wear glasses but none of us consider it to be a disability. Why? Because eyeglasses have been normalized, and this kind of vision impairment has been fully accommodated. Glasses have pros (shield you from flying debris) and cons (finding your glasses is very difficult if you're not wearing glasses), but they are an accepted, uncontroversial part of life. Eyeglass wearers are accepted in positions of power, and no one thinks twice about befriending (or even dating!) us. This is how all disabilities should be viewed and treated: as a part of life for some people that, though it shapes our every waking moment, can be easily accommodated. If we choose, we can separate the concept of disability from the stigma and ableism with which it has been imbued. Disability isn't inherently bad or tragic. Disability isn't a bad word. Disability is simply a state of being, and it's fine.

Book Overview

What follows is a collection of writings on disability, each by disabled authors. Some are humorous, others are sad. There is a mix of academic works with citations, and personal narratives that rely on experience rather than theory. Interspersed with these chapters are poems, artwork, and photography. There are also disabled

people's animal companions. All are authentic accounts of disability.
One of our goals with this volume was to model accommodation
and inclusion. Due to the stigma surrounding disabilities, some of
our authors chose to be anonymous or to use pen names instead
of their real names. We also had several authors who required
accommodation in the form of an interview or direct assistance
from care workers. We received entries from across the globe. We
retained the spelling choices of the authors to honor their own
cultures. Thus, in one entry readers might notice American spelling
of words, and in others see the European spelling of the same word.
Each entry has discussion questions, almost all provided by the
authors themselves. Where possible, we included content warnings
(indicated by cw). However, given the deeply personal nature of
trauma, it is not possible to account for everything that may distress
a reader. If you are assigning this book in a class, we ask that you
please communicate with students that they can skip over anything
that may cause harm. The order of chapters was decided with a
certain flow in mind, but we invite readers to plot their own path
through the text. If you are disabled, we hope you find yourself
reflected in these writings. If you are non-disabled, we hope you are
willing to learn.

Notes

1 Self-diagnosis is a controversial topic, as many non-disabled, especially medical
   professionals, question the ability of a person to accurately connect bodily
   experiences to official diagnoses, absent a trained expert. This is often seen in the
   quote, "Do not confuse your Google search with my medical degree." However,
   cost, transportation, stigma, and quality of care often interfere with the official
   diagnosis process, and going to a doctor does not guarantee a diagnosis (accurate
   or inaccurate). Therefore, we trust disabled people to interpret their bodies
   accurately.
2 Self-identification is different from self-dx, as some people with officially
   recognized disabilities choose not to identify as disabled.
3 There is widespread debate on which is the most appropriate term (neurodiverse
   vs. neurodivergent). Disagreement is primarily over who is centered (are you
   different from me, are we different from you, or are we all different?) and which
   conditions are being discussed (plurals, alters, and schizophrenics—disorders that
   often include departing from standard interpretations of the world—often claim
   neurodivergent as only referring to this subset of conditions).
4 See Gabel and Peters (2004) for an excellent breakdown of paradigms, models,
   and theories as they relate to disability studies.

References

ADA National Network. (n.d.). *What is the definition of disability under the ADA?* https://adata.org/faq/what-definition-disability-under-ada

BBC News (2021, February 11). *COVID: Disabled people account for 6 in 10 deaths in England last year – ONS.* https://www.bbc.com/news/uk-56033813

Becker, H. S. (2008). *Outsiders.* Simon & Schuster.

Centers for Disease Control and Prevention. (2020, September 16). *Disability inclusion.* https://www.cdc.gov/ncbddd/disabilityandhealth/disability-inclusion.html

Charlton, J. I. (1998). *Nothing about us without us.* University of California Press.

Clark, M. A. (2006). Adult education and disability studies, an interdisciplinary relationship: Research implications for adult education. *Adult Education Quarterly, 56*(4), 308–322.

Dirth, T. P., & Branscombe, N. R. (2017). Disability models affect disability policy support through awareness of structural discrimination. *Journal of Social Issues, 73*(2), 413–442.

Evans, N. J., Broido, E. M., Brown, K. R., & Wilke, A. K. (2017). *Disability in higher education: A social justice approach.* John Wiley & Sons.

Gabel, S., & Peters, S. (2004). Presage of a paradigm shift? Beyond the social model of disability toward resistance theories of disability. *Disability & Society, 19*(6), 585–600.

Geronimus, A. T. (1992). The weathering hypothesis and the health of African-American women and infants: Evidence and speculations. *Ethnicity & Disease, 2*(3), 207–221.

Goering, S. (2015). Rethinking disability: The social model of disability and chronic disease. *Current Reviews in Musculoskeletal Medicine, 8*(2), 134–138.

Goffman, E. (1963). *Stigma: Notes on a spoiled identity.* Jenkins, JH & Carpenter.

Gold, L. H., Anfang, S. A., Drukteinis, A. M., Metzner, J. L., Price, M., Wall, B. W., Wylonis, L., & Zonana, H. V. (2008). AAPL practice guideline for the forensic evaluation of psychiatric disability. *Journal of the American Academy of Psychiatry and the Law Online, 36*(Supplement 4), S3–S50.

Green, S., Davis, C., Karshmer, E., Marsh, P., & Straight, B. (2005). Living stigma: The impact of labeling, stereotyping, separation, status loss, and discrimination in the lives of individuals with disabilities and their families. *Sociological Inquiry, 75*(2), 197–215.

Hussain, A., Ali, S., Ahmed, M., & Hussain, S. (2018). The anti-vaccination movement: A regression in modern medicine. *Cureus, 10*(7).

Jung, K. E. (2002). Chronic illness and educational equity: The politics of visibility. *NWSA Journal, 14*(3), 178–200.

Korn, J. B. (2003). Crazy (mental illness under the ADA). *University of Michigan Journal of Law Reform, 36*(3), 585–652.

Ladd, P. (2003). *Understanding deaf culture: In search of deafhood.* Multilingual Matters.

Linton, S. (1998). *Claiming disability: Knowledge and identity.* New York University Press.

Longest, K. C., & Thoits, P. A. (2012). Gender, the stress process, and health: A configurational approach. *Society and Mental Health, 2*(3), 187–206.

Menzies, R., LeFrançois, B. A., & Reaume, G. (2013). Introducing mad studies. In *Mad matters: A critical reader in Canadian Mad Studies* (pp. 1–22). Canadian Scholars' Press.

Nielsen, K. E. (2012). *A disability history of the United States* (Vol. 2). Beacon Press.

Oliver, M. (2004). The social model in action: If I had a hammer. In C. Barnes & G. Mercer (Eds.), *Implementing the social model of disability: Theory and research.* The Disability Press.

Olkin, R. (2002). Could you hold the door for me? Including disability in diversity. *Cultural Diversity and Ethnic Minority Psychology, 8*(2), 130.

Parrish, C. (2020, December 28). Some California hospitals rationing care due to spike in COVID-19 hospitalizations. *ABC News.* https://www.cdc.gov/ncbddd/disabilityandhealth/disability-inclusion.html

Retief, M., & Letšosa, R. (2018). Models of disability: A brief overview. *HTS Teologiese Studies/Theological Studies, 74*(1).

Shakespeare, T. (2006). The social model of disability. In L. J. Davis (Ed.), *The disability studies reader* (pp. 195–204). Routledge.

Singer, J. (1999). Why can't you be normal for once in your life? From a 'Problem with no name' to a new category of disability. *Disability Discourse,* 59–67.

Smith, P. (2018). *Writhing writing: Moving towards a mad poetics.* Autonomous Press.

Tapper, J. (2021, February 13). Fury at 'do not resuscitate' notices given to COVID patients with learning disabilities. *The Guardian.* https://www.theguardian.com/world/2021/feb/13/new-do-not-resuscitate-orders-imposed-on-covid-19-patients-with-learning-difficulties

Thomas, C. (2004). Rescuing a social relational understanding of disability. *Scandinavian Journal of Disability Research, 6*(1), 22–36.

United States Census Bureau. (2021, February 23). *How disability data are collected from the American Community Survey.* https://www.census.gov/topics/health/disability/guidance/data-collection-acs.html

Vickers, M. H. (2017). Sick organizations, rabid managerialism: Work-life narratives from people with invisible chronic illness. *Public Voices, 4*(1), 59–82.

Volker, S., Levingston, R., & Seslja, E. (2021, April 28). Disabled car parks 'discriminatory to able-bodied people,' man in wheelchair told. *ABC Canberra.* https://www.abc.net.au/news/2021-04-29/disabled-car-parks-discriminatory-to-able-bodied-people/100103488

World Bank. (2021, March 19). *Disability inclusion.* https://www.worldbank.org/en/topic/disability

Zadrozny, B. (2019, May 21). Parents are poisoning their children with bleach to 'cure' autism. Theses moms are trying to stop it. *ABC News.* https://www.nbcnews.com/tech/internet/moms-go-undercover-fight-fake-autism-cures-private-facebook-groups-n1007871

CHAPTER 1

Existing in a Mortal Form and Other Disabling Experiences

E. J. K. Bremner and R. McGuire

As any abled person can tell you, disability begins in the doctor's office. Either the X-rays and blood tests have conclusively proven that you have an anxiety disorder, or a team of experts have worked tirelessly for months before diagnosing you with an extremely rare parasite you got from eating tuna.

There is, however, one minor flaw in this system: what if you live in the post-apocalyptic wasteland where doctors are scarce, but you still want to work out if your problems are caused by a disability or by the zombie horde outside your house? For that reason, and that reason alone, we (your kind hosts, E and R) think it might be valuable to try a different approach.

As it stands, the definition of disability is so intricately tied up in diagnosis that it often glosses over the experience of being disabled. We propose to redefine disability by centering experience over diagnosis, which can be a long, painful, expensive, and sometimes unhelpful process. It also involves So Many Blood Tests, and we only have so much blood.

Our definition of disability is related to the Social Model, but we hope it will be more accessible to disabled people who have had to sit in a doctor's office and be told that there's absolutely nothing wrong with them, despite the fact that they Can't Do Things, or are In Pain. Disability is a feature of society, but for us it is also a feature of our bodies.

The experiences we're talking about here could all be called problems, but we don't mean to say that disability is exclusively a problem. Disability has brought much joy into our lives. Even more than that, it has brought us-ness into our lives: it has made us the weird, funny, caring people that we are. We wouldn't trade our disabilities away, although we'd be happy to sell our migraines on the black market.

This chapter focuses on problems—because disabilities come with problems, both the ones inherent to our bodies and the ones built into our society. It is hard for us to stand for half an hour in the way it is hard for some people to climb a cliff. There are some people for whom both these things are easy, but probably more for whom they are both difficult. Everything is difficult for someone.

Disabilities are also hard because the Western world has chosen to make them hard.[1] Few of us are expected to climb cliffs in our daily lives, but we are often expected to stand for hours at a time. Society makes some people disabled, or makes them more disabled than they would be otherwise.

This might be why defining disability is so hard. Everything is difficult.[2] Sometimes it's more difficult because of your body, sometimes it's more difficult because of society's response to your body. How do we disentangle those things and identify the specific kinds of difficulty that we want to discuss?

The answer for us was to grab the handful of experiences that annoyed us the most. Anger has proven to be a very useful muse. Our choices have also been informed by the fact that we're formally educated white Australians and generally perceived as women. We are neurodivergent and have chronic illnesses, and we do not consider ourselves to have visible disabilities at this time. With that in mind, the disabling experiences we'll explore include:

1. Wanting a test, any test, that says there's something wrong with you so you'll finally know why your knees hurt. Alas, your blood is perfection.
2. Being given bad advice by friends, family, doctors, colleagues, enemies, strangers, and unfortunate others. At some point you'll be told to drink bleach because you can't be sick if you're dead.
3. Dealing with the mental load of your disability, people's reactions to your disability, the entire medical and insurance system surrounding your disability, and the effort of trying to Be A Person.
4. Seeking Reasonable Accommodations for your disability so that you can Be A Person. This experience is obviously Good and Easy, and doesn't involve asking your doctor to fill out seven forms, each a slightly different invasion of your privacy.
5. Some things are just harder for you, and it can be difficult to explain why. Such things can include Cleaning, Concentrating, Standing, Walking, Talking, Sleeping, Eating, and Existing in A Mortal Form.

Wanting Your Blood Tests to Show Something Wrong

One day you wake up with a sore knee. It hurts when you walk, when you sit, when you brush it against something. It doesn't hurt when you press against it with your fingers. And it doesn't hurt when anyone else does that, either. But it's still there, still sudden and persistent and ruining your life one inconvenience at a time.

If your Sudden And Persistent Knee Pain begins before the inevitable zombie apocalypse and the subsequent wasteland of medical intervention, you might go to your doctor. Your doctor might then perform a number of tests to ascertain the cause of your new symptoms, including, but not limited to, physical examinations, X-rays, ultrasounds, full blood tests, Latin blood tests, Vulgate Latin blood tests, exorcisms, and gastroscopies.[3]

If you're like E and R, every test is fine. According to all these tests, you're the veritable picture of health. But every time you walk, every time you stand, every time you sit with your knees even slightly pressed against something, you know that your knees are not fine. Knees don't just suddenly become allergic to normal functioning without a reason.

Your doctor explains, very kindly, that Sudden And Persistent Knee Pain is a symptom of the anxiety that you definitely have, despite the fact that you weren't feeling anxious before you got Sudden And Persistent Knee Pain.

Unless you're fat, in which case the doctor will inform you that your Sudden And Persistent Knee Pain is caused by your being fat, as are your migraines, depression, literal cancer symptoms, and your skin's tendency to glow purple at sunrise every Saturday morning ever since you found yourself in possession of a mysterious amulet of ambiguous origin.

Your doctor suggests a diet so complex it's impossible to follow, a psychiatrist you can't afford, and medication you're allergic to. Your parents tell you to drink bone broth. Your university or workplace asks you for your complete medical history dating back to the Norman invasion, which is how you end up telling a stranger that teenage pregnancy runs in your family. The pain spreads and gets worse, and you do not go back to the doctor.

No one believes you when you say anxiety isn't the answer. A doctor looked at your many, many blood tests, and they looked at your x-rays, and they might have even looked at your knee. And they told you it was a product of your brain chemistry. It's not until you see a different doctor, someone who specialises in Sudden And Persistent Knee Pain that appears out of nowhere with no known cause, that you discover all those tests can be completely normal when your body isn't.

Unfortunately, it's not until you see this doctor that the people around you start to understand this, either. And by this point they've probably had a couple of years to believe you're just lazy and like to complain.

It may seem antithetical to the point to start our list of disabling experiences with one that talks about diagnosis; we are, after all, trying to decenter diagnosis. Our point is this: a diagnosis is not what makes someone disabled, but the search for answers, no matter how successful, is an experience that unites many disabled people. For many of us, it isn't enough to know that our knees hurt. We want to know why.

A Litany of Bad Advice

Through our Extensive and Exhaustive Research (simply being alive), we've found receiving Truly Terrible and Unhelpful Advice on a regular basis to be one of the cornerstones of disabling experiences. This advice can come from anyone—including doctors, fitness coaches, and Martha in 12B who thinks a good juice cleanse will cure your explicitly incurable zombie infection.

Sometime during the Too Many Blood Tests phase of Trying To Understand Your Condition, you might mention to your doctor that you're having trouble exercising because your knees hurt, to which your doctor's usual reply is that you should do more exercise. You might decide to take the doctor's advice and join a gym, so that someone can yell at you for being weak and in pain. We have done diligent research on the subject, and so far, found no evidence that being yelled at stops you from being weak and in pain.

Upon visiting another doctor, you're threatened with leeches and bloodletting. It's at this point that you realise you took a wrong turn and ended up in the thirteenth century, and back out of the room before they start talking about your wandering uterus. You never learn how you ended up in the thirteenth century, which is a pity: as historians, we would love to know the secrets of time travel.

When you return to your apartment leech-free and in possession of no extra holes in your head through which the demons can escape, you're confronted by your neighbour. She tries to talk you into a juice cleanse and suggests fifteen different yoga poses that you technically could do, if you were willing to spend a full week in bed trying to soothe the ghosts that yoga awoke.

At some point you might decide to get a walker so you can sit down whenever you want, or a wheelchair so you can sit down whenever you want, or a shower chair so you can sit down whenever you want. These things measurably improve your life. But as soon as any abled person learns of your accommodations to the demons that live in your bones, they scold you for "Giving In" to Being Disabled.

All you'll hear from these people for the next 6 months is why you should avoid looking disabled and calling yourself disabled At All Costs. Calling yourself disabled is a Great Moral Failure and, thanks to Martin Luther, we can no longer pay for our moral failures to disappear. This advice is so bad that it might actually be making you more disabled.[4]

Good advice, in our experience, mostly comes from other disabled people. That's how we found out about shower chairs, eating lots of salt, and the kind of physiotherapy where they don't ask you to exercise at home in your precious free time. One of the advantages of being disabled is knowing more disabled people who are passionate experts on the topic of feeling better.

Trying to Think Everything at Once

There are a lot of things to think about in life. Like, did the ancient Romans like ghost stories? Or why is philosophy so obsessed with the trolley problem? And of course, is wireless internet actually just magic? But when you're disabled, you often have to think about a lot of other (and, in our opinion, less interesting) things that abled people generally don't have to think about. This results in a heavier mental load and an ardent desire to drink an entire bottle of gin.

The mental load, sometimes called *cognitive labour*, is the mental work of managing life's tasks. It's about "anticipating needs, identifying options for filling them, making decisions, and monitoring progress" (Daminger, 2019, p. 609). Most often this is discussed in regard to taking care of the household and family, where women are usually expected to bear a heavier mental load than men.

But simply getting through each day alive requires labour, both physical and mental. The physical component of self-care usually consists of eating, exercising, and bathing, while the mental component is deciding what to eat, what exercise you can do, and when to bathe.

Carers can assist disabled people with both physical and mental self-care, but most of us still have to do a lot of our own self-care in areas where others are not supporting us. Disabilities can make self-care almost insurmountable, to say nothing of caring for a household and loved ones.[5]

Chronic pain has introduced us to new and exciting mental labours to complete every day. First, we must constantly Ignore The Body's Desperate Alarm Signals: all the pain and dizziness and anxiety it produces as a result of illness. But we must also Stay Aware of those symptoms, so that we can Describe Them Accurately To Doctors and Notice If Something Concerning Happens.[6] It turns out that most abled people do not have to constantly micromanage their awareness of their body.

Visibly disabled people have to field countless undesired interactions with strangers about their disability. This can mean picking a spot on the train where people will see you less, cultivating your resting bitch face in an effort to Deter Complete Strangers and Other People You Don't Want to Talk To, and rehearsing your response if any of these people ask you invasive questions. It can mean wondering what you could change about your wheelchair or your service animal's uniform or about yourself that would get people to Leave You Alone.

Such tasks pile up endlessly. Even if you get through your day without a problem, you've had to expend a lot of effort on things abled people don't have to. That's less energy and willpower left over for deciding what to cook for dinner, when to shower, and how to rid your house of the demon you summoned to help with your Latin homework.

Disabilities can also come with entire new tasks that need to be managed. For the two of us, university requires not just study but a constant trade of emails about what support we're entitled to, how exactly it can be applied, and what paperwork we have to fill out. Every assessment comes with the added work of making sure our accommodations are applied correctly. There are doctors' appointments to be managed, triggers to track, prescriptions to fill. Actually Going Out seems nearly impossible: we have to know how long we'll be there, if there's seating available, if there's food we can eat, and if there are bathrooms nearby.

Brain fog, confusion, fatigue, forgetfulness, and indecisiveness can all be symptoms of the illnesses that made us disabled—but they could as easily be symptoms of a too-heavy mental load. We cannot pinpoint which forgotten appointments and misaddressed emails are the result of medical symptoms and which are the result of this mental burden; it all feels the same.

Getting Accommodations (Which Is Good and Easy)

Both authors have this year sought accommodations at our university. It's not a new experience to us, but changing degrees and changing disabilities bring exciting new elements to the process.

R has discovered that despite the university recognizing that migraines make her completely incompetent two to four times a week, she cannot reschedule exams without going to the doctor. Her doctor books appointments 2 weeks in advance, which her migraines sadly don't. The appointment involves waiting for 10 or 20 minutes in a waiting room (loud, bright rooms are the ideal place to be during a migraine) so she can tell her extremely busy doctor "I have a migraine." Her doctor writes this down on a piece of paper and gives it to R to give to the university—who already knows that R has migraines multiple times a week.

When R informed the university that this is a terrible system, she was told that they couldn't possibly use the information they already had to just give her extensions whenever she wanted. After all, R only experiences migraines *half* the time. It would be wholly unfair on the other students if R got an extension for her exam on a day when she wasn't experiencing a migraine, because obviously all the time spent in pain and wholly unable to absorb new information has put her at an unfair advantage.

E asked the university to make her degree and scholarship part-time, so that she was able to do them. The university is theoretically fine with this. They only require letters from E's two specialists and general practitioner. Both of those specialists cost $300 per appointment and have months-long waiting lists. The university then wanted to know E's entire medical history, failed treatments, current treatments, and side effects, presumably so they could sell her identity on the black market.[7]

For many people with chronic illnesses, accessing accommodations means sharing information about their family, their sex lives, their mental health. Maybe the university now knows that we were once suicidal, that we stopped taking Celexa because it made us unable to orgasm, that our father is adopted, that our grandparents have dementia, and that our entire family line has been cursed by a witch.

The powers that be insist this is a good, fair, and effective system. However, the preposterous difficulty of asking that our basic needs be met will likely be the end of our years-long relationship with this university—unless they decide to pursue arson charges against us.

Most disabled people go through this at some point. Society creates disabilities by failing to meet some people's needs, and then those people have to go through life asking for the failures to be corrected. The barriers to their participation are rarely removed because they're built into our material and immaterial culture on every level. They are instead expected to ask that the barrier be lowered each time they need to get past it and they are lucky if asking is ever easy.

Some disabled people apparently do not feel a constant screaming resentment about this situation. We're not sure what's going on in their lives that makes that the case. For us, a major part of this experience is managing the fury and despair it elicits. Hopefully it has made us funny, but funny doesn't pay for the therapy we need.

Telling jokes about our very real desire to do arson has, however, brought us to a community of other funny, furious disabled people. It's a strange blessing to be united with others by suffering, but the experience is very human.

Everything Is Hard

Things are hard for everyone, but they've become decidedly harder since our nerves became the favoured habitat for a herd of tiny goats, our feet were filled with bees, and our wrists were possessed by the ghost of Julius Caesar (who doesn't appreciate our talking shit about him). Our bodies are ecosystems that no longer want to function as bodies usually do.

As we've mentioned, people can be kind of weird about the fact that our bodies are a tiny haunted forest now, and they can go out of their way to make sure that experience is as bizarre and difficult as possible.

Probably the most disabling experience in the Everything Is Hard, We Would Simply Like to Lie Down category is that when we find simple accommodations to make things easier, abled people (including doctors) tell us to be ashamed of them. This includes using mobility devices, taking medication, and hiring a cleaner.

E has often expressed the desire to pay someone else A Lot Of Money to clean her house, because it is Decidedly Not Clean and she wants that to change. E has never liked cleaning, because E's brain is full of dust bunnies who don't want their habitats to be destroyed. More recently, E has discovered that the ghost of Julius (who is inhabiting her wrist) is strangely against the idea of having a clean bathroom sink. For E, cleaning is both emotionally distressing and detrimental to her physical well-being.

Apparently, wanting someone else to do this Extremely Difficult, Distressing, And Often Painful Task is classist. But house cleaning and maintenance is as much an accessibility issue as any other. Being able to prepare a meal is an accessibility issue, as is being able to shop for groceries or go out with friends. Many people who support accessibility in theory are opposed to the reality that people may need help to clean and maintain their homes, to prepare meals, or to go out with friends. Accessibility isn't intended for real people living their lives: it's intended for an idealized concept of disabled people.

Attempts to place the burden of justice on individuals rather than communities often hurt disabled people first. Everyone in a society depends on other people, but the way disabled people depend on others is seen as an innate moral failure. People believe this even when they're disabled themselves, and they go through their lives thinking they are failures when they just need accommodations no one's been willing to suggest or implement.

Many things have become more difficult for us during the progression of our illnesses, including physical and emotional self-care, having hobbies, making friends, maintaining relationships, going out, understanding our gender, having a sexuality, having sex, being queer, trying to engage with religion (especially Christianity), looking after our pets, talking to doctors, talking to abled people in general, and, of course, work.

These difficulties progress further than that. The ecosystems inside our bodies have decided that we can't eat the foods we love, that the medications that help our migraines will also make us horribly depressed, and that standing for more than 5 minutes may simply make us want to die. Existing in a mortal form is the hardest thing we've ever done, and we've both worked hospitality. What makes this even harder is being told that if we just worked harder, if we tried better, if we did more exercise or ate healthier food or if we were just better in general, then we could succeed in all of these things. Sometimes these things are just impossible without help. No amount of "bettering" ourselves will fix our problems if we're too burnt out, depressed, and disappointed in ourselves to actually live.

A lot of what society means by "disabled" is "unable to do the kind of work we expect them to do." It often feels like we can't Be A Person or Do Person Things. The fact is that society's definition of both of the above is prescriptive when it ought to be descriptive. There are many more people who can't cook, clean, drive, or work than our society's narrow definition of "personhood" or "adulthood" would suggest. No one deserves to have their lives devalued because they need help to walk, shower, or cut up their vegetables. Yet that's exactly what's happening, and people are dying because of it.

Conclusion

Disability is a thousand different experiences, and we've only covered five. The family resemblance theory of categorization proposes that a group doesn't have to be connected by one thing they all have in common. In a family resemblance, it's not one single feature everyone has that makes them look the same: it's the grey streak some of us have, the sticking-out ears others have, or cousins with the same blue eyes. Disability is the same way: we don't all have one experience in common. We have lots of experiences that we share with other people, who share other experiences with yet other people. These overlapping experiences extend throughout society, but there's a cluster of them we call disability.

These experiences are happening all the time. Someone might wake up unable to get out of bed, someone else might trip and break a leg. Someone might just be told to inject bleach into their veins to kill the demons in their blood.

We're writing this at the tail end of 2020, when many more people have and will become sick and disabled thanks to a virus and greedy politicians who value money over people. Many of these people will be brushed aside because they don't look sick, because doctors can't say why they stayed sick, or because this was all a hoax anyway.

But disability is always happening. It doesn't start in the doctor's office, and it doesn't start when you get a diagnosis stamped and sealed and sent off to your workplace or place of study. Disability happens before and around all of that. It happens from the moment your well-meaning uncle tells you to eat only pears, or a stranger asks for your entire medical history, or the day you wake up with Sudden and Persistent Knee Pain and the ghost of a tyrant in your wrist.

Disability happens.

Yours in chronic illness,
E. and R.

Discussion Questions

1.   What disabling experiences have you had? What made them disabling for you?
2.   How would you differentiate between a disabling experience and a difficult or unpleasant experience? How is the definition influenced by cultural norms?

Notes

1   As historians, this kind of development of cultural prejudices is very interesting to us. As disabled people, we're reminded that being on the receiving side of history sucks.
2   We are reminded of advice we once read for small talk: that when someone tells you what their job is, you can always respond with "That must be hard." Even puppy stylists have bad days.
3   We honestly don't know how we still have any blood left after this process.
4   It has been scientifically proven by Researchers Who Cannot Be Named that advice of this kind feeds the ghosts residing in your blood and encourages them to invite along more friends. House parties are much less fun when your body is the house.

5   Neither E nor R are required to provide daily care for other people, and it will not be our focus in this chapter. We recognize that many disabled people are also parents and carers.
6   We should point out that we still don't really know when something concerning is happening, because we were told for months that hardly being able to walk for pain is completely fine, but the transient arm pain we experienced upon taking migraine medication is Very Concerning. We are Understandably Confused by this.
7   E wrote this as a joke but is honestly questioning why the institution needs a copy of her driver's license, her medical history, and her mortal soul if not to steal her identity.

Reference

Daminger, A. (2019). The cognitive dimension of household labor. *American Sociological Review 84*(4), 609–633. https://journals.sagepub.com/doi/10.1177/0003122419859007

CHAPTER 2

Disabled Humans and Our Non-Human Animal Companions

Paul D. C. Bones

Pets, fur babies, animal companions, furry friends, whatever you choose to call them, non-human animals have a special relationship with disability. Although not all disabled people have animal companions, or even like animals, they often serve an integral function in our lives. Some disabilities include the use of service animals to help navigate an inaccessible world. Emotional support animals, while often ridiculed and exploited by non-disabled individuals, can help bring calm to otherwise stressful situations. For disabled people who are fully or partially homebound, animal companions provide socialization and love. After a year in which many disabled people were further cut off from society, due to the COVID-19 pandemic, the editors decided to acknowledge the cross-species bond by including photographs of disabled people's animal companions, along with a short description about how they make their lives better.

Each image comes with an image description. Although image descriptions are not common with physical media, we decided to use this opportunity to demonstrate inclusive accessibility. Image descriptions (also known as alt text) are short explanations of images, designed for screen readers. These are vital for blind and visually impaired individuals, and should be embedded in social media posts, course materials, and anywhere you share digital images. Keep in mind that image descriptions are intended to be short and descriptive, not as a place for hidden jokes.

Charlie

Aparna Nair

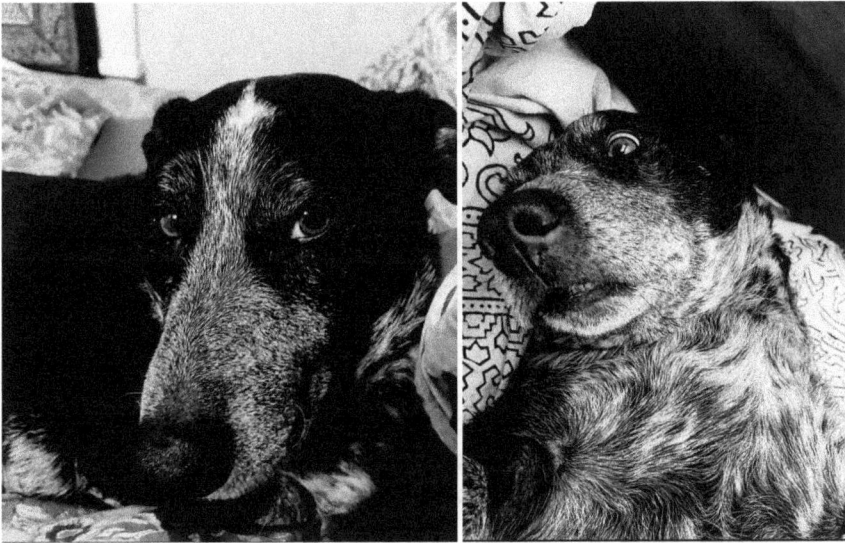

ID: A black and white dog looks expressively at the camera (left), and then shows his goofy side laying on his back (right).

• • •

Charlie was initially a rescue dog, but a year into his coming into my household, he started sensing my auras/seizures and warning me about them. It took me a while to realise what he was trying to tell me, and since then he has served as my seizure alert dog. (He has received additional training to ensure that he is safe to be in public spaces.) When I get close to an aura, he usually lets me know, and with him I have been able to better manage my epilepsy, which had become quite a problem at the time. More than that, he gives me the confidence and heart to leave my house after a seizure, which usually leaves me with some mild to severe agoraphobia. He's the most excellent boy.

CHAPTER 3

Disability Discourse Stuck in a Black/White Binary

Embodying a Black and Disabled Identity as a Mixed-Race Person

Cassandra Lovelock

Within social theory, questions of disability and disabled identity present themselves within debates such as structure versus agency or biology versus social dualism. Identity, however, is a complex concept to navigate, with the word being used across disciplines to signify different things. In this essay, the word *identity* is used in a reflexive sense—in terms of identifying oneself, which is about staking a claim to membership of a collective or a wider group—and in terms of what membership someone is pushed into based on their social and physical credibility. Foucault (1995) suggests we are made into subjects through surveillance and control operating through the state, through schools and other agencies, whereas we make ourselves into subjects through the processes of confession and communication, i.e., people "speaking the truth about themselves" (Taylor, 1984).

Building on Crenshaw's (1991) work, which defines intersectionality as a tool for understanding as opposed to a theory, this essay will discuss the invisibility of the mixed-race disabled experience in activism and academia. It will examine the disparity in social and physical credibility between Black and White disabled people, and how that credibility links to their capital, as well as discussing how this credibility and capital aids the formation of the Black and White disabled identity. Moving forward, this essay will echo Crenshaw's (1989) argument that Black women have multidimensional experiences of discrimination and oppression that a single axis of analysis cannot fully comprehend. It will argue that mixed-race disabled people's oppression cannot be fully understood within the current limits of disability activism and academia and cannot be accurately applied to our current theories and analyses of disabled or racial identity, thereby illustrating the need for a mixed-race-specific understanding of the intersections between disability and racial identity.

There is a significant body of literature illustrating that Black mixed-race people tend to be racialised to view themselves as Black people, experiencing similar social, health, and educational limitations as their Black counterparts (Song & Aspinall, 2012; Joseph-Salisbury, 2018). The majority of Black mixed-race people tend to identify as Black due to their close proximity to Black culture while growing up (Campion, 2019). However, there is little research into the experiences of Black mixed-race people who do not participate in, or feel rejected from, the collective Black identity. Especially for mixed-race people who have grown up in a white-dominant environment, which then influences our identity formation, it is an uncomfortable truth that we don't fit into Black culture. This is despite the fact that we potentially face higher rates of discrimination from multiple groups, including White people and people of colour (Brackett, Marcus, McKenzie, & Mullins, 2006).

Disabled identity, on the other hand, has received less attention in academic and activist spaces. Disabled identity is often defined by a loss of independence, being under the gaze of others, the need for employment, and shame within sex and sexuality (Gallagher, 1998; Galvin, 2005; Murphy, 1990). It appears reactive, being constantly co-created between the environment the disabled person finds themself in and their interactions with objects and people. It is less of a banner, as Blackness appears to be, and more of a fluctuating identity that changes depending on how disabling one's environment is (Paley, 2002).

Disclaimer: Throughout this essay, the term mixed-race will be used as the preferred label, instead of biracial, dual-heritage, or multiracial. This should be understood as a purely ascriptive label that has been chosen largely on the basis of the author's own ideological choice of self-identification (mixed-race Black Caribbean/British). However, I acknowledge that the label of mixed-race is becoming increasingly problematic and untenable. I will be using the term mixed-race in this essay exclusively to refer to Black mixed-race people. In terms of disability, the author is living with Hereditary Neuropathy with Liability to Pressure Palsies, Postural Tachycardia Syndrome, and Complex Post-Traumatic Stress Disorder. Where I am using the first person, it is to refer directly to my experience as a mixed-race disabled woman based in the UK.

Disability, Race, and Credibility

How a person conceptualises their identity is multifaceted, drawing on physical appearance, forms of oppression, dramaturgy (Goffman, 1956), stigma (Goffman, 1963), and interaction. Those with intersectional marginalised identities have learned to balance conflicting levels of social, cultural, and physical credibility and capital within themselves and different situations. Crenshaw (1991) states that people with several marginalised intersectional identities experience oppression on multiple socially situated axes that, although they often correlate, cannot be comprehended by people who are not members of that social group. For mixed-race disabled people, any understanding of our experiences is limited to a Black/White binary of how we currently understand disability; this is a conundrum, as we experience being racialised and disabled differently.

Social Credibility and Identity

Within disabled identity theory, social and physical credibility are intrinsically tied to the disabled person's capital and subsequently their identity and sense of self. Credibility and capital are terms used within social theory and are inherently linked to a person's perception of their own identity and societies' perception of the person. In this essay, the term *credibility* is loosely based on the concept of social acceptability as defined by Goffman (1963), who stated that social acceptability is parallel to stigma, with stigma being the situation of the individual who is disqualified from full social acceptance (1963). *Capital*, on the other hand, is used in the classic sociological sense—as defined by Bourdieu and Passeron (1977), capital is made up of economic capital, i.e., the command of economic resources, and social capital, i.e., the actual and potential resources linked to the possession of a durable network (p. 56).

The association between social credibility and disabled identity lies within stigma and social acceptability. Prior to becoming disabled, certain privileges and status are taken for granted; in much the same way that "Whiteness" is an invisible insignia of the norm, "able-bodied/non-disabled" is also the unquestioned, unremarked-upon state, which only becomes notable when the individual deviates from it (Thomson, Rosemary, & Garland, 1997). Where someone's identity is the assumed norm, they possess more social credibility and have a more broadly accepted status in wider society. More social credibility leads to better social capital—a type of capital gained by having a wealth of social connections and networks (Bourdieu, 1984).

White disabled people, due to having a "norm identity," possess more social credibility than Black disabled people with the same disability/symptomatology. As they are viewed as more socially acceptable, their reports, treatments, and experiences of illness and disability are treated as more severe (Whitson et al., 2011) compared to the experiences reported by Black disabled people. A White person's experience of existing in and navigating a disabled body will differ from a Black person's due to the social credibility that Whiteness grants them. For example, discrimination often leads to Black disabled people being excluded from any meaningful social opportunities (Harley et al., 2015). Furthermore, Black disabled people experience significant amounts of medical racism, leading to poorer treatment and worse health outcomes (Paradies, 2006). This point is not aiming to minimise the experiences of white disabled people who struggle within various systems, but rather to illustrate that the privilege that comes with their whiteness remains very much intact in the way that it influences those experiences and grants them more social credibility.

Further evidence that White disabled people experience less oppression than their Black counterparts can be found in the areas of activism and academia. Historically, disability activism and academia have been dominated by Whiteness; by disabled people who "become" disabled, as opposed to those born disabled (Bell, 2017). This may be partly because the loss of the privileges previously afforded by a norm identity is driving study and success in academia. For Black disabled people, this process of losing privileges and credibility can often be subtle. As they are already accustomed to holding inferior positions in society due to their racial or ethnic identity, it can take longer for them to recognise that they are experiencing further oppression as a result of their disability. This hinders the formation of the Black disabled identity and makes it the sole responsibility of the individual psyche.

Although the loss of one's comparatively privileged position may be very sudden and momentous, depending on the particular nature of the accident, illness, or injury, the overall arrival at a new level of identification is a gradual process, whereby the doubts from within, the stares and snubs from without, and the lack of access to previously available social locations and resources erode one's prior claim to social acceptability. In sum, White disabled people possess more social capital compared to Black disabled people, and their Whiteness influences their experience of being disabled as they possess one socially "normal" identity trait.

Physical Credibility and Identity

The body as the site of disabilities is often excluded from narratives about disability—particularly in the Social Model of disability—which repeatedly neglects the role of the body in being disabling (Hughes, 2000; Patterson & Hughes, 2000). A disabled person's body is always stigmatised, with limited physical capital and credibility—the term *physical capital* in this instance is taken from the work of Bourdieu (1990) and refers to the body itself as a form of physical capital—with the capacity to accumulate various "resources" and convert them into economic, cultural, emotional, and/or social capital. When a disabled person is unable to work, whether due to disability or lack of adaptations, their physical capital is limited as their body is unable to produce. Often, disabled people struggle to recognise themselves in this linear understanding of the values and uses of the body (Loja, Costa, Hughes, & Menezes, 2013). In this context, I am defining physical credibility as the extent to which the physicality of the person is oppressed or limited by society.

The capacity of disabled people to generate physical capital is limited by our ability, and that of societies, to adapt to our needs, along with our own physical credibility. I have identified some examples below:

1.   Visibly disabled people's bodily signals are often unique, deviating from the norm to expose something unusual, imperfect, and negative about their moral status. The stigma of bodily difference is interpreted as a moral deficit (Goffman, 1963), resulting in a reduction in physical credibility and, subsequently, a reduction in capital.
2.   Physical barriers often constrain work performance and social relationships, leading to a perception of weaker professional competence and economic capital, while architectural barriers also limit a disabled person's capacity to have physical capital—the classic example would be ramps for a wheelchair user.
3.   Architectural barriers also undermine social credibility. For example, when social or public spaces are made inaccessible, it

limits disabled people's capacity to forge and maintain social relationships.

4. The difficulties encountered in accumulating capital and sustaining credibility, which respondents refer to above, impact negatively on disabled people's desire to venture into public space. It is not just architectural barriers that present a form of confinement, but also the recognition of the inhospitality of public space. In public, disabled people are regarded as "unable," incapable of being "active doers." In the ableist or non-disabled imagination, disabled people are a dilemma of negotiation, reorganization, and reconfiguration of social relations (Papadimitriou, 2008).

Navigating These Issues as a Mixed-Race Person

Whether it is recognised or not: when you're mixed-race, people privilege one ethnicity over the others. Our ethnic identities are ranked as a matter for debate—often, we are seen as "too much" or "not enough" of one identity (Thomson, 2008), with one specific ethnic identity being valued more highly than others. With "Blackness" being increasingly gatekept to prevent Black mixed-race people from entering Black spaces—either physically or socially (Campion, 2019)—and micropolitics and anti-Blackness ensuring we are less welcome in white spaces for being "Black," we find ourselves caught in between.

As Black mixed-race people, we possess more social credibility than our Black counterparts, as we do not experience racism in the same way nor to the same extent. Given the extent to which we benefit from colourism, we are often viewed as weaponising our "privileged" ethnic identity to gain more credibility in different situations (Campion, 2019). Our markers of oppression make us the ideal candidates for "positive discrimination:" we are Black but not "too Black," or disabled but not "just" disabled. In order to successfully embody a mixed-race disabled identity, we find ourselves:

1. Moving within Black and White communities and disabled communities simultaneously.

2. Code-switching according to the social context—adapting a Whiter or Blacker demeanour depending on dramaturgy; a concept used in micro-sociology to describe changes in behaviour during human interactions attributed to time, place, and audience.

3.   Figuring out a monoracial identity while making journeys into
      each community as and when it's necessary.

Being a mixed-race disabled person primarily means figuring out
how to navigate our own value in systems that tie our worth to
our own credibility, whilst experiencing rejection from whichever
community we attempt to enter. Often, we feel forced into accepting
our minority ethnic identity to ensure the continuation of the
monoracial system we live in (Gillem & Thompson, 2004). But this
acceptance comes with struggle. Mixed-race disabled people cannot
"claim" the same oppression as the Black disabled community. We
are prone to experiencing identity invalidation (Edwards, 2008); our
identity is questioned and we experience rejection from both white
and Black communities, and this racialised experience also bleeds into
our disabled experience.

A Mixed-Race Disabled Identity

There is no one community for mixed-race disabled people to inhabit.
Instead, we exist on the fringes of multiple activist and academic
communities. There is no established mixed-race disabled identity;
instead, we typically see racialised mixed-race people identifying as
Black or non-racialised mixed-race people identifying as disabled,
something I still grapple with frequently.

When discussing disabled or racialised identities, an essentialist
model is commonly adopted. Master Identity Theory (Scott &
Hoonardm, 2016), sometimes known as master status, suggests
that there is one dominant "status" or characteristic about a person
that "has exceptional importance for social identity, often shaping a
person's entire life" (Macionis & Gerber, 2011, p. 141). A master identity
is something that can be achieved, such as becoming a parent or
making a career choice, or something that is ascribed, such as race,
sexual orientation, or disability. Norm identity traits rarely constitute
a person's master identity; people do not consider "whiteness," "able-
bodiedness," or "heterosexuality" as part of their identities, whereas
being "Black," "disabled," or "homosexual" can figure largely into
one's perception of self. However, assuming that one characteristic
of a person such as race or ethnicity determines their experiences

and life chances inexplicably ties that person's identity and future trajectory to that group. For example, disabled essentialism would view a person's disability as the paramount feature of their identity, and therefore as having the most significant effect on their future trajectory.

Navigating this as a mixed-race disabled person is tricky. A mixed-race identity is messy, changeable, and often negotiated for personal gain or loss (Campion, 2019). As reported by Franco, Katz, and O'Brien (2016), mixed-race people experience rejection from Black identities when our phenotype does not match our racial identity, when our behaviours do not match racial stereotypes, and when our ancestral heritage does not match our personal racial identity. Therefore, while we often feel forced to adopt a Black identity by wider societal pressures, it is common to feel like an outsider.

Similarly, adopting disability as our master status is a trial. There are few Black disabled activists and academics who embody both identities in their totality, as the majority of Black disabled people tend to embody their Black identity before any other (Aspinall & Song, 2013). Disability movements tend to be dominated by white (passing) people who can easily fit into the already perceived narrative of disability and whose experiences are difficult to relate to as a mixed-race person. With nobody to speak for our experience, mixed-race disabled people are often left at the fringes of activism and academia.

Experiencing rejection from activist spaces is isolating. Despite being a discipline and social space that prides itself on being accepting, activist spaces are often thorny and difficult to navigate for people who do not "entirely" fit the criteria that the space was set up for. These marginalised communities cannot score privileges against one another and yet we often find them trying to do so. For example, within disabled spaces, white disabled people sometimes feel exempt from conversations about whiteness and disability, as though their disability negates their white privilege. Experiences of ableism are not the same as experiences of racism, or vice versa, and yet they are often implicitly pitted against each other.

For mixed-race disabled people, therefore, a decision has to be made. What is your master status? It is often obvious to people what their master status is; for mixed-race disabled people, the master status seems to be caught in limbo between Black and Blackness or disability. Do I attempt to embody a Black identity in a culture that has rejected me or a disabled identity in a space where no one shares my experiences?

Conclusions

The aim of this essay is not to criticise, belittle, or invalidate Black or White disabled activists and scholars. It is not to force competition between different types of oppression nor to discredit the struggles of any one group. Being White and disabled doesn't equate to being Black and non-disabled; these experiences aren't comparable and it is toxic to keep forcing comparisons between them. This essay is merely to illustrate that non-racialised mixed-race people are unable to fully relate to White or Black disability academia and activism and to suggest that the mixed-race disabled experience requires its own axis of understanding. In the same way that socioeconomic influences cannot be ignored in disability discourse, neither can the racialised experiences of mixed-race disabled people.

Navigating the line between disability and race as a mixed-race disabled person is complex and often lonely. Having to choose between a racialised or disabled identity, as we are often forced to do, can put us in a difficult ethical position. Our social and physical credibility is higher than our Black counterparts but lower than our White ones. In white spaces, we are uncomfortably tokenised, lauded as a sign of progress, or the "ending of racism" simply by virtue of being mixed-race (Campion, 2019) without any real space being made for our experience. While in Black spaces, we often fear rejection. We need to stop feeling obliged to choose which identity trait "fits" us best; we need a space where we can simply be. Because the truth is, mixed-race people are constantly told to "stay in our lane," but I am yet to find a lane that accepts us in our entirety.

Discussion Questions

1.   How does disability relate to race? How does race relate to disability activism?
2.   Where do mixed-race people fit into disability studies?

3. The Black Panther Party was very supportive of disability rights and the disability rights movement, in large part due to the work of Brad Lomax. Using the internet, search for Brad Lomax and the San Francisco 504 sit-in.
4. Although there are no official statistics on this, it is believed that between 25% and 50% of African Americans fatally shot by police in America are disabled. How is racial violence also a disability issue?

References

Aspinall, P., & Song, M. (2013). Mixed race identities. *The Kelvingrove Review, 13*, 218–223.

Bell, C. (2017). Is disability studies actually *white* disability studies? In J. Davis (Ed.), *The disability studies reader* (5th ed.). Routledge.

Bourdieu, P. (1984). *Distinction: A social critique of the judgement of taste.* Routledge & Kegan Paul.

Bourdieu, P. (1986). The forms of capital. In J. Richardson (Ed.), *Handbook of theory and research for the sociology of education.* Greenwood.

Bourdieu, P., & Passeron, J. C. (1977). *Reproduction in education, society and culture* (R. Nice, Trans.). Sage.

Brackett, K., Marcus, A., McKenzie, N., & Mullins, L. (2006). The effects of multiracial identification on students' perceptions of racism. *The Social Science Journal, 43*(3), 437–444.

Campion, K. (2019). "You think you're Black?" Exploring Black mixed-race experiences of Black rejection. *Ethnic and Racial Studies, 42*, 16.

Crenshaw, K. (1989). Demarginalizing the intersection of race and sex: A black feminist critique of anti-discrimination doctrine, feminist theory and anti-racist politics. *University of Chicago Legal Forum, 1*(8).

Crenshaw, K. (1991). Mapping the margins: Intersectionality, identity politics, and violence against women of colour. *Stanford Law Review, 43*(6), 1241–1299.

Edwards, L. (2008). Working with multiracial clients in therapy: Bridging theory, research, and practice. *Professional Psychology: Research and Practice, 39*, 192–201.

Foucault, M. (1995). *Discipline and punishment: The birth of the prison.* Vintage Books.

Franco, M. G., Katz, R., & O'Brien, K. M. (2016). Forbidden identities: A qualitative examination of racial identity invalidation for black/white biracial individuals. *International Journal of Intercultural Relations, 50,* 96–109.

Gallager, D. J. (1998). The scientific knowledge base of special education: Do we know what we think we know? *Exceptional Children, 64*(4), 493–502.

Galvin, R. D. (2005). Researching the disabled identity: Contextualizations of the identity transformation which accompany the onset of impairment. *Sociology of Health and Illness, 27*(3), 393–413.

Gillem, A. R., & Thompson, C. A. (2004). Introduction: Biracial women in therapy: Between the rock of gender and the hard place of race. *Women & Therapy, 27,* 1–18.

Goffman, E. (1956). *The presentation of self in the everyday.* Doubleday.

Goffman, E. (1963). *Stigma: Notes on the management of spoiled identity.* Preface.

Harley, D. A., Mpofu, E., Scanlan, J., Umeasiegbu, V. I., & Mpofu, N. (2015). Disability social inclusion and community health. In E. Mpofu (Ed.), *Community-oriented health services: Practices across disciplines.* Springer Publishing Company.

Joseph-Salisbury, R. (2018). *Black mixed-race men: Hybridity, transatlanticity and "post-racial" resilience.* Emerald Group.

Loja, E., Costa, M., Hughes, B., & Menezes, I. (2013). Disability, embodiment and ableism: Stories of resistance. *Disability & Society, 28*(2), 190–203.

Macionis, J., & Gerber, L. (2011). *Sociology (Seventh Canadian edition with MySocLab)* (7th ed.). Pearson Education Canada.

Murphy, R. (1990). *The body silent: An anthropologist embarks on the most challenging journey of his life: Into the life of the disabled.* W.W. Norton.

Paley, J. (2002). The Cartesian melodrama in nursing. *Nursing Philosophy, 3*(3), 189–192.

Papadimitriou, C. (2008). Becoming en-wheeled: The situated accomplishment of re-embodiment as a wheelchair user after spinal cord injury. *Disability & Society, 23*(7).

Paradies, Y. (2006). A systematic review of empirical research on self-reported racism and health. *International Journal of Epidemiology, 35*(4), 888–901.

Rockquemore, K. A., & Brunsma, D. L. (2004). Beyond Black? The reflexivity of appearance in racial identification among Black/White biracials. In C. Herring, V. Keith, & H. Horton (Eds.), *Skin deep: How race and complexion matter in the 'color blind' era* (pp. 99–127). University of Illinois Press.

Scott, L., & Hoonardm, D. (2016). The origins and evolution of Everett Hughes's concept: 'Master status.' In *The anthem companion to Everett Hughes.* Anthem Press.

Song, M., & Aspinall, P. (2012). Is racial mismatch a problem for young 'mixed race' people in Britain? The findings of qualitative research. *Ethnicities, 12*(6), 730–753.

Taylor, C. (1984). Foucault on freedom and truth. *Political Theory, 12*(2), 152–183.

Thomson, R. G. (2017). *Extraordinary bodies: Figuring physical disability in American culture and literature*. Columbia University Press.

Whitson, H., Hasting, N., Landerman, L., Fillenbaun, G., Cohen, H., & Johnson, K. (2011). Black-White disparity in disability: The role of medical conditions. *Journal of the American Geriatrics Society, 59*(5).

CHAPTER 4

Plum Tomato

Solanum lycopersicum

Ellen Samuels

Your body should be mute
as this globed fruit
in a hollow of leaves
heavy and red.

What you wish
sometimes
when the night draws deep
is for someone else
to be able to hear you.

What you wish sometimes
is for anyone else
to lay a hand
across your back and feel
its thrumming.

It is either pain
or the absence of pain
that defines you. You forget
sometimes how to
tell the difference
between stem and root.

Your body should be
a part
of the world, or
the world should be a part
of your body. You forget

sometimes how to tell
the difference
between pulp and skin.
Both over so soon,
so sweet.

Discussion Questions

1. How does pain shape our interactions with others? With
    ourselves?
2. How can one still love their body when it causes them pain?

CHAPTER 5

Disability Aesthetics
A Crip Artistry Manifesto

Aurora Berger

Aesthetic:
Adjective: concerned with beauty or the appreciation of beauty
Noun: a set of principles underlying and guiding the work
of a particular artist or artistic movement (Oxford Learner's
Dictionary)

I grew up nearsighted, eyes focused within a few inches of my face. The perfect distance for reading. I had dislocated lenses (which glasses don't fix), so at a young age I fell in love with cameras. I used them like binoculars to help me see what my own eyes could not. I loved that a photograph could be printed out, lifted into focus, and show me things that I had experienced in person but had never been able to see clearly. Today, my camera still operates as an extension of my visual field, one that can be adjusted and manipulated, focusing for me when my own eyes do not.

I love the form of the human body, the softness of the skin and the fragility of the bones. Inspired by the works of artists like Francesca Woodman and Robert Mapplethorpe, I began to photograph my own body. It took years for me to begin to break through the ableism that I had internalized, to begin feeling at home in my body. Seeing my body in photographs, in the same plane as the rest of my world, enabled me to see it for what it was, disabled, but thriving.

My work is an expansive self-portrait. Sometimes literally—photographs of my body—documentations of my life. Others build on environmental cues that place the viewer in my position through fragmented imagery and visual confrontation. Together these photographs tell my story from my own perspective. My work is an investigation of capacity, normalcy, disability, agency, visual acuity, and interpretation.

When I had surgery on both eyes at 18, I gained distance vision in my left eye, creating a new dichotomy of space. My eyes are set—programmed in a cyborgian sense—to focus at two completely different distances. Left eye 15 feet, right eye 2. Everything else is guesswork.

•••

Here's the thing: a visually impaired photographer makes for good inspiration porn, and even though I didn't know that was what was happening, I knew it felt icky. Every time that my vision was brought up in relation to my art, I would try to laugh it off as inconsequential or irrelevant. But, as many disabled people know, I was wrong. My disability is important—it changes the way I work, think, and exist. I had pushed away my disability for so long, ignored it and dismissed it, and for the first time I began to wonder if I should try to give myself a little bit more credit.

Inspiration porn is a term that was coined by Stella Young in 2012. Young wrote, "Inspiration porn is an image of a person with a disability, often a kid, doing something completely ordinary—like playing, or talking, or running, or drawing a picture, or hitting a tennis ball—carrying a caption like 'your excuse is invalid' or 'before you quit, try'" (2012, para. 5). To expand on Young's definition, inspiration porn is any state of holding up a disabled person as what Rosemary Garland-Thompson called *wondrous* or *sentimental* (2002, pp. 59–65). *Hey, this photographer is blind and she won an award.* Young continues:

> Inspiration porn shames people with disabilities. It says that if we fail to be happy, to smile and to live lives that make those around us feel good, it's because we're not trying hard enough. Our attitude is just not positive enough. It's our fault. Not to mention what it means for people whose disabilities are not visible, like people with chronic or mental illness, who often battle the assumption that it's *all* about attitude. And we're not allowed to be angry and upset, because then we'd be "bad" disabled people. We wouldn't be doing our very best to "overcome" our disabilities. (2002 para. 25)

I have an invisible disability. At the moment the only visible signifier of my disability is a pair of bifocal glasses. Eyeglasses also happen to be the only form of adaptive technology that has ever been "normalized" into mainstream fashion and culture. This normalization then continues to render my disability as invisible. I live my life under the pretense of being able-bodied. It's an illusion, one that is created by an ableist model that requires a normative body in order to succeed. I grew up socially conditioned to see my own body as failing. Invisible illnesses bring their own sets of stigmas and complications, within able-bodied and disabled communities alike. This is not an endorsement of the Social Model of disability—which situates disability as a construct of society—but rather a statement of my reality. I personally struggle with the Social Model's refusal to acknowledge the lived experience of having a disability, the experience of feeling pain, the physical existence of being disabled.

•••

In the medicalized world, my body is broken and must be fixed. Mainstream culture teaches people with disabilities that our success is intrinsically tied to rejecting our bodies. In order to succeed we must "overcome" our own existence. The medical process is one of surrendering control. It breaks you down into a summation of parts, fragmenting your body and your identity. Every intervention brings new negatives with it, but these are quickly minimized, and favored for the positives in the quest for a "cure." Disability positions the body as a passive object, a problem that must be solved. Being disabled, being sick, I've spent a lot of time in doctor's offices. I'm beginning to collect the ephemera and charts that these visits generate and work with them in my art. I love that these documents and images are a medical portrait of my disabled body, one that contrasts sharply with the normal, abled person that society believes I am.

   I'm thinking about the way that W. E. B. Du Bois wrote of a "double consciousness" when speaking of race. I feel that something similar can be used to examine the double lives that many disabled people lead. As a marginalized group, we are imbued with a "second sight" that allows us to see ourselves within the socially constructed ideology of the disabled (1897, para. 3). We see ourselves through the eyes of others, and we feel ashamed. This socializing of disability is fascinating to me.

   Crip culture has grown from this dichotomy and actively works to change public perceptions and reclaim disabled identities. It feels important to me here to clarify what I mean when I write crip. Carrie Sandahl explains, "The term cripple, like queer, is fluid and

ever-changing, claimed by those whom it did not originally define...
The term crip has expanded to include not only those with physical
impairments but those with sensory or mental impairments as well"
(2003, p. 27). While there are some who feel that the term crip should
be restricted to those with physical impairments, I use it in this essay
to mean disabled bodyminds with a wide range of disabilities, as
Sandahl suggests.

•••

We all have our own versions of what disability looks like. These
images come from popular media and people we know. Disability
looks like Jillian Mercado at New York Fashion Week and Selma Blair
at the Oscars. It's *One Flew Over the Cuckoo's Nest* and the *Fault
in Our Stars*. For me, disability looks like long blurry walks in the
woods. It looks like Lucio Fontana's slashes and Tracey Emin's bed.
It looks like Bob Flannigan hanging from the ceiling above a hospital
bed and Viktoria Modesta's glowing prosthetic leg. It looks like the
Venus de Milo and her forgotten arms; it looks like hospital visits and
disheveled beds and abstract Crip joy. It looks like friendship. Scars.
Soft curves. Hard edges. It looks like my bed.

My point is, no aesthetic ideal is singular. My visual understanding
of disability will always be unique to my experience. I am a disabled
artist, so I see disability in art even when it was not intended.
Wandering through an art book fair with another disabled friend,
we find disability aesthetics in places they were never meant to
be: a book on the design history of chairs called *Be Seated*, a book
about cognition titled *Blind Faith*. This essay is not intended to be a
directive; this is not the definitive way of understanding Disability
Aesthetics, but rather a personal manifesto of how I view art,
disability, and the world around me. To that end, I have developed a
list of guidelines for disability art and aesthetics.

Guidelines for Disability Aesthetics:
- Work does not need to be visual.
- Work does not need to be aesthetic.
- Work does not need to be made by a disabled artist, but must
  be informed by, or in reference to, the lived experience of being
  disabled (not a secondhand experience, i.e., a caregiver or family
  member to a disabled person).

- Not all art by disabled artists is disability art.
- Not all art that relates to disability is disability art.
- Disability art is underpinned by the experiences of being disabled.

I struggle with this word *aesthetic* because I don't know how to make it fit the Disability Art that I know and love. Disability is intrinsically beautiful, but beauty is not a tenet of disability art. Disability Art transgresses beauty; it is bigger, more complicated than that. Disability Art grows from a lineage of ugly laws, physiognomy, the very basis of the medical system, remnants reminding us that beauty is not a sociological framework for disability.

This is not to say that disability cannot be aesthetic, only that beauty is not intrinsic to Disability Art. Disability aesthetics can be downright ugly. I frequently think of the work of Otto Dix for example: Dix's paintings interrogate the disabilities of World War I veterans. His work often features men with disfigured faces (*Skin Graft, Transplantation*, 1924). His paintings may not be pretty, but they are realistic. Do these works not demonstrate an ugly aesthetic of disability?

These aesthetic ideas can be further complicated. Ugly, vulgar, violent, repulsive. Words that have been used to describe disabled bodies for centuries. This language requires us to ask: Whose bodies are legitimate? Whose bodies are triggering?

This is an aesthetic that is constantly evolving, and resists being pinned down. Disability itself is an experience that is constantly changing, socially, medically, and artistically. In 1937 Joseph Goebbels, the Nazi minister of propaganda, ordered the creation of an art show titled *Entartete Kunst* (Degenerate Art). This exhibition was to be a contrast to the Aryan curatorial masterpiece, The Great German Art Exhibition (*Große Deutsche Kunstausstellung*). The Degenerate Art collection comprised more than 16,000 works that the Nazi party deemed "degenerate," that is modern art, as well as any work depicting bodies that betrayed the Aryan ideal (disabled, people of color, different body types, and of course, Jewish). Reality is, in curating this show, Goebbels created his own aesthetic ideal of disability.

It feels intrinsically wrong to credit Goebbels with doing anything remotely worth valuing (and mind you, his aesthetic was a distinctly problematic one), but as a disabled Jew, I know that power is often born of trauma. This is one of those cases. In the catalog for *Entartete Kunst* the works containing disabled bodies were described as a "spiritual or racial idea envisioned by 'modern' art...the idiot, the cretin, and the cripple." The pamphlet goes on to read: "Where these 'artists' have depicted themselves or each other, they have always chosen to portray themselves with cretin-like faces and figures" (Kaiser, 2012, p. 56). This collection of art is what I like to call Disability Art. Capital D, capital A. I use this capitalization of the term as a signifier of disability art that was always supposed to be disability art. Work that was made, as the *Entartete Kunst* collection was, with disability as a central tenet of its creation.

•••

I wonder how an artist or a work of art can become part of the canon, who decides what will become history and what will float away. But I also believe that canons are not stagnant, that they can evolve and change as society does. The canon of disability art is not based on the works of disabled artists. It has grown from a lineage of disabled bodies and disability aesthetics. The aesthetics of pain, of disfigurement, of caregiving. The aesthetics of difference, access, and community. The aesthetics of change. Disability aesthetics are built from a multitude of visuals and languages.

Disability and art are so deeply intertwined for me that I can't separate them. Art history, cultural history, personal history, all twist together and bind into a single trajectory that leads through the shadows of disabled history to the artist that I have become. I'm not interested in the common narratives of disability in art: the stories of overcoming, the tortured artists isolated by their illnesses. These stories are flat, one-dimensional clichés. The story that I want to tell is my own, one of reckoning with mortality. I approach my work with a sense of morbid optimism. Life is short; make art about the things that you care about.

I feel that a facet of my role as a disabled artist and writer is to bridge the divide between the private disabled spaces that I inhabit and the public spaces that I share with other people. As an artist I do this by creating documentation of these private moments, forging insight, a visual guide to navigating my experience. My practice is always, foremost, about creating the work that I need. Some days it is a need for expression, a visual answer to a question that has worked its way into that part of my brain that I can't ignore and desperately seeks a formal solution. Other days my work is a form of therapy, the act of photographing, allowing me to work out my own thought processes. Much of this work will never see the light of day and that is okay. My work has never been about production, just processing. My photographs are, for me, a method of self-forgiveness.

As a photographer I am immersed in the visible. As an invisibly disabled artist I am constantly searching for the edges of that vision. Frida Kahlo painted her pain, depicting her spine as a shattered Ionic column, ripping her heart from her own chest for all to see. Bound to the existing visible world, I work in a quieter manner. I cannot rip out my own heart, as much as I might like to some days, so I use medical imaging—X-rays, MRIs, sonograms, EKGs. These images are a new kind of self-portrait. One without the sentimentality of a photographer and editor. One where I literally lay myself bare. Stories about my life in a language I cannot understand. A scientific exploration of the fragility and power of the human body.

•••

I am fascinated by the idea that the disabled body is somehow incomplete, somehow less than human. I like that tearing my printed photographs instantly connotes a traumatic experience, jagged white lines against dark paper. I began doing this in my studio out of frustration. I desperately sought perfection and I tore the work that did not meet my own high standards. It was only when I saw the torn pieces on my floor that I began to understand the power that they hold. In one finished piece, my own naked body mimics the twisted torso of the Venus de Milo. The print has been torn diagonally from left thigh to right ribcage, acknowledging the interior break and the history of disability in my work. The Venus is often praised for being the "epitome of graceful female beauty." There is no question of whether her long lost arms make her any less complete.

Linda Nochlin describes fragmentation as "a loss of wholeness, a shattering of connection, a destruction or disintegration of permanent value" (2001, pp. 23–24). She was speaking of modern art, but her analysis is spot on in a different regard: the medical industrial complex does these exact things to disabled bodies, breaking us down and devaluing us. Disability art flips (and crips) this definition, asking why a body must be whole to have value, why fragmentation must mean a severing of connection. Perhaps the most well-known example of this is Frida Kahlo, painting her own fragments into reality. In pieces like *Henry Ford Hospital* (1932) or *The Two Fridas* (1939), she takes her internal physical pain and renders it into a visual realm. Marta Zarzycka writes, "By performing a dissection of the live body, by pulling internal organs, bones and veins outside, Kahlo became a fragmented assemblage of parts and their malfunctions" (2006, p. 81). This fragmentation mirrors our lived crip experiences, Zarzycka notes, because "pain in Western medical science often invites fragmentation: the body is dissolved into the representation of its parts, one or more of them hurting. Only when these parts hurt do we recognise their autonomy and separateness as heart, liver, kidneys or stomach" (2006, p. 81).

This fascination with fragmentation has led me to new territories. I am interested in the materiality of photographs. The files, the raw data, offer endless potential for manipulation. As with the torn prints, I also work with transforming the image through different media. I print the photographs on plastic and fabric, I hide them from view behind translucent curtains; I project them through space. I take the digital negatives and make cyanotypes from them, letting the material dictate the final product. I love the way that Sally Mann lets the chemicals on her wet-plate collodion negatives infiltrate her images, and I do the same with my cyanotypes. I destroy things and I let nature do the same.

In one of my most expansive projects, I created a durational work of art in the forest surrounding my childhood home in Vermont. At the beginning of summer, I placed black and white fabric prints of my body in the forest, and documented over the next few months as they slowly disintegrated. I feel most comfortable in this place: barefoot, muddy, scratched, and raw. I know the way that the rocks shift beneath my weight, the strength of the tree roots I used to climb. I know which plants are poisonous and under what conditions. I know the feeling of the air before a storm. Being disabled usually negatively affects the way that I negotiate space, but in this place where I first learned how to walk and how to see, many of those barriers vanish. As the summer ended, I retrieved my photographs from the trees and streams where they had become embedded. I had watched them as they changed from pristine blacks and whites to faded browns and greys. Edges frayed and coated in pine sap, the work finally felt whole.

To me these works are about the restoration of body and place. My body can never be restored, only conserved. To quote Eli Clare,

"[Cure] grounds itself in an original state of being, relying on the belief that what existed before is superior to what exists currently...but for some of us, even if we accept disability as damage to individual body-minds, these tenets quickly become tangled, because an original non-disabled state of being doesn't exist" (2017, p. 15). These photographs represent more than their physical forms. They are wind-battered and torn, but they are still me.

Disability art, crip artistry, disability aesthetics...these ideas haunt me. They hover around me like ghosts, begging for their problems to be resolved. But the deeper I fall down the black hole of theory, of questioning, the more entangled I become. The reality that I am just beginning to accept is that perhaps I have no solutions, that perhaps there are none to be found. This is the gift and the curse of a constantly evolving culture and language, that there is no right answer. For now this is the best that I can do and perhaps, for this disabled body-mind, that can finally be enough.

Discussion Questions

1. What does "disability aesthetics" mean to you?
2. How do you personally define the idea of disability art?
3. Do the terms "disability art" and "crip art" mean different things to you?
4. Practice making some alt-text image descriptions. What words do you think are vital to understanding the image? What words are not?

References

Clare, E. (2017). *Brilliant imperfection: Grappling with cure*. Duke University Press.

Du Bois, W. E. B. (1897, August). Strivings of the Negro People. *The Atlantic*. https://www.theatlantic.com/magazine/archive/1897/08/strivings-of-the-negro-people/305446/

Garland-Thompson, R. (2002). The politics of staring: Visual rhetorics of disability in popular photography. In S. L. Snyder, R. Garland-Thomson, B. J. Brueggemann, & Modern Language Association of America (Eds.),

Disability studies: Enabling the humanities. Modern Language Association of America.

Kaiser, F. (2012). *Degenerate art: The exhibition catalogue guide in German and English*. Ostara Publications.

Nochlin, L. (2001). *The body in pieces: The fragment as a metaphor of modernity*. Thames & Hudson.

Oxford Learner's Dictionary. (n.d.). Aesthetics. www.oxfordlearnersdictionaries.com/us/definition/english/aesthetic_1

Sandahl, C. (2003). Queering the crip or cripping the queer? Intersections of queer and crip identities in solo autobiographical performance. *GLQ: A Journal of Lesbian and Gay Studies, 9*(1–2), 25–56. https://doi.org/10.1215/10642684-9-1-2-25

Young, S. (2012, July 2). *We're not here for your inspiration*. Ramp Up. https://www.abc.net.au/rampup/articles/2012/07/02/3537035.htm

Zarzycka, M. (2006). Now I live on a painful planet. *Third Text, 20*(1), 73–84. doi:10.1080/09528820500472555

CHAPTER 6

Life on the Line

Aurora Berger

ID: A nude woman sits with her arms crossed over her body against a black background. Only part of her face and body are visible.

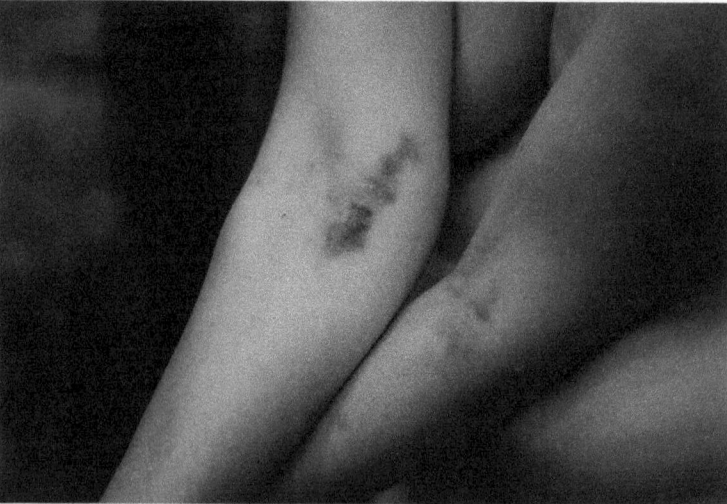

ID: A nude woman's arms and torso. Her arms are turned up, showing bruises in the creases of her arms.

© AURORA BERGER, 2022 | DOI:10.1163/9789004512702_008

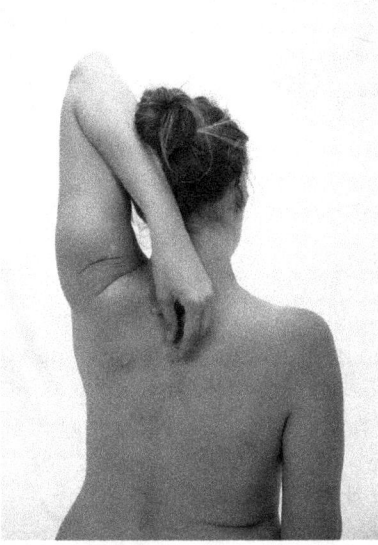

ID: A nude woman's back against a white background. Her left arm is raised, bending behind her back.

ID: A woman's hair against a black background. Her hands are running through her hair, and she has a ring on her right ring finger.

CHAPTER 7

Finding My Way in a Society Where I Don't Fit

Jill Richardson

The root cause of my disability is trauma. When a person feels they cannot save themself from a threat by asking for help, fighting, or fleeing, they experience trauma. Trauma is, at its core, an experience of powerlessness and lack of control. At first one feels powerless during the trauma itself, and later they feel powerless over their symptoms while they attempt to reclaim control. The brain and body respond to the world around them as if the danger is still ongoing long after it has passed.

People with disabilities live in a world designed to fit other people, but not them. It's like trying to walk in shoes three sizes too large for you, while everyone else tells you they are the right size and you should make yourself fit in them. In these shoes, I am clumsy and I have blisters, but I would not have either problem if I could only get shoes in my size. Unfortunately, they don't make shoes in my size.

My difficulty or inability to function in society is not simply caused by my impairment—Post-Traumatic Stress Disorder (PTSD). As noted by the Social Model of disability, it's an interaction between my impairment and the society I live in (Shakespeare, 2010). However, I am healing from trauma and reclaiming my own agency. Here's how.

My Family: The American Dream, Kind Of

I grew up with a lot of privilege, and my story would not have the happy ending it has without that privilege. My family was white and upper middle class. My parents both have graduate degrees. They had two kids, two cars, a house, and a dog. We went on family vacations, to Broadway musicals, baseball games, and museums, and my parents came to every swim meet, soccer game, and recital. I had a lot of stability as a child: my parents are still married, they do not drink or use drugs, and there was no physical or sexual abuse in my home. I was hugged and told "I love you" often. They tried hard to be great parents.

Families are supposed to help one another when they get sick; mine exacerbated my illness. Based on the work of Heller and Lapierre (2012), I believe my trauma began in utero or at birth. I was born a month premature and I spent 6 days in an incubator. My birth was extremely stressful to my mother, who had medical complications, and I don't know how even the best mother could have fully been there for her premature infant while suffering so severely herself.

Based on their behavior and symptoms, I suspect my parents and grandparents suffered trauma too, and that each generation, along with life's normal bumps and bruises (like my premature birth), inadvertently traumatized the next. I don't think my parents were equipped to raise a child who came into the world with a compromised nervous system from trauma like I did. Babies rely on the regulation of their primary caregivers' nervous systems to develop a well-regulated nervous system of their own, but my parents' nervous systems are extremely dysregulated. I know my parents did the best they could with the tools they had to parent my brother and me, but the tools they had traumatized us. The abuse came out of their desire to make us into perfect children because they so badly wanted to protect us from a world that scared them. After 23 years of verbal and emotional abuse, my brother died of a heroin overdose. I, on the other hand, channeled my feelings into my body where they manifested as physical symptoms like insomnia, fatigue, and pain.

I have a somatoform disorder—a real physical disease with psychological origins. People who suffer from somatoform disorders grow up in families where they are unable to be heard when they express feelings of sadness and anger, so they learn to suppress the feelings instead (Lind et al., 2014). Looking back, I remember learning how to hide my emotions, learning how to not even feel them, and how to freeze or dissociate. Sometimes I want to make myself invisible by being as still or as neutral and unobtrusive as I can. Sometimes it feels like I am making myself mentally not exist so I don't have to experience what I am going through. I remember a lot of random, unexplained aches in my arms and legs starting around age 5. One day I woke up and my whole body hurt around age 10, and then daily headaches began at age 14.

While I was getting good grades and college scholarships, I fell asleep all the time during the day, but couldn't fall asleep at night. I constantly thought I felt hungry (it turned out to be emotions I was interpreting as hunger), felt pain all over my body, and could not dance, take deep breaths, meditate, or do any form of exercise more strenuous than walking. As a child, my teachers, coaches, and parents thought I was lazy. My teachers gave me lower participation grades because I fell asleep in school. My mom nagged me constantly to stop napping. I couldn't. I knew I wasn't lazy because I knew how hard I tried to stay awake and couldn't, and I knew how much pain I was in every day. I was powerless to communicate that in a way that would be heard so I stopped trying—as people with somatoform disorders tend to do (Lind et al., 2014).

My family is not unique. More than 60% of U.S. adults reported experiencing one or more of Adverse Childhood Experiences (ACES), and nearly a quarter reported experiencing three or more ACES (Merrick et al., 2018). ACES can include physical, emotional, or sexual abuse; physical or emotional neglect; or household dysfunction, much like a parent experiencing intimate partner violence or living with adults who are mentally ill or abusing substances. The more ACES a child experiences, the more likely they are to develop a host of physical and mental disorders throughout their lives, just like I did. Families like mine where children experience trauma are not normative, but we are the majority.

Diagnosis: Unknown

In our society, doctors are supposed to know how to diagnose and treat illness. Mine didn't know how to help me. My doctors believed I was telling the truth about my pain, but they had no idea what was wrong. Some managed to fix other problems along the way (they checked my vision and I got glasses at age 18) or ruled out other problems (I don't have a brain tumor). It's terrifying to realize that your doctor has no idea why you hurt or how to make the pain stop.

My doctors were not bad. Rather, they are a part of a system that is not set up to treat people like me (Jutel, 2010). The health care system separates physical and mental health, but the two are intricately related. Trauma occurs in the autonomic nervous system, which affects every part of the body. Trauma can lead to autoimmune disorders, gastrointestinal problems, fatigue, insomnia, and chronic pain, like headaches or fibromyalgia (Schwartz et al., 2018). And trauma is common: more than 70% of adults experience a traumatic event in their lifetime (Kessler et al., 2017). It's accepted that childhood trauma is correlated with a long list of diseases, both physical and mental, including somatoform disorders.

Some trauma experts believe there is another way our health care system is not designed to treat childhood trauma like mine. They criticize the *Diagnostic and Statistical Manual of Mental Disorders* (DSM), which is the official classification of all mental health diagnoses, because "the diagnostic criteria for PTSD is not sensitive to developmental issues and therefore does not adequately describe the effect of ongoing early trauma, abuse, and neglect on child development" (Heller & Lapierre, 2012, p. 119). In other words, many people who suffered trauma as children will never get diagnosed with PTSD because the diagnostic criteria do not describe their symptoms. Psychiatrist Bessel van der Kolk led an effort to add a new diagnosis, Developmental Trauma Disorder, to the newest edition of the DSM-5, published in 2013, but it was unsuccessful.

Perhaps because my problem was both physical and mental and because my trauma occurred in childhood, it took me 20 years of headaches to get a PTSD diagnosis. Between ages 14 and 25, I tried explaining what I sometimes called headaches, but often referred to more honestly as "eye aches" because back then it often felt like the pain was in my eyes. You get some funny looks when you tell people you have eye aches. I would try to find the right words to describe different types of pain, but could never make myself understood by others.

Patients without a diagnosis don't just lack the proper treatment, they also lack a way to explain themselves or legitimize their disease (Jutel, 2009). With no diagnosis, patients feel like other people think they are lazy or crazy, and they have no clear course of treatment or prognosis (Nettleton et al., 2005). Without a way to communicate and be understood, they sometimes stop trying. They miss opportunities where they could have been heard and validated, and they also miss out on a lot of life because they are avoiding it (Lind et al., 2014). I sought medical care in fits and starts because I would give up, often for years, every time I attempted it and failed to receive help. It hurt less to stay home and have headaches than to go to a doctor who could do nothing for me.

As the patient with the undiagnosable condition, I was a problem. Nobody, including myself, knew how to understand me. My existence disrupted everyone else's safety and order in the world. I was proof that disease cannot always be understood and treated by doctors. That thought frightens people and they don't want to consider it. For doctors, patients with undiagnosable, untreatable conditions threaten their professional identity because they don't know what to do with us (Sarradon-Eck, Dias, & Puchain, 2020).

The "medical gaze"—the objectifying perspective through which the doctor views the patient that separates the body from the patient's mind—precludes one from understanding my problem (Foucault, 2012; Mol, 2003). One is a person in the shape of a body, and mind and body are separate, according to Cartesian dualism. Medicine is rationalized accordingly, into specialties, ancillary and alternative therapists, and mental and physical health almost entirely separate, treated by different people. Over two decades, I went to an optometrist, ophthalmologist, podiatrist, sports medicine doctor, neurologist, physical therapist, occupational therapist, and a psychologist for different symptoms of the same problem (usually pain nobody could observe) and nobody put all of the pieces together. It was kind of a relief when I broke my foot because at least the doctor knew how to help me for a nice change.

The prevalence of somatoform disorders—some estimate they account for 50% of doctor visits (Farkas, 2017)—shows that the split between mind and body is an imaginary one. Relationships between doctors and patients with psychosomatic symptoms can be tense. Patients can get angry because they believe "psychosomatic" either means "making it up" or "crazy" (Farkas, 2017). After about 6 months, my first neurologist timidly suggested I see a mental health practitioner. When I was 26, one of my neurologists made an offhand remark that I appeared to have PTSD symptoms, but then he never followed up on it (and I went another decade before getting diagnosed). I later asked why and he told me it would have been unethical to practice medicine outside of what he was trained to do. Meanwhile, mental health practitioners have their own limitations. None of the psychologists I saw had been to medical school; they were trained to understand the mind, but not the body. They did what they could, but as neither neurologists, nor psychologists, diagnosed me with trauma, and nobody ever referred me to anyone trained to treat it. Nothing worked.

Diagnosis: Migraines

My second neurologist finally gave me a diagnosis: migraines. When I got the diagnosis at age 25, it was a relief—but not because the doctor stopped my headaches. Instead of trying to explain "eye aches," I could tell people "I get migraines" and receive immediate understanding. Finally, nobody thought I was faking it, and at long last I could be "officially" sick with a "real" recognized disease. Doctors told me that migraines are genetic, and all migraine patients have triggers that cause their migraines, but beyond that, the actual causes of migraines are unknown. The drugs they prescribed gave me plenty of side effects, but no relief.

At this point in my life, I needed a diagnosis mostly to satisfy my employer. Without a diagnosis from a doctor, according to my employer, I was an able-bodied person who should stop complaining about headaches and do her job if she wanted to keep it. With a diagnosis from a doctor, I was a legally protected employee with a disability entitled to reasonable accommodation under the law.

Parsons' Sick Role

Diagnoses and power are linked. Having a diagnosis is empowering— even a diagnosis that never leads to adequate treatment—because it helps you understand yourself, explain yourself to others, and find a community of other people with the same diagnosis who share similar experiences with you (Jutel, 2009). Only certain people and institutions have the power to license people to diagnose patients, and to define and classify diseases. Even though some trauma experts believe that Developmental Trauma Disorder is a real disease, the people with the authority to write the DSM decided it is not. Therefore, officially, it isn't. Only people with licenses to practice medicine or psychotherapy can diagnose patients. That's why, when I was 25 and a massage therapist suggested I had suffered trauma because of how my body felt, I did not believe her: she had a license to give me a massage, but not a diagnosis.

In the mid-twentieth century, sociologist Talcott Parsons (1951) defined the *Sick Role* as two rights and two responsibilities. The patient (1) does not have to fill their normal social roles (like working) and (2) they should not be blamed for their condition; in return they (1) must get better as quickly as possible and (2) do whatever the doctor tells them. I needed a doctor's diagnosis to access the rights of the sick role: disability accommodations, treatment, and insurance reimbursement (Jutel, 2009; Mol, 2003).

In the end, I got better by violating the responsibilities of the sick role. When doctors pressured me to take medications I had already tried that did not work, I said no. When they continued to prescribe drugs that did not work and clearly had no idea how to help me, I stopped going to neurologists altogether. In my late twenties, I began mental health treatment with a psychologist. I learned a lot from her, but my health did not improve. I began reading voraciously on my own, until one day, at age 34, I found a book that described me: *The Body Keeps the Score* by Bessel van der Kolk (2015). It was about PTSD.

From van der Kolk's book, I found Peter Levine, who created a type of therapy called Somatic Experiencing (SE). SE is a gentle type of therapy that works with the body's natural ability to heal itself and it uses the calm nervous system of the therapist to help regulate the nervous system of the patient. It is based on the theory that our bodies are able to naturally resolve a trauma, but we often do not allow that to happen and so we get stuck. SE practitioners guide patients to manipulate their autonomic nervous systems to allow that natural process to occur. A session usually feels mostly like a regular conversation that flows naturally, but the therapist occasionally asks questions or instructs the patient to do something like notice how their body feels or the surroundings around them. Occasionally, intense emotions arise, and the therapist guides the patient to allow their bodies to process them and return to a feeling of safety without becoming overwhelmed.

SE and other, related therapy methods in the field of somatic psychology understand trauma differently from how most people see it. For most people, the word *trauma* sounds extreme. They assume trauma refers only to unthinkable acts of violence and abuse or horrific accidents. With this point of view, trauma is often inflicted by people—a violent attacker, an abusive relative, a terrorist, a drunk driver, etc. It's hard to imagine a world so ugly that trauma is common, and harder still to accept that the people who traumatize others walk among us. It's more comforting to think of trauma as extreme and rare than mundane and common, and to imagine the people who cause it as monsters, not the normal people we interact with daily.

Somatic psychology focuses more on trauma as an internal experience based on how one's nervous system perceives one's safety, regardless of whether one was ever actually in mortal danger. For example, my nervous system reacted like I was going to die at age 11 when our family watched a movie with a sex scene together and my dad joked that I was "taking notes." (I was *not* taking notes; I was trying to blend into the couch because I was so mortified.) My physical safety was never in any danger, but my body reacted as though it was. My dad is not a bad guy, even if he's a bad comedian. When most people think of trauma, they don't think of dad jokes. Focusing on the internal experience of trauma provides a better understanding of trauma because it's more accurate and because it allows us to understand how common trauma is without simultaneously believing the world is filled with an equivalent amount of evil, violent, or deranged perpetrators.

Somatic psychology teaches that trauma is simply what happens when a person feels they cannot save themselves by asking for help, fighting, or fleeing, so they freeze. If their body does not discharge the energy from the freeze response after the fact, they retain it as trauma, and it continues to impair them until it is resolved. In the short term, it is protective; our ability to freeze can save us. In the long term, it can be debilitating if left untreated. The amount one is disabled by trauma depends on when the trauma occurred, how much cumulative trauma the person has experienced, and other factors in their life that help or hinder their resilience. Someone can live a mostly healthy, happy life but still experience some trauma.

This view not only provides a path to resolving trauma, but it also normalizes it. My SE therapist does not want me to over-identify with my diagnosis; she wants me to focus on building an identity around what I *can* do. She reminds me that everyone's nervous systems work the same. Her attitude shifts trauma from the horrific and unthinkable to an everyday part of life. Therefore, I am not someone who suffered from a uniquely terrible past, I'm just another person living life like everyone else, and life is hard. She educates me about how nervous systems work and how I can help mine heal. This is work that I must do myself; she's not "fixing" me.

Instead of receiving a doctor's diagnosis, I first found the diagnosis myself and had it confirmed by a therapist, and then the diagnosis became unimportant. Whereas in the past I was a passive recipient of doctors' and therapists' medical care, now I am an active agent in my own recovery. I went from powerless to empowered, unheard to heard, unseen to seen, *and I am getting better.*

After 4 years of SE, my migraines are less frequent. I stopped confusing emotions with hunger and I lost 30 pounds without trying. Unlike before, now I fall asleep easily at night and wake up naturally in the morning. For the first time in my life, I am able to dance. When things get hard, I know what to do to help myself feel better. Because I have more control, everything is getting easier. I never knew life could be this good! Parsons assumed doctors were infallible and patients should act like well-behaved children and obey them. In my case, Parsons was wrong.

Disabled as a Socially Constructed Category

Our society is set up with socially constructed categories that I simply don't fit, like poorly fitting shoes. You can be able-bodied or have a disability, but be able to complete your job with "reasonable accommodation," or you can have a disability and hardly be able to work at all. If you fit in the last category, you can receive government payments to support you, but you will live in poverty. I can work a lot—but until I began healing in the last 4 years, I couldn't fit into any of the predefined categories that society offered me as my only choices.

Employers want "reasonable accommodations" to fit into a few categories too. A few options that would have helped me during the years that I was sicker, such as working part-time or working from home, are often unavailable because employers don't think they are "reasonable" enough. What I need is the ability to feel like I have enough control to keep myself safe. I need to feel I can trust the people around me, or I can act independently from them if I don't trust them. Sometimes I need to be able to let my nervous system recover when it's overwhelmed. I don't pick and choose when that happens, and it's not always at a convenient time. The more flexibility an employer can give me, and the more we can have an open dialogue about my needs, the better. That, in itself, helps me feel safe. The accommodations offered are usually more like a list of concrete options for people with more "traditional" disabilities: wheelchair access, Braille, large print books, sign language interpreters, and so on.

Until I got my first job after college, I did not identify as a person with a disability. I was just me, with headaches every day. I had learned about the Americans with Disabilities Act (ADA) in a college class, and I realized pretty quickly that it gave me the legal right to ask for what I needed at work. My ability to get the accommodations I needed to do my job rested on calling my health problem a disability. So, fine, it's a disability.

The binary categories of disabled and non-disabled feel artificial to me, especially with regard to mental illness. We all share the same brain and nervous system, and many things fall more on a continuum than a binary. A certain amount of anxiety is healthy, but too much isn't. Trauma is remarkably common. At what point is the anxiety or trauma interfering with your life so much that you call it a disorder? Diagnostic criteria require you exhibit a certain number of symptoms from a list. What if you're one symptom short—then are you fine? And many people who are severely impaired by these problems don't go to (or don't have access to) a doctor or a therapist, so they are never diagnosed. I find it odd that I have a disability because I chose (and could afford) to go to a person with a license allowing them to diagnose me and they did and then I chose to call my impairment a disability. Someone who is far more impaired than I am might not do the same things and make the same choices. Do they not have a disability then?

I finally found my place in the world where I'm less of a mismatch, and found therapy that helps me get better. Given how fast I'm improving, I'll be fine. I find it concerning, however, that after 20 years of being failed by mainstream medicine, I found my way to diagnosis and therapy on my own. How many others are like me but never got help? How can we change our society to help all of the many people affected by trauma, not just the few individuals who are fortunate enough to get a diagnosis and treatment for it?

Discussion Questions

1.   What are the ways in which the author did not "fit" in the world? What strategies did the author use to navigate the world?
2.   What does it mean to be in a binary category? Why does the author mean when she says she feels the binary categories of disabled and non-disabled are "artificial"? Do you agree?
3.   How do we conceptualize "treating" a disability, and how does this relate to medicalization?

References

Farkas, C. A. (2017). Introduction: The psychosomatic as nothing, something, and everything. In C. A. Farcas (Ed.), *Reading the psychosomatic in medical and popular culture: Something. Nothing. Everything* (1st ed.). Routledge.

Foucault, M. (2012). *The birth of the clinic* (3rd ed.). Routledge.

Heller, L., & Lapierre, A. (2012). *Healing developmental trauma: How early trauma affects self-regulation, self-image, and the capacity for relationship.* North Atlantic Books.

Jutel, A. (2009). Sociology of diagnosis: A preliminary review. *Sociology of Health & Illness, 31*(2), 278–299. https://doi.org/10.1111/j.1467-9566.2008.01152.x

Jutel, A. (2010). Medically unexplained symptoms and the disease label. *Social Theory & Health, 8*(3), 229–245. https://doi.org/10.1057/sth.2009.21

Kessler, R. C., Aguilar-Gaxiola, S., Alonso, J., Benjet, C., Bromet, E. J., Cardoso, G., Degenhardt, L., de Girolamo, G., Dinolova, R. V., Ferry, F., Florescu, S., Gureje, O., Haro, J. M., Huang, Y., Karam, E. G., Kawakami, N., Lee, S., Lepine, J.-P., Levinson, D., … Koenen, K. C. (2017). Trauma and PTSD in the WHO World Mental Health Surveys. *European Journal of Psychotraumatology, 8*(5). https://doi.org/10.1080/20008198.2017.1353383

Lind, A. B., Delmar, C., & Nielsen, K. (2014). Struggling in an emotional avoidance culture: A qualitative study of stress as a predisposing factor for somatoform disorders. *Journal of Psychosomatic Research, 76*(2), 94–98. https://doi.org/10.1016/j.jpsychores.2013.11.019

Lind, A. B., Risoer, M. B., Nielsen, K., Delmar, C., Christensen, M. B., & Lomborg, K. (2014). Longing for existential recognition: A qualitative study of everyday concerns for people with somatoform disorders. *Journal of Psychosomatic Research, 76*(2), 99–104. https://doi.org/10.1016/j.jpsychores.2013.11.005

Merrick, M. T., Ford, D. C., Ports, K. A., & Guinn, A. S. (2018). Prevalence of adverse childhood experiences from the 2011–2014 behavioral risk factor surveillance system in 23 states. *JAMA Pediatrics, 172*(11), 1038–1044. https://doi.org/10.1001/jamapediatrics.2018.2537

Mol, A. (2003). *The body multiple: Ontology in medical practice* (Illustrated ed.). Duke University Press.

Nettleton, S., Watt, I., O'Malley, L., & Duffey, P. (2005). Understanding the narratives of people who live with medically unexplained illness. *Patient Education and Counseling, 56*, 205–210. https://doi.org/10.1016/j.pec.2004.02.010

Parsons, T. (1951). *The social system* (1st ed.). The Free Press.

Sarradon-Eck, A., Dias, M., & Pouchain, R. (2020). Ces patients « particuliers ». Comment les jeunes médecins (dé)médicalisent les symptômes médicalement inexpliqués ? *Sciences Sociales et Santé, 38*(1), 5–30. https://doi.org/10.1684/sss.2020.0160

Schwartz, A., Maiberger, B., & Shapiro, R. (2018). *EMDR therapy and somatic psychology: Interventions to enhance embodiment in trauma treatment* (1st ed.). W. W. Norton & Company.

Shakespeare, T. (2010). The social model of disability. In L. J. Davis (Ed.), *The disability studies reader* (pp. 266–273). Routledge.

van der Kolk, B. (2015). *The body keeps the score: Brain, mind, and body in the healing of trauma* (Reprint ed.). Penguin Books.

Mac

Valerie and Chase Novack

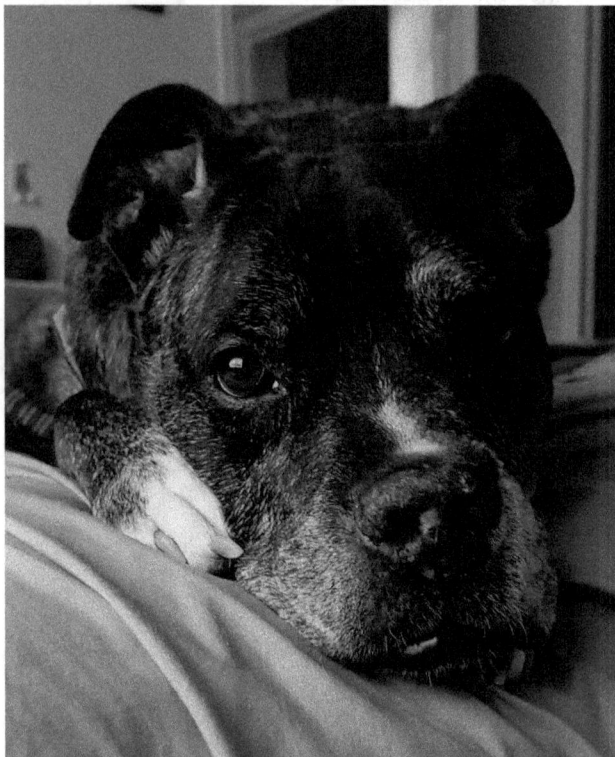

ID: Mac is a brindle mastiff mix with graying hair. He is laying on a sage green blanket with his paw near his face.

• • •

Mac was more aware of my (Valerie's) physical and emotional states than most of my doctors. He moves slowly alongside me on bad POTS and fibromyalgia days. When my depression is bad, he lays in bed with me all day and makes sure I can keep some type of routine because he needs it. Mac both makes living life easier and is a reason to persist even when it's hard.

He's my best friend.

© PAUL D. C. BONES, JESSICA SMARTT GULLION AND DANIELLE BARBER, 2022
DOI:10.1163/9789004512702_010

CHAPTER 8

Misfit in the Academy

Succeeding as a Visually Impaired Scholar in Australia

Sheelagh Daniels-Mayes

What has six legs, is Indigenous, has poor eyesight, is a woman, and works at a university? That would be me. I am an Australian Aboriginal/Kamilaroi woman who is visually impaired and I rely on a guide dog for my mobility and well-being. In other words, I am a "six-legged blacademic." To my knowledge, I am the only such person in Australia and I have experienced my presence and success as being epistemologically disruptive for those who still construct me as a misfit, a bundle of intersecting deficits. In this milieu of multiple forms of inequity, I focus in this chapter on the story of what it means to be a visually impaired scholar. While my identity of Aboriginality is undoubtedly significant, I choose here to stick to the task of re-defining disability privileged in this text. More specifically, I will critically reflect on my lived experience of being an academic with a disability that is fraught with highs and lows.

My research into higher education and disability revealed that the vast majority of scholarship relates to students living with a disability, and the reasonable adjustments they require to succeed at university. By comparison, the experiences of academics living with disability are underrepresented within worldwide scholarship (Kosanic et al., 2018; Williams & Mavin, 2015). Additionally, like Mellifont and colleagues (2019) and Waterfield, Beagan, and Weinberg (2018), I found there is a relative scarcity of university programs and policies to support academics with a disability. Recent coverage in higher education newspapers and social media platforms are therefore troubling, as they reveal that chronic illnesses and disabilities are becoming more prevalent amongst academics (Brown & Leigh, 2018). There is a clear and significant gap in the research and scholarship where the voices of academics with disability are largely absent, hiding the less comfortable and less palatable aspects of higher education experienced by many academics with disability.

The Power of Story

As a Critical Race Theorist, I have come to know the power of story and counterstory to reveal the lived experiences of the marginalised and minoritized, the excluded and silenced, based on the racialisation of the othered (Daniels-Mayes, 2016). Duncan (2006) contends that the ability of stories is that they allow others to get into the mindset, or see the world through the eyes of those who are oppressed or subjugated. As such, the method of storytelling, for those silenced and ignored due to disability, likewise need to take a critical approach, privileging the lived experiences—the emic perspective—of those living with disability. Disability studies is an interdisciplinary, multidisciplinary field. Disability studies disrupts the idea that disabled people should be defined primarily through their disabilities by others; instead, it advocates for the right for people with disability to define their own relationships with disability (Dolmage, 2017). I offer in this chapter a personal narrative that represents a storied way of knowing and communicating (Hinchman & Hinchman, 1997) that disrupts how my ability has been defined and constructed politically, socially and culturally for generations by governments, institutions, social movements and—yes—higher education, but largely not by me. As stated by Langellier (2001):

> Embedded in the lives of the ordinary, the marginalized, and the muted, personal narrative responds to the disintegration of master narratives as people make sense of experience, claim identities, and "get a life" by telling and writing their stories. (p. 700)

But "getting a life" as a six-legged blacademic is fraught with difficulty. I need to push back against the master narrative that, as I will share, constructs me primarily as a problem to be fixed, excluded, or silenced; or, strangely enough, at times exemplified and respected. In this chapter, I use narrative enquiry as it requires us to listen deeply and then engage in a process of critical reflection that enables me to go beyond the telling of my story to a place of understanding what it takes to succeed in the academy as a visually impaired academic, an anomaly, and a misfit.

Misfit Theory

In this chapter, I draw upon the work of Garland-Thomson (2011) who uses the critical concept misfit "in an effort to further think through the lived identity and experience of disability as it is situated in place and time" (p. 591). Scholars from fields of study such as feminism, Critical Access Studies, Critical Disability studies, and Critical Race Theory, have increasingly attempted to disrupt pernicious historical understandings of deficit, excess, or fault located in bodies to a relational construction of disability as a social construct whose meaning is determined primarily through discourse (Garland-Thomson, 2011). Accordingly, disability oppression originates from embedded narratives that are given form in the world through social, architectural, and digital barriers, as well as the unequal distribution and access to resources and exclusionary institutions (Davis, 1995; McCall, 2019; Thompson et al., 2007).

My recent discovery of misfit theory came at a time when the struggle against ableism in the academy was almost too much for me to tolerate. My area of research at the time was not disability studies—that was my lived experience and not my passion. I was establishing myself as a Critical Race Theorist in Aboriginal education, which had been the focus of my doctoral instigation. But events at work pushed me down the proverbial "rabbit hole" of disability scholarship in an attempt to understand (and possibly disrupt) how I was being positioned and why. Misfit theory offers an account of a dynamic encounter between flesh and world, a consideration of how the particularities of embodiment interact with their environment in its broadest sense, to include both its spatial and temporal aspects (Garland-Thomson, 2011). In other words, how does my "sight deprived" flesh interact with a "sight dependent world" and who is constructed as having the problem? Garland-Thomson (2011) simply says:

> Fitting and misfitting denote an encounter in which two things come together in either harmony or disjunction. When the shape and substance of these two things correspond in their union, they fit. A misfit, conversely, describes an incongruent relationship between two things: a square peg in a round hole. (pp. 593–594)

For centuries, the "disabled" have held an incongruent and disharmonious relationship with society's dominant narratives of what is the accepted norm. Accordingly, people with disabilities have been constructed as the "square peg" through narratives of outcasts, lepers, or misfits (to name but a few). Or, for me as a child incarcerated in an institution for the "handicapped," I was constructed as society's misfit in need of being hidden from the public gaze.

Universities are implicated, very deeply, in this history-having a legacy of using people with disabilities for research fodder, objects of curiosity; people with disability are not to be the researchers and teachers, the producers or purveyors of knowledge (Dolmage, 2017). Students and teachers alike are expected to accentuate ability, valorise perfection, and stigmatize anything that hints at intellectual (or physical) weakness (Dolmage, 2017). As a six-legged-blacademic, I am a misfit; unsuitable and inconsistent with the traditional purpose and form of higher education (Garland-Thomson, 2011).

The Narrative of Economics

Higher education is generally known to champion values like autonomy, freedom of expression, and creativity. Too often, however, the economic purpose of education is ignored or justified in a myriad of taken-for-granted ways. Undoubtedly, higher education is an industry that, beyond the surface, is dominated by economic considerations, but prefers not to be seen as a business (Dolmage, 2017). Political scientist Wendy Brown advises that, more than a set of policies, an ideology, or a relation between state and economy, neoliberalism is "a normative order of reason developed over three decades into a widely and deeply disseminated governing rationality," which "transmogrifies every human domain and Endeavour, along with humans themselves, according to a specific image of the economic" (Brown, 2015, pp. 9–10). This understanding of imbalanced benefit and harm, then, must be used to analyse the workings of academic ableism.

In a neoliberalist world, economic competitiveness is central, individuals are expected to compete with one another, taking the necessary steps to earn success, regardless of social adversity. Embedded is the view that all individuals begin on an equal playing field and are thus able to participate equally within higher education (Waterfield, Beagan & Weinberg, 2018). Accordingly, difference is understood as an individual responsibility, frequently leaving academics living with disability navigating exclusionary spaces and processes without institutional support (Brown & Lee, 2018). Academics with disabilities are required to strategize and negotiate the exclusionary institution of higher education so as to compete, participate, and succeed. So, while neoliberal performance standards are increasingly affecting all academics, they affect academics with disability uniquely as they are embedded with ableism experienced in overt, covert, aversive, and laissez-faire ways (Keller & Galgay, 2010) that remind us that we are misfits in the academy, trespassers in a system never designed for anyone less than perfect or anyone defined as weak. Put simply, as an academic with disability, I do not belong and am regularly reminded of my misfit status through a myriad of ways, too many to fully story here. Instead, I will highlight two stories, one of ableism and one of anti-ableism.

Personal Narrative 1: Applying for Promotion

Applying for promotion within my institution is a highly competitive and arduous process, not to be taken lightly for if you are unsuccessful, you cannot re-apply for another 2 years. Significantly, I noted that structural disadvantages are recognised. That is, you can make your case for your research achievements relative to research opportunities. Technically, therefore, expectations for number of publications (among other aspects of being an academic such as grants and impact on policy) all reduce commensurate to how much time you have had to do research. The impact of disability on research outputs is one such structural disadvantage. Or is it? When I met with my manager to discuss my promotion application, I was told quite simply that I did not have enough "research outputs" and therefore my application would not be supported. Now, I could have agreed with this if they had even spent 30 seconds reading my "Relative to Opportunity" narrative or my Curriculum Vitae that demonstrated the myriad of Governance, Leadership, and Engagement (GLE) undertakings in the academy or the success I was having in my teaching.

Notably, this was not the first or last time this comment had been made. Sure, I did not have a huge number of publications in high-ranking journals (as is smiled upon within the competitive environment of higher education). But why not? Could it be because as a vision-impaired academic I am relentlessly needing to overcome ableism in the academy such as digital inaccessibility (i.e., websites, learning systems, PDFs, and PowerPoints not being readable with screen reader software)? Or could it be that being the only person with my lived experience, I am constantly having to educate those around me and therefore spend an inordinate amount of time creating an environment in which I, and hopefully others coming through the ranks, can undertake my job—time that is generally not recognised in my workload hours?

For academics with a disability, career progression is slowed when we are trapped in the neoliberalist world of having to perform to the same (or better) standards than able-bodied peers, despite the constant ableist challenges put before us. Understandably, people with disabilities may make self-limiting decisions which restrict career options such as avoiding promotion (French, 2001), to manage work and maintain control over—for example—workloads (Harlan & Robert, 1998; Shah, 2005). Or in my case, are not deemed worthy alongside my able-bodied peers. The example provided here of how ableism plays out in the academy, is not intended to denigrate, but rather enable the reader to get into the mindset of the neoliberalist-driven academy that insists on perpetuating a myth that there is an equal playing field for all.

Studies on people with disabilities suggest that work processes and practices reflect the organising requirements of non-disabled people, requiring disabled people to strategize to negotiate inaccessible or non-inclusive contexts in order to participate and succeed in their work (Harlan & Robert, 1998). For some, this may involve requesting that employers accommodate impairment within their work remit. For others, disability-related requirements are negated, or strategies are developed, to meet normative expectations shaped around the assumed ideal (non-disabled, non-weak, non-imperfect) worker (Harlan & Robert, 1998). Frequently, work practices are premised upon assumed non-disability standardisations that limit options, such as promotion, available to academics with disability (Williams & Mavin, 2015).

Personal Narrative 2: Digital Accessibility

But there is a counterstory amongst this ableist debris. There are those who, as I say, "get it." Those individuals who, for largely unknown reasons, understand the extra demands placed upon disabled academics shoulders and work toward success and change. These are the people who understand that being a "misfit" is a positive attribute, and work toward making the academy function for those with disabilities. Within my institution there exists a Digital Accessibility Lead whose primary focus is students with a disability. However, it is to this person and their small team that I, and the wider university, frequently turn when digital barriers arise. Academia is print- and website-dependent, two domains fraught with misfit potential (McCall, 2019; Thompson et al., 2007). There is a common misunderstanding that if something is in print, or if it is on a computer screen, then it is accessible.

However, digital environments or content are not currently inherently accessible or easily navigable to people who are blind or who have vision, learning, cognitive, or print disabilities (McCall, 2019). When computer engineers, computer programmers, or document authors do not design digital content using universal design principles for accessibility, unintentional barriers are created and require retrofitting that, in my experience, frequently does not occur. In digital environments, higher education at all levels makes extensive use of digital textbooks, Learning Management Systems (LMS), online ethics, whiteboards, digital collaboration, PowerPoints, surveys, and other support materials, such as websites.

Accessibility, navigability, and inclusion are often not thought of at the time of design, due to a lack of knowledge and understanding of potential digital barriers. Additionally, adaptive technology and software is rarely designed by those with disabilities. Two comments I often hear when I engage with the designers are enlightening: (1) "We didn't know blind people could be academics;" and (2) "There aren't enough blind academics to justify the cost." I am clearly a "jarring juxtaposition" (Garland-Thomson, 2011, p. 593) to the construction of who can be an academic. In most higher education institutions, training in accessible document design exists on an ad hoc basis with mandatory training programs largely absent (McCall, 2019). Embedded in this approach is the hidden message that accessibility of digital content and the inclusion of those with disabilities is of low priority, if needed at all. Beyond my assigned workload or job description, I frequently undertake work that primarily educates the institution, and those who work within it, about the need and benefit of digital accessibility for all. But as noted earlier, such activities are rarely recognised or valued by those who do not "get it," those whose mindsets have been formed by the inhuman agenda of neoliberalism.

The Political Dimension of Disability

Disability has a political dimension within the academy through which competing views are contested. On the one hand, disability is received with an open and willing mind. On the other, disability is understood as problematic (Mellifont et al., 2019). Garland-Thomas (2011, p. 593) states that "The utility of the concept of misfit is that it definitively lodges injustice and discrimination in the materiality of the world more than in social attitudes or representational practices, even while it recognises their mutually constituting entanglement." The concept of "misfit" is a relatively new critical keyword that seeks to defamiliarise and to re-define dominant constructions of disability as deficit, imperfection, and weakness; of no value or an unwarranted cost.

As an Aboriginal/Kamilaroi woman I am Crow the trickster whose responsibility it is to disrupt, disturb, and destabilise the taken-for-granted (Daniels-Mayes, 2016). In recent times, I have come to understand that this responsibility extends beyond that of racism borne out of two centuries of dispossessing colonisation. Rather, my responsibility is to disrupt normalised and often invisible forms of discrimination that result from disharmonious interactions between flesh and world, between body and environment, that occurs in a diversity of often intersecting ways. Through my stories and subsequent critical reflection, I have illustrated that while many may construct me as not belonging in the academy, as a misfit I am successfully disrupting persistent discrimination that would have me excluded from the elite and neoliberalist-driven academy. As I have come to know misfit theory, I have come to embrace being a square peg despite its many dramas and traumas, despite its exhausting demands. Re-defining myself as a misfit in the academy enables me to locate the problem, the exclusion, squarely within the materiality of the world that would dematerialise if social and architectural barriers no longer disabled me and others living with disability (Garland-Thomson, 2011).

Final Thoughts

Ultimately, the chapter has sought to open discussion surrounding the experiences of academics with disability and how, although universities are becoming more diverse, academics with disabilities are still having to prove that they are "good enough" (Waterfield, Beagan, & Weinberg, 2018). Being a "misfit" should be celebrated and valued for the knowledge they produce and teach, and for the ways in which they disrupt the normalised fit.

Discussion Questions

1. How much visual media (images, videos, digital or print text, etc.) do you consume every day? How would your day be different if you did not have access to these materials?
2. Indigenous beliefs about disability are often very different from Western colonized conceptions. Using the internet, find what group(s) originally inhabited the land where you live. Can you find any information about how they view disability?
3. Disability is often left out of Diversity and Inclusion. What role, if any, should it take in the larger conversation about diversity and marginalization?

References

Brown, N., & Leigh, J. (2018). Ableism in academia: Where are the disabled and ill academics? *Disability & Society, 33*(6), 985–989. https://doi.org/10.1080/09687599.2018.1455627

Brown, W. (2015). *Undoing the demos: Neoliberalism's stealth revolution*. Zone Books.

Daniels-Mayes, S. (2016). *Culturally responsive pedagogies of success: Improving educational outcomes for Australian Aboriginal students* [Unpublished doctoral dissertation]. University of South Australia.

Davis, L. J. (1995). *Enforcing normalcy: Disability, deafness, and the body*. Verso.

Dolmage, J. T. (2017). *Academic ableism: Disability and higher education*. University of Michigan Press.

Duncan, G. A. (2006). Critical race ethnography in education: Narrative, inequality, and the problem of epistemology. In A. D. Dixson & C. K. Rousseau (Eds.), *Critical race theory in education: All God's children got a song* (pp. 191–212). Routledge.

French, S. (2001). *Disabled people and employment: A study of the working lives of visually impaired physiotherapists*. Ashgate.

Garland-Thomson, R. (2011). Misfits: A feminist materialist disability concept. *Hypatia, 26*(3), 591–609.

Harlan, S., & Robert, P. (1998). The social construction of disability in organizations: Why employers resist reasonable accommodation. *Work and Occupations, 25*(4), 397–435.

Hinchman, L. P., & Hinchman, S. K. (Eds.). (1997). *Memory, identity, community: The idea of narrative in the human sciences*. State University of NY Press.

Keller, R. M., & Galgay, C. E. (2010). Microaggressive experiences of people with disabilities. In D. W. Sue (Ed.), *Microaggressions and marginality: Manifestation, dynamics, and impact* (pp. 241–267). John Wiley & Sons.

Kosanic, K., Hansen, N., Zimmermann-Janschitz, S., & Chouinard, V. (2018, September 1). *Researchers with disabilities in the academic system*. American Association of Geographers. https://doi.org/10.14433/2017.0042

Langellier, K. M. (2001). Personal narrative. In M. Jolly (Ed.), *Encyclopedia of life writing: Autobiographical and biographical forms* (Vol. 2). Dearborn.

McCall, K. (2019). Identifying and eliminating digital barriers. In C. McMaster, B. Whitburn, & M. Oliver (Eds.), *Disability at the university: A disabled students' manifesto* (pp. 159–166). Peter Lang.

Mellifont, D., Smith-Mary, J., Dickinson, H., Llewellyn, G., Clifton, S., Ragen, J., Raffaele, M., & Williamson, P. (2019). The ableism elephant in the academy: A study examining academia as informed by Australian scholars with lived experience. *Disability & Society, 34*, 7–8. https://doi.org/10.1080/09687599.2019.1602510

Riessman, C. K. (1993). *Narrative analysis*. Sage.

Shah, S. (2005). *Career success of disabled high-flyers*. Jessica Kingsley.

Thompson, T., Burgstahler, S., Moore, E., Gunderson, J., & Hoyt, N. (2007). International research on web accessibility for persons with disabilities. In M. Khosrow-Pour (Ed.), *Managing worldwide operations and communications with information technology*. Information Resources Management Association.

Waterfield, B., Beagan, B. B., & Weinberg, M. (2018). Disabled academics: A case study in Canadian universities. *Disability & Society, 33*(3), 327–348.

Williams, J., & Mavin, S. (2015). Impairment effects as a career boundary: A case study of disabled academics. *Studies in Higher Education, 40*(1), 123–141.

Mudkip

Ari

ID: An axolotl (an amphibian with three pairs of gills covered in filaments that look like fringe) smiles at the camera in a tank.

• • •

My axolotl's name is Mudkip. She is an incredibly cute little pet who absolutely makes my day. She cheers me up when I'm feeling down and is low-maintenance, which is perfect for dealing with high fatigue and pain levels.

DOI:10.1163/9789004512702_012

CHAPTER 9

Justice vs. Injustice

Poetic Dialogue about the Meaning of Disability Justice among People Labelled/with Intellectual Disability

Anonymous 1, Anonymous 2, Anonymous 3, Nicholas Herd, Anonymous 4, Doreen Kalifer, with support from Erin Kuri and Ann Fudge Schormans

The DiStory project is a multi-year, multi-generational inclusive project in which co-researchers labelled/with an intellectual disability have been collaborating with non-labelled academic and community-based co-researchers to design, develop, and conduct a project whose primary purpose is the co-production of knowledge and development of teaching materials for postsecondary students about the lives of people labelled/with intellectual disabilities. (We use the language *labelled/with* in recognition of the heterogeneity of people understood to have intellectual disability and of the hurtful impacts being labelled can have on people's lives.)

Co-researchers labelled/with intellectual disabilities include survivors of Ontario's large-scale institutions, as well as younger generations of people labelled/with intellectual disabilities. This was by design. It is a means of preserving and sharing survivors' history of institutional "care" with younger generations of people labeled/with intellectual disabilities who, while never incarcerated in these institutions, nonetheless experience institutionalized care and ongoing experiences of discrimination and violence. It was intended as well to challenge perceptions that the closure of institutions has meant that life is now "better" for people labelled/with intellectual disabilities. Instead, it makes plain that while large-scale institutions may, at this moment, be closed in Ontario, institutions and such forms of care continue, and living "in the community" is no guarantee of a "good life" of one's choosing.

In what follows, the co-researchers labelled/with intellectual disabilities re-define disability using a framework of disability justice. They do so by using a form of poetic dialogue to contrast meanings of disability (in particular, "intellectual disability") as articulated

in their understandings of "disability justice" and its converse—
"disability injustice."

Justice vs. Injustice[1]

	someone seems different	*We are all human beings but we were born differently*
	but really are the same as you and me	*We want to be treated the same as everybody else*
	as me and you	
	is this a reason?	*I'm talking about dignity,*
it's not right what they did to us	**not to accept who they are?**	*pride and our comfort*
	does this make it justified	*the right to live our lives the way we want to live them*
	to make	
	remarks that are snide?	*We have to feel heard and respected because all of us have a voice*
		justice is when you get treated equal like everybody else then it feels like I'm
	I think not	*a member of society*
it's not fair, it's very sad	**not by far**	*but society doesn't treat me*

that way

**everyone is
different**

And it's
heartbreaking

*We do belong
like everywhere, like
anywhere
in the world
because We're
important
We're human beings
We're important*

in their own way

does this mean

the government
doesn't care

*that means finding
the right job
having people
to help you find the
right job
We should be able
to live
where We want
the right to live our
lives the way We want
to live them
and so on and so on and
so on*

**we should turn
everyone away?**

**does this make it
justified**

they don't want
to give up power

to make

**remarks that are
snide?**

*it means Our voices
are understood*

My life wasn't that
good to tell you the
truth
I got abused a lot

**some people don't
talk**

*Everybody deserves
to have a good
family life*

I never forget
I don't trust people
keep your damn
hands to yourself

**some people don't
walk**

*Our voices should
be heard*

**some people
cannot hear**

*We want to feel
heard and respected*

I couldn't tell
anybody
about what went on
in the institution,
not even my own
parents

I was dis-cluded
from everything else
because of my
disability
and me being gay
I did not feel like I
belonged

you know what
someone said?
he said NO
I'm not cute
because I have a
disability
and even if he was
gay
it wouldn't be Me
[he would choose]
because I have
down syndrome

What happened in
the institution
there was no justice
when I was there

some people have
too much fear

some people
cannot see

some people are of
a different race or
creed

some people are
queer and
transgender

does this really
make them the
offender?

does this make it
justified?

to make

remarks that are
snide?

someone seems
different

really they are the
same as me and
you

so we can explain
Our own
experiences
all of Us have a
voice

We shouldn't be
treated any different
because of our
disabilities

We learn differently
all we need is a
little extra hand
along the way
not to be picked on
and that
because of it

it's not Our fault
it's like a punishment
picking on Us
for something
We can't even do
anything about

I feel good
when My rights are
respected
I feel happy about it
if Our rights are
respected
We can do better in
life
and live up to Our
full potential
instead of being
robbed of it

I had no choice
I wasn't old enough
to have a say in the
matter

is this a reason

the system should
be corrected
so that none of this
ever happens again

not to accept who
they are

people in the
professions
like psychologists
and social workers
should understand
what people with
disabilities
are going through

I was only a child

I think not

We had no rights

not by far

Disability Justice
means that We are
fighting
for disability rights

We're sad because We
didn't get justice

I think this world
has too much
fights

We are fighting
for Our voice to be
heard more

and crime

we have to get the
government
to realize that
to realize
what they have done
to us

it's not right
what they did to Us

perhaps we can
learn not to justify
injustice

it's up to Us
to get people to
understand

in time

Disability Justice is
important
for Our lives

Discussion Questions

1. Where do you see the role of people labeled/with intellectual disability in conversations about disability?
2. Disability Justice culture values both aesthetic and practical ways of doing and knowing. How do you understand the importance (and interdependence) of arts-based ways of sharing knowledge, along with traditional forms of academic scholarship?
3. Many English-language insults invoke people labeled/with intellectual disabilities. How do you think this community feels about this? And what are some alternative, non-ableist ways to critique people?

Note

1   The poem is composed from the words of the co-researchers labelled/with intellectual disabilities. Ann and Erin supported the mechanical construction of the poem in conversation with Doreen.

CHAPTER 10

Inspiration Porn and Desperation Porn
Disrupting the Objectification of Disability in Media

Kara B. Ayers and Katherine A. Reed

Disability is underrepresented in all forms of media, from newsprint, magazines, and advertisements, to cinema, television, and social media discourse. This pervasive underrepresentation results in the salience of the portrayals of disability that emerge. One of the most harmful amongst these themes of disability portrayal is one of personal tragedy and impairment. Non-disabled people typically hold the dominant perspective and overshadow actual members of the disability community. They view the problems that emanate from disability as results of an impairment of the individual, rather than society's failure to meet that person's needs in terms of support, accessibility, and inclusion. From this perspective, it can be nearly impossible to understand how a person might characterize disability as a positive part of their identity. Repetitious and harmful media portrayals of disability further complicate developing a positive disabled identity.

Using the word *porn* to describe these dehumanizing communication strategies related to disability is intentional yet controversial. The word pornography, or porn, is not confined to its sexualized meaning. More recently, alternative variations of porn, including "trauma porn" (Shackelford, 2016), "disaster porn" (Recuber, 2013), and "feminist porn" (Whisnant, 2016), have been described in literature. Porn objectifies one party or group for the self-satisfaction of another. It is devoid of art or nuance. The spread of these images or portrayals is often difficult to contain because they reinforce power structures that oppress disempowered groups. While traditional forms of sexual pornography typically objectify women and promote sexist attitudes, the forms of porn discussed throughout this chapter objectify disabled people and promote ableist attitudes.

Inspiration Porn

One specific form of problematic representation has been described as inspiration porn. Inspiration porn promotes ableist views of people with disabilities. The late Stella Young (2014) popularized the term in disability culture in her renowned TED Talk, in which she describes the negative ramifications for disabled people objectified by these messages. Movies, television shows, advertisements, online memes, and news articles that invoke inspiration porn portray disabled people as one-dimensional, stereotypical figures whose primary value and purpose lie in a superficial mood boost for non-disabled people. Inspiration porn reinforces to non-disabled people the central idea that disability is a tragedy to overcome, and a plight that non-disabled people are grateful to avoid. Common tropes that are displayed about disability include the *supercrip*, the concept that a disabled individual must not only overcome their disability, but also strive to achieve goals far beyond their disabled and non-disabled peers alike. A burdensome view of caregiving is also emphasized as a common trope perpetuated by objectifying images and commentary that portray disabled people as incapable of caregiving themselves or otherwise unable to contribute to society.

These media portrayals of disability are criticized for lacking substance, underrepresenting disability, and reinforcing stereotypes. While many people remain entirely unaware of the existence of inspiration porn, disabled people have been articulating the reasons why these characterizations perpetuate ableism and stereotypes about disability for years. Carly Findlay, an Australian disability advocate and writer, has written: "Disabled people are often called inspirational because expectations are so low. When we do something ordinary, we are seen as conquering our disability...I don't want to be an inspiration just for existing, or to make non-disabled people feel better about their own lives" (Findlay, 2019, para. 4).

Inspiration porn captures these low expectations and packages them in a seemingly positive message with significant viral spread capacity. Paternalistic and inspirational forms of ableism were found to be among the most pervasive forms of ableism because we misinterpret them as benevolent (Nario-Redmond, Kemerling, & Silverman, 2019). Infantilism, the persistent view of disabled people as perpetually childlike, is also a notable theme among examples of inspiration porn. Gagliardi (2017) leveraged this theme to analyze the sentiment of Facebook captions to identify inspiration porn. The use of childish terms, like "sweetie," were often invoked in comments discussing disabled adults. Other forms of media mirror these trends with 90% of autistic characters in fictional books and 68% of autistic characters in film depicted as children (Stevenson, Harp, & Gernsbacher, 2011). While perpetrators of sharing inspiration porn online span a large spectrum in background, parents of disabled children are the most likely to share a variation of objectifying online material...desperation porn.

Sharenting: Parents Seek Support and Look for Community

The birth and burgeoning of social media platforms have offered new avenues for parents of children with disabilities, a group that has historically reported feelings of isolation and uncertainty in charting the unknown waters of raising a disabled child. Parents of disabled children often desperately seek connection and understanding that can only be shared with other parents in similar situations. While it is essential to give extra support to these parents, it is equally imperative that we recognize the often-unhealthy underpinnings that this outlet creates; a platform that openly allows harmful, ableist views. The singular focus on the burdensome aspects of disability and caretaking often takes center stage in these forums. This online narrative leads to further unhealthy concepts, such as the able-bodied savior. The non-disabled parent is portrayed as a hero or even a martyr for assuming even basic parenting responsibility of their disabled child. All the while, these concepts are not only propagated on public display on social media, but also greatly impact the mental health of the disabled community as they often are forced to be voiceless observers of said content. When identified, called out, or disputed by a disabled person, the response is often not apologetic but a doubling down of ableism by labeling the disabled individual as "too sensitive."

"Sharenting" is a form of communication privacy management in which parents decide what information and images to share broadly online about their children's lives (Goggin & Ellis, 2020). While the general practice of sharenting has its critics among those that believe children shouldn't be depicted online until they are of age to consent, it also offers the positive benefits of learning together and a sense of togetherness for families of disabled children, including those with rare conditions who may otherwise feel alone in their experiences. Sharenting has even grown into a profitable pursuit for some online influencers, sometimes called "mommy bloggers" (Hunter, 2016). With the move to commercialization for some, sharenting across various social media platforms, like Facebook and Instagram, has seen an uptick with little regard for privacy or confidentiality concerns (Rogers & Green, 2015). These issues have relevance for disabled children who are almost always unknowing and without consent the subjects of their parents' public postings (Goggin & Ellis, 2020).

Sharenting of content about disabled children is also complicated by the non-disabled gaze, which invalidates disabled bodies and considers a curiosity about disability as reason or even a right to intrude (Loja et al., 2013). This curiosity may manifest in intrusive questions from strangers (i.e., "What happened to her?") or uncomfortable stares. The erosion of privacy and autonomy begins early for the disabled child, whether it be through the intrusion of medicalized care or the charitable disposition that demands disabled people be the objects of benefaction (Loja et al., 2013). The broad online sharing of personal moments related to disability fuel these curiosities and remove what few barriers may avert the gaze in face-to-face situations.

Desperation Porn: Ratcheting up Cries for Help with Graphic Images or Calls for Attention?

Families who engage in sharenting typically cite a desire to provide support for others and build a community as the motivation of their posts (Morrison, 2011). Because social media communities are propelled to growth from likes and views, posts that generate high degrees of interest are the formula for a successful sharenting profile. Some parents have exploited this reality further by sharing graphic images of children in distress related to their disability. This has been termed *desperation porn* due to its similarity to inspiration porn in objectifying the disabled experience to hotwire an immediate and sudden response of attention and sympathy to the poster (Ayers, 2012). Desperation porn was coined to describe a troubling trend observed within online communities for people with Osteogenesis Imperfecta (OI) and their families. OI causes bones to break easily.

With the growth of large, online social media groups composed of parents of children with OI, some parents began sharing graphic images of their children mere moments after fractures/injuries. In these photos, their limbs were visibly misaligned by sometimes compound fractures. It is typical for families of children with OI to splint a fracture at home. Many of these images capture children's agony prior to splinting. The children are visibly distraught, and the adult is out of frame capturing the photo instead of providing physical comfort. The photos are usually captioned with pleas for help, prayers, and descriptions of the family's distress.

Desperation porn is not specific to OI, a brittle bone disorder; it is equally disempowering for other types of disabilities. Several parents of autistic children maintain high-profile social media accounts with content depicting their children experiencing meltdowns. Other parents have shared images of teenagers with disabilities shown in various stages of undress on the floor of a public restroom because there are too few changing stations large enough to accommodate their needs. With the intention to advocate for better accessibility in public restrooms, the reality remains that the photos are publicly available via Google Images detached from original commentary describing the advocacy effort.

Parents of disabled children are typically non-disabled. While intimately connected to disability, their disabled child's disability is a horizontal identity (Solomon, 2012). These non-disabled parents, like most in society, have deeply held beliefs that associate sympathy and pity with disability. Ableist beliefs do not resolve immediately with the birth of a disabled child. In addition to parenting a child with an identity different from their own, these parents seek support. Nearly all women (98%) between the ages of 18 and 29 years old and across racial and socioeconomic lines in the United States have a mobile phone and access to social media, where these online communities reside (DeHoff et al., 2016). Access to online communities is prolific and far exceeds access to in-person support sources. For parents of disabled children, empowerment is gained from social support that provides both information and an emotional buoy in a shared experience (DeHoff et al., 2016). While these online communities offer parent-to-parent support, they are also frequently rampant with examples of inspiration and desperation porn.

Desperation porn may be a knee-jerk reaction to share a moment of agony without consideration of long-term implications.

Sometimes images or videos fitting the criteria of desperation porn are shared in an effort to advocate for better access or inclusion of disabled people. Parents may also fail to note the differences between developing an identity as a parent of a disabled child and developing an identity as a disabled person. As one blogger wrote, "The problem, for me, is that my story, for better or worse, is completely intertwined in my son's" (Stephanie, 2015). Desperation porn differs from inspiration porn because the former claims to seek immediate help; it generates a sense of urgency and pity. While these posts claim to seek support for parents, they rarely showcase images or videos of the parents themselves in a state of vulnerability or distress. The objectification of the disabled person is central to this type of media.

Disclosing Disability

Privacy and preservation of identity should be a concern for all parents sharing information about their children online. Protecting information like full names, birthdates, and addresses is important. Parents who share information online about their disabled children may overlook the complexity of disability disclosure in later phases of life, which further promotes the infantilization of disabled individuals. Today's generation of young people are the first to grow up with an online history, only part of which may have been self-created, but all of which is searchable by nearly anyone.

Some disabled adults have attempted to educate parents about the risks of outing someone's disability. One young adult with Osteogenesis Imperfecta urged parents in a Facebook group of more than 6,000 parents to refrain from posting intimate details about their child's disability, "If you think long term, it's better for your child when he/she goes into the job market. I was in a sorority for years in my undergrad and let me promise you, if people are diligent enough, they WILL find everything online; possible employers will be looking and find it all, closed group or not...Disclosing disability is very complicated and discrimination while hiring (while technically illegal) is still very much a problem" (Sofia, 2017).

The dynamics of such a discussion with a potential employer could be irreparably changed if the interviewer uncovered the employee's image online with objectifying messaging aimed to elicit pity. Both desperation and inspiration porn complicate the already precarious experiences and decisions around disclosing disability. Disabled people themselves are often strategic and intentional about the degree to which they disclose specific aspects of their disability (Furr, Carreiro, & McArthur, 2016). Both desperation and inspiration porn complicate these already precarious experiences and decisions around disclosing disability.

Triggering Medical Trauma among Disabled Adults

Negative consequences of sharing images of desperation porn can extend beyond potential harm or embarrassment for the subject of the image to other adults with disabilities, whose histories of medical trauma may be triggered by seeing graphic, usually unexpected pictures or videos of bodily harm similar to what they may have experienced. Little is known, overall, about the role of graphic media exposure in the response to news or a collective tragedy. One adult with Osteogenesis Imperfecta explains:

> I have two simultaneous reactions when I see parents post pictures of fractures. First, I can almost feel the child's fracture having had so many myself. Second, as an employment lawyer I get very angry because I know that photo may be used against those children in all sorts of ways, as a justification of discrimination. Parents are clearly not thinking of those of us that have had similar trauma and they definitely don't think about how they are actually hurting the future opportunities of that child. (M. Duprey, personal communication, February 1, 2021)

Tensions between Disabled Advocates and Non-Disabled Parents

As noted previously, it is often disabled people who point out the problematic nature of inspiration and desperation porn. These images, stories, and portrayals may be posted by parents, friends, or family members of disabled people. The response of the original poster or person sharing the information is often characterized by defensiveness. Because society is so steeped in a medicalized and tragedy model of disability, it can be difficult for most people to consider why these portrayals are dehumanizing. Many are outright shocked that a cure is not a universally adopted goal for disabled people. A disabled advocate who attempts to educate others about these issues is often outnumbered, characterized as overly sensitive or bitter. They are often ostracized and accused to be set on ruining a feel-good moment or a desperate cry for support.

Repetition of these online interactions persist and further the divides and tensions between disabled adults and non-disabled parents of disabled children. Many parents who have a disabled child report little to no experience or knowledge about disability prior to their child's surprising birth. Ableism is pervasive in our society, yet we assume that parenting a disabled child somehow remedies stereotypical and oppressive ways, or thinking or behaving related to disability. Until we address it, the ableism within the non-disabled parent community continues to stymie the need for united progress toward disability acceptance.

Carey, Block, and Scotch analyze the complex relationships between disabled advocates and parent advocates in their 2020 book *Allies and Obstacles: Disability Activism and Parents of Children with Disabilities*. They discussed the imbalanced distribution of power between these groups: "Parents tended to wield greater political and economic capital to influence disability policy, and their relationship with disabled activists [is] thorny. Although parents always argue that they are fighting to improve the world for their child, the goals they espouse at times differ dramatically from those of disabled activists" (p. 4). A similar trend is observed in creating online support communities for parents of disabled children. These communities and online narratives are typically established by and for the non-disabled parents, who remain a member of the dominant culture despite the affiliation and parenthood of a disabled child. Goggin and Ellis (2020) describe how the disability narrative is once again controlled and framed by the non-disabled narrator:

> In effect, in this dominant view, parents assume the role as the active and important agents in the discussion, with children with disabilities serving as widely accepted key site of social anxiety. The sum total of this arrangement is a reinforcement of pervasive social assumptions that "other" and stigmatize people with disability. (p. 222)

Proposed Solutions to Reduce Dissemination of Inspiration and Desperation Porn

A just and inclusive society is hindered by the perpetuation of ableism. As such, reducing the creation and dissemination of inspiration and desperation porn holds promising benefits for both disabled and non-disabled communities. A need for support or solidarity is the most identified reason for sharing inspiration or desperation porn. Perhaps most unfortunate about the persistent nature of these flawed forms of communication is their failure to accomplish what may be the intended goal. Inspiration porn worsens, not betters, attitudes about disabilities. Desperation porn may quickly accumulate thousands of views while failing to offer any real help beyond vaguely supportive messages from strangers. Amassing more effective avenues for community-based support to parents of disabled children is essential. Also, among these priorities should be an integration of disabled voices into spaces in which disability is central to the discussion.

Just as parents are educated about how to change a J-tube, facilitate speech, or splint a broken arm, they should learn about ableism and its multiple deleterious effects on their children. The medical aspects of disability often change over time. For some individuals, symptoms may stabilize into adulthood. Ableism persists. Teaching parents about ableism from a social dominance perspective may increase rapport building between non-disabled and disabled communities, leading to more equitable interactions (Kattari, 2015). The potential for more non-disabled parents to be powerful anti-ableist allies exists.

Media platforms also hold accountability for the harm perpetuated by these objectifying images and commentary. Broad censorship of disability-related content is problematic, but some platforms allow dissemination of images with children who are nude or in various states of undress *because* they are disabled. Such images of non-disabled children would almost immediately be flagged for their potential exploitation. Disabled adults have also been met with resistance from platforms when they've asked that objectifying images taken without their consent be removed. Media platforms that aspire to be anti-ableist should show this commitment by enacting policies to respond to the most egregious examples of user-created ableist content. They should affirm the diversity of bodies and minds by increasing disability representation overall across all forms of media.

While it has been emphasized that inspiration and desperation porn differ from the more commonly known sexualized forms of media, perhaps there are lessons from efforts to reduce the distribution of porn through media literacy education. When 13- to 25-year-olds were taught how and why sexually pornographic portrayals of women objectified women and contributed to sexism, their own sexist view became weaker (Vandenbosch & van Oosten, 2017). Teaching allies the connection between images objectifying disability and ableism may have the same promising effect.

Finally, it's important to maximize the efforts to reduce these harmful images by teaching people to identify them in the first place. In the age of misinformation and disinformation, it's increasingly difficult to decipher underlying messages from the media. Many people who share forms of inspiration or desperation porn do so with intentions to spread awareness or increase the disability representation they see missing in much of our mainstream media. When actions further marginalize an already oppressed group, intention matters less than impact. Teaching people at an early age to understand ableism, how to identify ableist messages, and what to say in response would significantly improve the accuracy and inclusivity of disabled perspectives in media.

Further empirical research needs to explore the impact of various media portrayals on ableism. It's not always clear what classifies as inspiration or desperation porn. Clarity and consensus around common elements would allow better identification and response to these portrayals. As advocates call for more and better disability representation, we must also widen and diversify the network of support to non-disabled parents raising disabled children. Tensions between these groups detract from a shared goal of a more just society for future generations of people with disabilities. Balanced and fair portrayals that center the disabled experience empower instead of objectifying. Too often, the actual story is lost because repetitious re-workings of the same inspirational story are told over and over again. The true story of the disabled experience is often so much more interesting and richer. If given the chance, these stories, too, could have viral potential.

Discussion Questions

1. Where is the line between inspiration porn and positive disability representation in media?
2. Why does inspiration porn often spread virally on social media? What makes it so popular to share?
3. What are strategies to educate people about the harms of inspiration porn and stop its spread?
4. How can parents with disabled children combat the issues mentioned in this chapter?
5. How can you be an ally to the disabled community via the internet?

References

Ayers, K. B. (2012). Desperation porn: The impact of graphic medical images on the disability community. *Audacity Magazine*. https://www.audacitymagazine.com/desperation-porn-the-impact-of-graphic-medical-images-on-the-disability-community/

Carey, A. C., Block, P., & Scotch, R. (2020). *Allies and obstacles: Disability activism and parents of children with disabilities*. Temple University Press.

DeHoff, B. A., Staten, L. K., Rodgers, R. C., & Denne S. C. (2016). The role of online social support in supporting and educating parents of young children with special health needs in the United States. *Journal of Medical Internet Research, 18*(12), e6722.

Findlay, C. (2019). *On being called an inspiration*. Retrieved May 1, 2021, from https://carlyfindlay.com.au/2019/02/03/on-being-called-an-inspiration/

Furr, J. B., Carreiro, A., & McAurthur, J. A. (2016). Strategic approaches to disability discloser on social media. *Disability and Society, 31*(10), 1353–1368.

Gaghardi, K. (2017). Facebook captions: Kindness or inspiration porn? *M/C Journal, 20*(3).

Goggin, G., & Ellis, K. (2020). Privacy and digital data of children with disabilities: Scenes from social media sharenting. *Media and Communication, 8*(4), 218–228. doi:10.17645/mac.v8i4.3350

Hunter, A. (2016). Monetizing the mommy: Mommy blogs and the audience commodity. *Information, Communication & Society, 19*(9), 1306–1320.

Kattari, S. (2015). Examining ableism in higher education through social dominance theory and social learning theory. *Innovative Higher Education, 40*(5), 375–386. doi:10.1007/s10755-015-9320-0

Loja, E., Costa, M. E., Hughes, B., & Menezes, I. (2013). Disability, embodiment and ableism: Stories of resistance. *Disability & Society, 28*(2), 190–203.

Morrison, A. (2011). "Suffused by feeling and affect": The intimate public of personal mommy blogging. *Biography, 34*(1), 37–55. http://www.jstor.org/stable/23541177

Nario-Redmond, M. R., Kemerling, A. A., & Silverman, A. (2019). Hostile, benevolent, and ambivalent ableism: Contemporary manifestations. *Journal of Social Issues, 75*(3), 726–756. doi:10.1111/josi.12337

Recuber, T. (2013). Disaster porn! *Contexts, 12*(2), 28–33. doi:10.1177/1536504213487695

Rogers, J. M., & Green, F. J. (2015). Mommy blogging and deliberative dialogical ethics: Being in the ethical moment. *Journal of the Motherhood Initiative for Research and Community Involvement, 6*(1).

Shackelford, A. (2016). "Orange is the new black" is trauma porn written for white people. *Wear Your Voice.* Retrieved February 21, 2019, from wearyourvoicemag.com

Sofia, K. (2016). I was in a sorority for years in my undergrad and let me tell you people are diligent [Osteogenesis Imperfecta (OI) Community Forum group post]. *Facebook.* http://www.facebook.com/groups/43935368633/search/?=sorority%2C%20disclosing%2C%20undergrad.

Solomon, A. (2012). *Far From the Tree: Parents, Children and the Search for Identity.* Simon & Schuster.

Stephanie. (2015, July 7). *Sharing our stories on social media: How much of my story is mine to tell?* The Road We've Shared. http://theroadweveshared.com/sharing-our-stories-on-social-media-how-much-of-my-story-is-mine-to-tell

Stevenson, J. L., Harp, B., & Gernsbacher, M. A. (2011). Infantilizing autism. *Disability Studies Quarterly, 31*(3). dsq-sds.org/article/view/1675/1596. doi:10.18061/dsq.v31i3.1675

Vandenbosch, L., & van Oosten, J. M. F. (2017). The relationship between online pornography and the sexual objectification of women: The attenuating role of porn literacy education. *Journal of Communication, 67*(6), 1015–1036. doi:10.1111/jcom.12341

Whisnant, R. (2016). "But what about feminist porn?" Examining the work of Tristan Taormino. *Sexualization, Media, & Society, 2*(2). doi:10.1177/2374623816631727

Young, S. (2014). *Inspiration porn and the objectification of disability.* TEDxSydney. http://tedxsydney.com/site/item

Scribbles

Melanie Coughlin

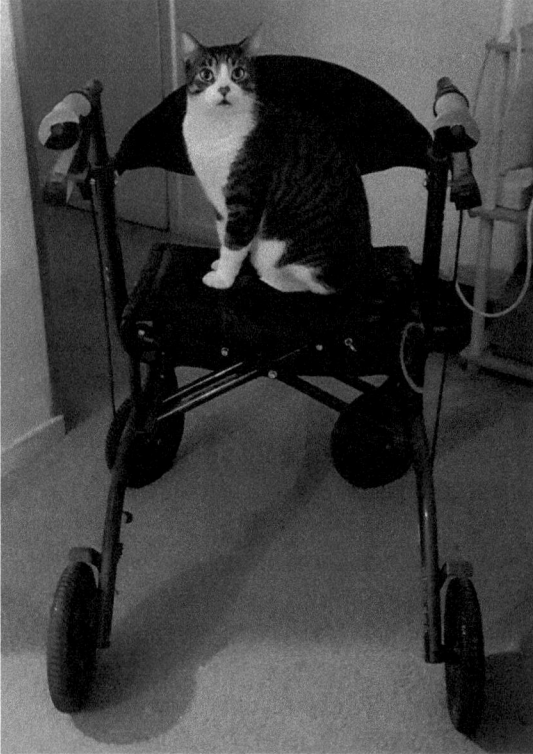

ID: A brown tabby with white tuxedo sits on his owner's rollator (a device that provides support and a place to rest for standing/walking).

• • •

I adopted Scribbles when I first became consistently reliant on mobility aids. Hardships of his earlier life in a roadside ditch had created in him nutritional needs that took time to resolve, and my own challenges were buoyed by the enjoyment of life that rioted within the expanding energy of his movement. To this day, Scribbles enacts a distinctly unprejudiced and thoroughgoing appreciation for the possibilities offered by my precious mobility aids.

© PAUL D. C. BONES, JESSICA SMARTT GULLION AND DANIELLE BARBER, 2022
DOI:10.1163/9789004512702_015

CHAPTER 11

Tap Tap Tap

Marie Gagnon

"Olivia! Stop that!"

I cringed. My mom hated when I tapped—when I tapped—when I t—tuh—tuh—tuh—tapped—my fingers, but I had to keep going. I had to keep tapping until it felt right, until the world told me *fine. Enough.* I couldn't stop until then.

If I did, the world would burn.

"Olivia!" she snapped. "Cut it out! You're going to give yourself arthritis."

I squeezed my eyes shut, as if my scrunched-up face could block out her voice. I couldn't lose track of the beat—the beat—the beat of my finger on my thigh, or I'd have to start over. I felt the smoke pouring into the corner of the room, hot and roiling, and I bobbed my head in time to the rhythm.

Mom huffed, and went back to flicking through her magazine.

I felt tears edge at my eyes. I'd told her that it just makes it worse when she complains about my tapping, that I already lived in fear of my joints locking into crooks of charred and splintered bone, the smoke swelling inside my body like puffy bruises.

What I hadn't told her is my wrist already aches from the tapping, and that I ice it every night so I can fall asleep. If she knew, she would just try to stop me even more. Snatch my wrist at the dinner table. Make me carry her bags at the store, so maybe I wouldn't be able to keep tapping. But I had to.

I had to keep tapping.

It wasn't time to stop yet, but a pain jabbed through my forearm, like a spark melting into my skin. My hand felt heavy and dense, like it was hardening into coal as the smoke edged closer, wisps starting to seep into my pores. I tried to imagine my hand breaking free from the hardened talons of coal, but it wouldn't soften into skin. My fingers continued to harden, the space around each molecule in my hand filling with ash. It crystallized its way up my arm, a crunching mass of carbon. I tapped faster.

© MARIE GAGNON, 2022 | DOI:10.1163/9789004512702_016

The world hissed at the change in rhythm and I tried to return to the old, steady beat. It didn't feel right anymore. I thought I saw a fleck of orange light outside the window—a spark—but when I looked again it was gone. Maybe a reflection from a passing car. I was tapping, after all. I was tapping. Nothing could burn while I tapped. While I tap-tap-tap-tapped.

I muttered the word as quietly as I could, hoping Mom wouldn't hear me. I had to aspirate the t and the p, the t and the p, the t and the p the t and the p. The snap of my tongue against the back of my teeth for the tuh—tuh—tuh—t, like the flick of a thumb over the wheel of a lighter. The strike of a flint, the t as hard a sound as I could make. Tuh—tuh—tuh—tuh like the sound of stilettos clicking on marble floors.

The smoke was thick now. I could feel it curling around me. It pricked at my eyes, but that sensation could have just been my tears.

How could my mom not feel it? It unfurled into our living room, all around us, ready to devour, but she just kept flipping through that magazine like it wasn't about to smolder in her hands.

I tap-tap-tapped, and tried to calm myself. But I didn't want to breathe in this air. I held my breath and tapped as fast as I could, as if I could wave away the smoke if I could just move my hand faster.

"Stop that tapping!" my mom snapped.

I pressed my hands flat against my thighs. I clutched at my legs, digging in my nails, and watched as a spark alighted on the potted lily by the window. As its soil turned into embers and its petals shriveled in flames.

A wisp of black smoke unfurled from the blossom, and I grabbed my mother's glass of iced tea.

"Olivia! What are you doing? Give me my tea."

A spark popped from the flower, and my mom shrieked. She stumbled getting up from the couch, and lunged for the phone.

I walked over to the flowerpot, and tipped her iced tea onto it. The flames disappeared in a curl of smoke, and I started tapping my fingers on my thigh.

Tap-tap-tap-tap.

Discussion Questions

1. Why do you think the author chose not to name or diagnose the source of Olivia's repetitive behaviors? What do you think the tapping signified/represented?
2. A major component of this story is Olivia's relationship with her mother. What message do you take away from this relationship/story?

CHAPTER 12

Adaptation from the Margins
Toward a Crip Theatre

Christopher Bryant

It's 2019. I hold a script development for my Crip-led adaptation, *Factory*. Early on in the process, one of the actors asks about my experiences making theatre while navigating an acquired brain injury. She works at the intersection of cognitive disability and performance. She wants to know how I've personally found the experience of creating from a place of difference.

"What we used to do was just pick out a play for our outpatients to perform and hand it down, but it never went well. And, fair. Not everyone wants to be a munchkin in *The Wizard of Oz*. Now we ask which character they most want to play in all the world, and devise a show around, 'What if these characters met?' Of course, then you end up with Terminator meeting Mary Poppins, but I think that's kind of exciting, honestly. I was just telling one of the cast members that I'd be at rehearsal on Friday but not today; just to reassure him I'd find a place in the script where he can sing 'Feed the Birds.'

He really loves that song."

• • •

This story clearly illustrates the discussion at the heart of this chapter. When a text is adapted by and for people outside the traditional majority, it may offer new insights into a well-worn story. Adaptation holds the potential to subvert the theatre industry's undue focus on ablebodiedness; thereby allowing disabled artists to reclaim what we've previously been excluded from. By actively including those left out of popular narratives, an adaptation may raise questions around the voices included and excluded from theatre, in particular from the adaptation's source-text.

In *Redeeming the Text*, Charles Martindale (1993) writes that "the interpretation of texts is inseparable from the history of their reception" (p. xii). This claim speaks to the root of a problem found often in theatre (and exemplified by *Marat/Sade*—but more on that later). That is, as the world changes, a piece of theatre can change from "of the moment" to museum-piece to downright offensive. As an institution, Western theatre has historically told able-bodied stories at the expense of nearly all others. When disabled stories *are* told, the roles are usually given to abled actors. To date, this lack of representation has been broadly left unquestioned. I posit that if we take Martindale's provocation as even partially true—that a text is *often* inseparable from the history of its reception—a radically inclusive form of adaptation could be a way of slicing through this Gordian knot of representation.

The difference between inclusion and accessibility is simple but vital for a sense of belonging to permeate the theatre industry. Accessibility gives a disadvantaged party access to something that remains largely exclusive: like, say, the casting of disabled actors as munchkin characters in *The Wizard of Oz*, allowing them to access 5 minutes of group stage time where they won't get in the way. Inclusion, meanwhile, *includes* the disadvantaged party, building from the ground up. Where theatre is concerned, this means ensuring that diversity is inherent in the fabric of the final theatrical product, and that anybody involved can present their "full" and actual self. Working to actively increase theatrical inclusion is often deemed a niche concern attributed to marginal-specific companies, rather than an important task with far-reaching implications. But claiming inclusion is niche is essentially claiming that diversity is niche, rather than a direct agent of disabled agency and community.

Key Term: *Crip*

Crip is a term used predominantly by disabled people as a marker of self-identification. As with queer, Crips understand the significance of the disabled experience, and want to reclaim a term used to historically hurt them. Disabled artists "have been appropriating, inhabiting, theatricalizing, and re-signifying the very terms of extravagant abjection used to disqualify them" (McRuer, 2018, p. 125). By "Cripping" Peter Weiss' *Marat/Sade*, I aim to destabilise the negativity and cliche that runs through the play; addressing the problems in the way the text and production have treated disabled people and proving that said treatment was unnecessary and unimaginative.

Key Term: *Adaptation*

"Adaptation is repetition, but repetition without replication" (Hutcheon, 2013, p. 7). In just seven words, Linda Hutcheon manages to cut to the heart of the act itself. Despite the differences in adaptive approaches, most theorists agree: creative adaptation is the transposition of a work from one form into another form—as simple and as complex as that. This transposition can take many different forms, but even if source and target are the *same* form (play-to-play, film-after-film), a fundamental shift in the source-text's context occurs. Adaptation is "repetition" in the sense that it is ostensibly a "rewriting" of a preexisting story; it is a repetition with difference. Not a replication, but rather an expansion—an engagement with the source text as it is retold.

Defining Crip Adaptation

As Crip is a self-determined descriptor, so too is a Crip adaptation: defined as much by the intent behind the work as the orientation of the people who make it. Disabled people are excluded from able-bodied culture, and as a result we create new ways of relating to the world around us. Therefore, the intent behind a Crip adaptation is first to undermine the pervasiveness of able-bodied culture. This undermining acknowledges that textual interpretation—what a text means—is totally dependent on the context of audience, actor, adaptor alike, and so creates space for new interpretations by considering disability. While adaptation often sets itself up for failure by establishing a defined end-goal—to do justice to its source text—a Crip adaptation acknowledges the multitude of interpretation and meaning, and likewise, the multitude of social intersectionality surrounding any text.

As adaptation guru Linda Hutcheon writes, a "successful" adaptation should be "an engagement with the original text that makes us see that text in different ways" (Hutcheon, 2013 p. 16). The point of a disabled-led adaptation, then, is not just to transpose or update the source text with accessible characters, but instead to *reread* the story itself, with disability ingrained at a deeper dramaturgical level; an inclusive text, fundamentally rebuilt from the ground up. A Crip adaptation considers the representation and intent behind its source text in order to comment on the present—and perhaps the life and ability of its adaptor, director, cast, crew. What has previously been thought of as a linear transposition (adaptation as A to B) becomes something more rewarding and subliminal. This is all to ask: what does a previously closed-off source (play, book, film, song) look like when confronted with actual inclusion? Through deconstructing the power of presumed and compulsory ablebodiedness, both artists and audience alike see themselves represented on stage—a true intersection of ability, race, sexuality, age. To date, theatrical inclusion has largely been as a special case, with undue emphasis placed on the cast and crew's diversity. Instead, the aim here is to make diverse representation *on* stage as commonplace as it is in everyday life.

The point of making this definition is that these are not simple concepts. To Crip "is to adopt an orientation toward the world that asserts the potential for *radical transformation of so-called normative social scripts, desires, and ways of life*" (Godden & Hsy, 2013, p. 318, emphasis added). Disabled bodies and minds are cultural texts, source material in their own right, interpreted and given meaning by an audience suddenly asked to consider them onstage. The presence of disabled performers, playwrights, and adaptors in a Crip project underlines the importance of us performing the truth of our own stories, rather than an abled hypothetical. Moving disabled theatre out of a disability-specific space emphasises that disabled concerns speak equally to nondisabled people too.

Ablebodiedness is widely held as a societal norm. Able bodies and minds are socially presumed, and they are equally ingrained into the dominant mode of storytelling. But a Crip adaptation asks more of its audience and its creators alike. Disability is often seen as an identity that we would never want to have—although disability awaits everyone in one sense or another, even simply through the ageing process. Through the performance of the disabled body, a Crip adaptation draws attention to the construct of performance, questioning the idea of truth or coherence onstage. This is adaptation that embraces a "failure to be proper" (Ahmed, 2006, p. 543), where the monolithic standard of an able-bodied "proper" exists, and is shirked by the disabled community who live effectively outside of it. By refusing the proper standards of theatre past, a Crip adaptation remains open to both narrative and formal possibility. This openness results in larger implications for traditionalist form. It may reshape narratives into a more fantastical conceit, using the adaptor's disabled experience to reread a source text. It may blend together an array of disabled experiences to create a dream-like adaptive text. It may also find countless other methodologies for reorienting its source material. Through this shifting methodology, a Crip adaptation invites us to engage with the world around the adaptation itself; to look at what it might be responding to and how. By turn, this affects playwrights and theatre-makers without the immediate resources to see themselves in theatre. It speaks to the sharp difference between diversity ("we are here") and inclusion ("we are *present*") in playwriting.

Notes on *Marat/Sade* (1964)

The Persecution and Assassination of Jean-Paul Marat as Performed by the Inmates of Charenton Asylum under the Direction of the Marquis de Sade (otherwise known as *Marat/Sade*) is a political stage play written in 1963 by Peter Weiss. In 1808, shortly after the French Revolution, the Marquis de Sade—at the time locked up in Charenton Asylum—stages a play he has written about the recent assassination of radical Jacobin Jean-Paul Marat. All characters, aside from Sade himself and the hospital's regime, are played by the Asylum's patients, adding a metatheatrical layer to the piece and creating the revolutionary tension at the heart of the narrative. In Weiss' play, disability is deviance, and the asylum's inmates are posed as a genuine threat to the real-life audience. His characters are an oppressed mass; speaking and acting at inappropriate times, and victimised by the hospital's wardens. The play's characters regularly find themselves unable to commit to the roles they've been cast as, serving as a constant source of tension for Coulmier, the director of Charenton.

As the play makes clear, "the use of disability as a dramaturgical device tends to erase the particularities of lived disability experiences" (Sandahl, 1999, p. 15). By setting *Marat/Sade* in an asylum, Weiss robbed his inmate characters of any genuine power or agency. Characters are known only for their "in-play" historical figures (Charlotte Corday, Jean-Paul Marat, Jacques Roux), and their pathologies round this out; we never engage with the truth of the "inmate" below, only a set of signifiers for each illness. His unnamed characters are just generally "crazy," where "crazy" acts as a stand-in for "threatening" or "pitiful."

Directed by Peter Brook, the Royal Shakespeare Company debuted *Marat/Sade* in London in 1964, before transferring to New York in 1965. This production had substantial implications for the way that Weiss' play was received and reproduced in the Western world. Brook's production featured a chorus of crudely drawn disabilities performed by a largely abled cast, and the "horror" of disability, that is, characters unable to control their violent urges, often breaking the fourth wall to terrorise the real-life audience. Weiss' play infamously ends in a "disabled riot," the "insane" cast tearing each other apart before turning on the audience in the play's final seconds. Disabled vilification is equally in the written text and the way it was realised, raising questions around the performance of disability—who is it for? Why does someone have to perform at such a highly disabled level? Does a performance need to be so recognisably clichéd in order to be valid?

Every reason I have for adapting *Marat/Sade* stems from this one truth: that Peter Weiss' play itself is built around an inherently ableist proposition, and therefore raises extreme problems in terms of a Crip analysis. At no point in its production history does it appear to have engaged with the disabled community; not as Weiss wrote the text itself, nor as the initial production was being developed. This immediately calls to mind "nothing about us without us" (Charlton, 1998, p. 3), the rallying cry of the disabled community, itself later adapted by many other marginalised communities. Similarly, as an exercise adapting and subverting an actively ableist text (rather than inserting a Crip layer into an able-bodied or minded text) provides a deeper dramaturgical engagement with Crip theory.

Factory (2019)

> If our past and our present are written by death, then what does the future hold? How can we even say there'll be a future? When we're gone, we leave something behind: a history that's still being written. When all is said and done, I want to be on the right side of it.
>
> I want to look at my surroundings and ask: what's next? What's left?
>
> I want to ask: shall we find our way out of all expectations? (Bryant, 2019, p. 69)

My adaptation of *Marat/Sade* was written as part of a practice-led adaptation project with Monash University, Melbourne. As much as Crip theory broadened my thinking around disability and representation, it also provided an effective framework to approach Weiss' play. My writing was initially informed by a superficial similarity: in *Marat/Sade*, Corday comes to Marat's door three times. She gains entry on the third, and murders him. In 1968, Valerie Solanas came to Andy Warhol's door three times. She gained entry on the third, and so attempted to murder him. This similarity allowed me to play with an initial expectation held by the audience—that they knew what would happen as the play unfolded—and then spend the rest of the play dismantling it.

Character and Performance

The process of writing *Factory* was as a complex root system, with Valerie Solanas as the tree rising above the ground, and each character stemming off from her world and experience. I treated everything I consumed about The Factory and its stars as research for my adaptation; falling deeply in love with each of them as I worked. I loved them because ultimately, I related to them. Warhol was the world-famous artist without social skills, shunned by the harshness of the gay experience and his own near-death and disability experience. Solanas was the radical feminist who screamed that all men should die before winking at her audience, never quite letting on how much she believed, wrestling with a mental illness that would overwhelm her. Edie Sedgwick was the mean-girl supermodel with surprising depth, her fame belying a great internal disconnection, in turn cultivating her substance abuse. The outliers to the Warhol story were equally chosen for these values. First Anna Nicole Smith as a replacement for *Marat/Sade*'s Herald narrator, with the obvious iconography of Warhol's Monroe "gone wrong." Next, Kathy Acker as the female de Sade, who wrote iconic and controversial books in her time, and likewise held a tenuous link to Andy Warhol in life (as Sade did to Marat). My cast of characters were all frightened at the state of the world, and each had their own experiences of chronic illness (Acker, Solanas), disability (Warhol), addiction (Smith, Sedgwick). Finally, instead of Weiss' Coulmier, here I gave life to an imagined version of Peter Weiss himself—someone I had kept returning to as I wrote, whose source-text had (intentionally or not) hurt the community I belong to. This Weiss was the Author as metaphor; a representation of the theatrical ableism that has haunted *Marat/ Sade*.

Emulating the Weiss' play-within-play structure allowed *Factory* to exist largely free from concerns of accurate casting, and create space for disabled actors. In writing, it is impossible to predict the play's future, but at the very least I could insert a writer's note: "Cast this play with actors who fall within the Social Model of disability. Characters' pathologies have not been mentioned, and I encourage performers to explore their disability within the text as they see fit (if comfortable)" (Bryant, 2019, p. 1). My aim was to speak to the multitude of disabled identities in existence, and to speak to (or provide for) the multitude of disabled theatre professionals I personally know. Not stating (or "requiring") a certain type of disability to be performed acknowledges the shifting nature of disability itself—the fact that disabled bodies do not necessarily work (or "act") on cue. This allows for movement away from cliché, and provides space for actuality, encouraging performers to show pride in their disability. Notably, what is set down in the text version of the play could (and perhaps should) be thrown out or deconstructed in support of its disabled performers. A script is an imagined blueprint for a wider aim, and if *Factory* needs to be altered so that its creatives can perform it, so be it.

Place and Dramaturgy

With characters established, I began to consider setting, coming to Foucault's Panopticon prison as a Crip-iteration of Charenton. In the Panopticon—as in the lives of disabled people—a look is imbued with meaning and potential judgement as connections are made and broken, as people are vilified. Whenever someone is performing—in a Panopticon, and in our society—it is because they are being "seen" (or "watched," under Foucault's "unequal gaze"). My life with an acquired disability speaks to these notions of appearance and performance. As I explore my changed identity, I constantly question if I am "disabled enough" to make someone believe I have a disability, or if I look or act "disadvantaged" enough according to some judgmental Other. My body appears largely normal (but what does normal mean?), but both my physical and mental capacity shifts from day to day. One day I might be too tired to leave the house, another I might happily walk for 6 hours. One I might get vertigo and migraines, another I might have the balance of an abled person.

This adaptation, and I am all about performance—who is doing the performing, what marks they are hitting, how convinced whoever is watching might be.

A far cry from the physical violence of Weiss' Charenton Asylum, *Factory*'s Panopticon operates instead on mental violence, rules and regulations enforced by psychological compliance. "Visibility is a trap"—prisoners are placed around the outer rim of a circular institution observed by a guarded watch tower at the centre. This is dubbed the "unequal gaze," where "inspection functions ceaselessly." Prisoners remain unaware if they are being watched at any given time (Foucault, 1975). Inmates are motivated to act as though they're being watched at all times, and they are—if not by the watchtower, then by each other. From their respective cells, prisoners can see far out across the institution, but not to the compartments either side, they remain unaware as to who else is in the prison. Punishment seems random—sometimes not coming, sometimes overwhelmingly and without reason—leaving all in a state of hypervigilance. Because of this, the prison is run with minimal intervention as the prisoners "make real" their own compliance.

With setting and character established, Weiss' blueprint would naturally be altered as I wrote, by my own interests, and likewise by the addition of characters placed at the margins of society. Scenes and sequences began in imitation of Weiss' play, but quickly grew in their own direction. This direction was informed by their characters' intertextuality, and most featuring subconscious references to my disability, my queerness, and to Weiss' play (references I did not appreciate until reading it as a whole). Images call to mind and play with moments from *Marat/Sade*, but equally to my own experiences being in and out of hospitals, as well as in and out of recovery. Instead of building expectation for a simple retelling, the structure, dramaturgy, and casting of *Factory* are all designed to engender a disabled act of failure. As in *Marat/Sade*, here disability cannot appear as anything other than failure, because the characters they represent are already established in the collective audience's mind. But unlike *Marat/Sade*: this is failure that gives rise to enjoyment, rather than disappointment.

The Riot

Perhaps the most egregiously ableist moment of *Marat/Sade* is the riot that ends the play. Since the first moments of the text brutality has threatened to spill over. Dissenting patients are all controlled through the threat (or execution) of violence, to the point of complete normalisation; violence is simply how Charenton is run. In the final minutes, the patients finally fight back. Agitated toward their own revolution by Sade's monologues, a *"column of PATIENTS begins to march forward,"* the rhythm *"grow[ing] in power. Fully at the mercy of their mad marchlike dance,"* they attack the wardens, the administration, and their fellow inmates. *"Suddenly the whole stage is fighting"* (Weiss, 1965, pp. 100–102) before turning to the audience themselves. In the filmed production, the camera cuts outside of the asylum for the first time, allowing the real-life audience a moment of reprise as they are reminded they're watching a fiction. In the script, the play ends instead on this bleak image: an orgy of violence and disabled people brutalising each other as the able-bodied audience become "Crip victims." I had held this moment in my mind as I wrote *Factory*. I knew I was building toward the play's climax, and remained both conscious of Weiss' mistakes while understanding the basic rules of dramaturgy and narrative structure. For *Factory* to reach a satisfying resolution, *something* needed to occur. But what? In *Cruising Utopia*, José Esteban Muñoz writes: "The eventual disappointment of hope is not a reason to forsake it as a critical thought process [...] it is nonetheless essential," for creativity, for connection, and for the future (Muñoz, 2009, p. 10). This entire project emerged from an acknowledgement of theatre's present shortcomings, and my resultant hope for something better: to subvert an ableism that is so ingrained in our culture that it's often hard to properly acknowledge. Instead of ending on a replica of *Marat/Sade*'s violence, I needed to end with a version of this hope.

Minority stories alike are all-too-often sacrificial; characters are brutalised or killed, with the indication being if they had not been a minority, had experienced that oppression, they would have lived. But the bleakness of the world doesn't mean we should forget hope, an active hope that shapes our future in response to current inaccessibility. To this aim, the play ends with the cast moving out of this conflict together and exiting the stage to join the audience—sort of a ceasefire between audience and performer. The act of having disabled characters breaking the presumed hierarchy between audience and performer speaks to a hope for something better (as indefinable as this may be). This is not to say, "We are all the same," but rather "We are all different, human, *legitimate*, and we refuse to play by rules set down by somebody else." This is the hope that we, as a collective consumer, have had enough of these stories; that we can move past them into something better. Appropriately, Muñoz in part draws this belief "from Warhol's philosophy [...] the understanding that utopia exists in the quotidian" (Muñoz, 2009, p. 9). Utopia exists inside a coke bottle, inside an act of connection, or inside a disabled cast dismantling the walls between "us and them."

Conclusion

In 2017, disabled actor Kate Mulvany played Richard III for Australian company Bell Shakespeare, to critical acclaim, in part because of the opportunity to present her genuine self. "I've spent most of my life disguising my body, especially on stage [...] Playing Richard, I can walk the way my body wants to, rather than the way in which I usually present to the world. I'm very proud of my disabilities but no one has ever really seen them. It makes me proud to perform as Richard" (Mulvany, 2016). If this is the effect one Crip character has on one Crip actor, imagine the potential a wholly Crip play could have.

When the disabled community isn't even a consideration for most theatres, what does true disabled representation look like? Those at the margins of experience are often expected to work twice as hard for less gain and less opportunity. But constantly creating in a mode of resistance is not tenable; we need to embrace the mediocre, to allow ourselves to be human—to be okay to not be exceptional. In the context of this methodology, this might mean adaptation—or new plays entirely!—not focused on dismantling an actively ableist text, but instead cultivating an array disabled narratives where disability is included *in* the narrative, but is not the *focus* of it. Not Crip-as-inspiration and Crip-as-victim, but instead: Crip-as-*human*. By allowing disabled artists to be "mediocre," the world might then begin to take disabled art seriously—removing it from its own subcategory to readily engage with non-disabled artists and consumers. This works twofold, providing more complex representation for storytellers, actors, designers, directors. Secondly, imagining a more integrated future allows and encourages others to do the same. If the future can be made real through art, the possibilities are endless. We need a balance of new and old, so why not Crip the old as we return to it?

Discussion Questions

1. What other disabled representation can you think of—on stage, but perhaps in film, TV, or fiction? Can you identify why each example is positive or negative—what makes them so, and do their actions and character arc center on the fact of their disability?

2. What does a "disabled mediocrity" look like on a stage? How might makers tell disabled stories without centering a narrative on a disability "victim"?

3. In a group, identify a story that works against a marginalized group and adapt it from the perspective of this group—work out the dramaturgical beats and ways you can subvert the source text. Then, swap story outlines with another group. What worked? What didn't? Why?

References

Ahmed, S. (2006). Orientations: Toward a queer phenomenology. *GLQ: A Journal of Lesbian and Gay Studies, 12*(4), 543–574.

Bryant, C. (2019). *Factory* [Unpublished play script]. Monash University.

Charlton, J. (1998). Nothing about us without us. In *Nothing about us without us: Disability oppression and empowerment* (pp. 3–18). University of California Press.

Foucault, M. (1975). *Discipline and punish: The birth of the prison* (A. Sheridan, Trans., 2nd ed.). Vintage Books.

Godden, R., & Hsy, J. (2013). Analytical survey: Encountering disability in the middle ages. *New Medieval Literatures, 15*, 313–339.

Hutcheon, L. (2013). *A theory of adaptation* (2nd ed.). Routledge.

Martindale, C. (1993). *Redeeming the text*. Cambridge University Press.

McRuer, R. (2017). No future for crips: Disorderly conduct in the new world order; or, disability studies on the verge of a nervous breakdown. In A. Waldschmidt, H. Berressem, & M. Ingwersen (Eds.), *Culture – theory – disability: Encounters between disability studies and cultural studies* (pp. 63–77). Transcript Verlag.

McRuer, R. (2018). *Crip times: Disability, globalization, and resistance* (Vol. 1). New York University Press.

McRuer, R. (2020). Compulsory able-bodiedness. In G. Weiss, A. Murphy, & G. Salamon (Eds.), *50 concepts for a critical phenomenology* (pp. 61–67). New York University Press.

Mulvany, K. (2016). Kate Mulvany takes on villainous Richard III for Bell Shakespeare's 2017 season [Interview by Elissa Blake]. *Sydney Morning Herald.* https://www.smh.com.au/entertainment/kate-mulvany-takes-on-villainous-richard-iii-for-bell-shakespeares-2017-season-20160922-grm7fw.html

Muñoz, J. (2009). *Cruising utopia.* New York University Press.

Sandahl, C. (1999). Ahhhh freak out! Metaphors of disability and femaleness in performance. *Theatre Topics, 9*(1), 11–30.

Weiss, P. (1963). *The persecution and assassination of Jean-Paul Marat as performed by the inmates of the asylum at Charenton under the direction of the Marquis de Sade* (G. Skelton, Trans.; verse adaptation by A. Mitchell). John Calder Ltd.

Pepper

Brian

ID: A black, brown, and white border collie wearing a red leash looks up at the camera.

• • •

My pet is Pepper. She's a Border Collie pup. Her mother is a working sheepdog in Derry, Northern Ireland. Now she lives with me on The Black Isle in the Highlands of Scotland.

Pepper is helping me cope with life as a profoundly deaf person who is about to go through major surgery for another disability that I have—a colostomy. She's a bundle of kindness and fun.

© PAUL D. C. BONES, JESSICA SMARTT GULLION AND DANIELLE BARBER, 2022
DOI:10.1163/9789004512702_018

CHAPTER 13

Diagnosis Limbo

Danielle Barber

A hidden chronic illness can be defined as a health condition or disease that is experienced long term, and the associated symptoms are not always readily apparent or visible to others. Students living with a hidden chronic illness often choose to not disclose their illness in order to avoid stigma and discrimination (Åsbring & Närvänen, 2002; Moore, 2012; Riddell & Weedon, 2014; Vickers, 1997). Erving Goffman (1963, p. 42), explains the dilemma of stigma management as "to display or not to display, to tell or not to tell, to let on or not let on, to lie or not to lie, and in each case to whom, how, when, and where."

Disclosure becomes even more problematic when you have symptoms, but you do not have a diagnosis. For many people living with a hidden chronic illness, the road to diagnosis is anything but a short speedy process. For example, a diagnosis of multiple sclerosis (MS) can take days, but typically years, to receive. The reason for this is that there is not a single definitive test that diagnoses MS. Some can remember specific events 20 years prior to their diagnosis, that they now attribute to MS flareups (Strickland, Worth, & Kennedy, 2017). Often reaching a diagnosis of MS is a relief, as finally reaching a diagnosis legitimized their journey for medical help and confirmation that their symptoms were not just "in their head" (Strickland et al., 2017). Strickland and colleagues wrote that "Many people engage in active information seeking and arrive at a self-diagnosis of MS before it is confirmed by a physician. This stage is described as a prediagnostic limbo and is a stage which is common in other chronic conditions with symptoms described as 'nonspecific'" (2017, p. 1718).

I conducted a study on female college students with chronic illness (Barber, 2019). When I first launched the survey, I received two emails that I would like to share. The first read:

> Hi Danielle! I'm an undergrad researcher here at TWU and I just want to say how much I appreciate your study! I have several chronic illnesses and have spent my whole undergrad working

on getting the right diagnosis and treatments, which had a huge impact on my college experience. I will definitely take your survey!

The second email read:

> I hope you are well on this day! I am emailing you with interest in helping you with your study; however, I am not entirely sure I qualify. This is simply because I display symptoms of Irritable Bowel Syndrome but I have not been to a doctor to diagnose that problem. It is also a lengthy process to truly diagnose it, and so I have been avoiding doing so. If I am not able to participate, simply tell me so, but I thought it was worth asking because I know how hard it is to get participants for some studies.

Both of these emails resonated with me, as they both sounded strikingly similar to my own experience. Additionally, participants were asked to indicate any barriers they encountered to receiving accommodations once they disclosed their hidden chronic illness. Case 74 stated that a barrier they experienced was "financial because you need to pay a doctor for paperwork," Case 61 stated, "Refusal to offer what I need (absence forgiveness)," and Case 21 indicated they felt "humiliation discussing my illness with both Disability Support Services and Instructors" (Barber, 2019, p. 47).

Six years ago, I was working full-time and about to finish my associate's degree at community college. Just a few months prior, I had undergone a diagnostic laparoscopy for extreme chronic pelvic pain that my doctor suspected was endometriosis. Sure enough it was, and the tissue that was causing the pain, growing where it was not supposed to, was removed. The physical pain from endometriosis was one thing, but I was deeply upset that I was just 23 years old and worried that this would lead to infertility. However, more importantly, I was relieved knowing that there was finally an actual real cause for my pain and I was no longer a "hypochondriac."

A few months after the operation, I was in my trigonometry class, sitting in the front row intently listening to the lecture and taking notes when suddenly my hand could not write. It is hard to explain, but I had experienced temporary moments of weakness in my hands before when picking up a glass of water or trying to turn the key to start my car, but it never lasted long, and I always brushed it off.

But this time I was in class trying to take important notes. I looked around scared and kept trying to write. Everything I attempted to write was entirely illegible. I was so frustrated that I wanted to cry.

In the days and weeks following, these moments of weakness and inability to use my fine motor skills in my hands became more frequent. I had extreme fatigue, debilitating chronic pain, and developed a drop in my left foot that eventually tore up most of my left paired shoes from scraping on the ground when walking. One day I developed a pain in my eyes, and the vision in my left eye was blurry for a couple of weeks. I also experienced restless leg syndrome, muscle spasms, nausea, and vomiting. I told my primary doctor about my symptoms and he referred me to a neurologist that I would see for a couple of years. This neurologist would later diagnose me with transverse myelitis, multiple sclerosis, and fibromyalgia. Initially—and still to this day—I have a lot of trouble trying to accept the diagnosis of MS because even though nearly every autoimmune disease had been ruled out by my neurologist, I did not have any lesions on my brain in my MRIs or o-bands in my spinal fluid. Because a single definitive test to diagnose MS does not exist, all other conditions that mimic MS must first be ruled out through various testing. Aside from findings from physical neurological examinations, in order to be diagnosed with MS there must be lesions on the brain, optic nerves, or spinal cord depicted by an MRI in two different areas, as well as o-bands found in spinal fluid through a spinal tap.

Each time I had a flareup of these bizarre symptoms, my neurologist would send me for Solu-Medrol infusions. A Solu-Medrol infusion is 1,000 mg of steroids that cannot be taken orally because the dose is so high you have to go to the infusion clinic and get the Solu-Medrol through an IV, which takes an hour. You do this for 3 to 5 days in a row. This always improved my symptoms and would be the only treatment that I would accept for MS from my neurologist. Shortly after this time, I lost my health care coverage.

So there I was, 26 years old, finishing up my undergraduate degree, now at Texas Woman's University. My final semester, I was managing a spa full-time and taking an 18-hour course load. It was in this semester that I would have another flareup of symptoms. Up until this point in my academic career I had maintained a 4.0 grade point average and was looking forward to graduating Summa Cum Laude. Except my dream would not come to fruition. This very last semester,

I had received two Bs, and not because my coursework was suffering, but because two separate instructors had a policy that if more than two classes were missed unexcused, then this would result in an entire letter grade deduction in your final grade. During this time, the policy to get an absence excused at my university was to go through the Office of Student Life, and if you missed class due to illness, a doctor's note was required.

Requiring a doctor's note for those with chronic illness is problematic. First, I did not have any health insurance at this time. Second, most of the time, in my experience, there is little to nothing a doctor's visit can do to alleviate symptoms of a flareup. Third, going to the doctor costs time and money, both of which are in short supply for any college student. I suppose I could have emailed my instructors and explained that I have MS, but I was not entirely convinced that I had MS; I just knew something was wrong with my health. I could have gone back to my neurologist, uninsured, and had him send the documents to Disability Services for Students (DSS) at my university, as he had offered to do for me in the past. But did I really want a paper trail of such a stigma? Did I want all my professors automatically knowing this about me at the beginning of each semester, as this is how DSS works? No, I did not. Thus, my absences were not excused and even though the points I earned in both courses would have meant an A, I received a B in two classes for missing three classes that semester. Three classes, out of 27 sessions meant a drop in an entire letter grade. I did not miss class because I was out partying or hungover. I did not miss class because I was lazy or because I did not care. I love school and I can guarantee that I would have much rather been in class than feeling physically terrible. Needless to say, my perfect GPA that I had maintained for over 100 credit hours, was ruined and I did not get to graduate Summa Cum Laude.

So, here I am now, and I have been in graduate school for a little over 2 years and I am not any closer to figuring out what is causing my symptoms. I do have health coverage now, and I have gone for a second opinion to two different neurologists, both of which do not think that I have MS, but that I have fibromyalgia. They both recommended getting MRIs every 6 months to monitor that I am not developing lesions in my brain. Regardless of my diagnosis, the symptoms that I have experienced are real, real in their consequences (as the Thomas Theorem would say), and there is no doubt that these symptoms have—and continue to—impact my experience as a college student.

Even though I try my best not to, I constantly worry about my future. Will I be able to be independent or will I become a burden on others? When will I have another flareup of symptoms, and how will I handle it? If I do end up with MS lesions, will I lose my cognitive skills? I have also spent quite a bit of time grieving the person that I used to be 6 years ago, and I have had to rethink a lot of my plans for the future. But there are a few things that I am certain about. I wake up every day thankful, grateful, and blessed for the good health that I do have. I am especially grateful every day that I wake up and am able to walk. I have also come to realize, especially through this research, that even though everyone's experience is unique, I am not alone in my experience as a female college student living with a hidden chronic illness. Considering the two emails I received inquiring about my study, the road to diagnosis for many with chronic illness is a long and frustrating journey. I am grateful for the opportunity to contribute to chronic illness research, and with this research, I hope to raise awareness and influence universities to change their policies that disadvantage their students with invisible chronic illnesses.

Discussion Questions

1. How are compulsory attendance policies ableist? What are ways that professors could check for engagement, that allow for disability flares and other issues that affect attendance?
2. What are some barriers to receiving accommodations through disability support services in institutional settings, and how could these be changed?
3. What criteria, if any, should be used to obtain accommodations in organizational settings?
4. Self-diagnosis (self-dx) has been proposed as a cost-effective alternative to medical diagnosis for accommodation. Part of the argument for requiring an "official" diagnosis is that non-disabled students could claim to be disabled to get additional time on exams and other accommodations. If you are non-disabled, how likely would you be to apply for disability accommodations if you were not required to prove a disability?

References

Åsbring, P., & Närvänen, A. L. (2002). Women's experiences of stigma in relation to chronic fatigue syndrome and fibromyalgia. *Qualitative Health Research*, 12(2), 148–160.

Barber, D. (2019). *Hidden chronic illness in female college students* [MA thesis]. Department of Sociology, Texas Woman's University.

Goffman, E. (1963). *Stigma: Notes on a spoiled identity*. Jenkins, JH & Carpenter.

Moore, I. S. (2013). "The beast within" life with an invisible chronic illness. *Qualitative Inquiry*, 19(3), 201–208.

Riddell, S., & Weedon, E. (2014). Disabled students in higher education: Discourses of disability and the negotiation of identity. *International Journal of Educational Research*, 63, 38–46.

Strickland, K., Worth, A., & Kennedy, C. (2017). The liminal self in people with multiple sclerosis: An interpretative phenomenological exploration of being diagnosed. *Journal of Clinical Nursing*, 26(11–12), 1714–1724.

Vickers, M. H. (1997). Life at work with "Invisible" Chronic Illness (ICI): The "unseen," unspoken, unrecognized dilemma of disclosure. *Journal of Workplace Learning*, 9(7), 240–252.

Luther & Layla

Danielle Barber

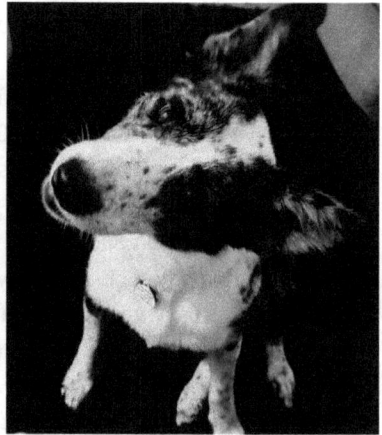

ID: (Left) A white dog with brown and black markings and blue eyes looks at the human just behind the camera. (Right) a black and white dog with spots looks up at the camera, head tilted to the side in confusion.

• • •

Luther came with that name because I rescued him from a previous abusive home. Luther and I have a bond like no other because we both have PTSD. I understand that you can't come up behind him because this spooks him and makes him jump (just like me). I understand that loud noises startle him and if I can control it, always warn him that there is about to be a noise. His safe place is underneath the bed, so I always make sure he has access to this spot. I never ever push him too far out of his comfort zone.

Layla just came into my life, so we haven't formed a disabled relationship, but she's too cute to leave out.

DOI:10.1163/9789004512702_020

CHAPTER 14

Successful Sad

Vanessa Ellison

She gives a wink and a thumbs up with her perfectly French manicured thumb to the teller at the window. After she flashes a confident smile, she turns to walk out of the building, and the storm cloud comes. There isn't an actual storm. The weather **is** sunny and **beautiful, but** she has a personal, metaphorical storm cloud that is **depression**. It **follows her** to her car. She tries to turn up the music to drown it out but it is too late. Rain in the form of tears is already flooding her face and down her suit jacket. Her phone rings and **she** inhales two big gulps of air, plasters on a smile, and answers in her best customer service voice.

"I'm having a breakdown right now. I can't help you!" she wishes she could say.

However, the conversation sounds more like

"Of course I can! Yes. Say no more. It is already done. You **can** depend on me. You're very welcome!" she says as she ends the call.

Great. Another project that she doesn't have time to add to her schedule. Why does she **overcommit**?

She is a successful sad person. They are the cheerleaders amongst us who smile and encourage others, but cry in the restroom in between classes and skip meals because they are too busy. It is the inside outsider. The person that everyone is acquainted with, **but nobody knows**. She doesn't get invited to private social gatherings because people see enough of her on websites and TV. She is envied and liked **at the same** time.

Her façade is her **perfectionism**. It **is her coping mechanism** to keep her getting out of bed each day. She's exhausted most of the time but always manages to follow through with her commitments. She is **that** girl. The one that is so **high-functioning** that no one believes that she is sad. It has taken many years of self-training for her to perfect her **act**. She studied actresses and starlets to learn how to hold back tears **in public** and to smile through rage. She coats her eyelashes with mascara and drinks water **to avoid crying** before she attends meetings where she knows she will be belittled and

© VANESSA ELLISON, 2022 | DOI:10.1163/9789004512702_021

discounted. T-E-A-M player! **She** is a pro at helping others navigate through their challenges but can't conquer her own. No one ever asks her how she is doing or if she is okay because she **appears** "fine." She's not. I promise. Sure, she's **successful** by societal standards, and **she is** also undoubtedly **depressed**.

Discussion Questions

1.   Are there social and/or cultural implications of revealing a disability to others?
2.   Are "invisible illnesses" such as depression trivialized? Why or why not?
3.   There are some aesthetic and popular culture trends based on sadness. Does this help or harm mental illness awareness (i.e., Japanese Yami-kawaii, sick cute, emo)?
4.   What do you think depression "looks like"? Can you be depressed but look "normal"?

Monkey

Emily Dall'Ora Warfield

ID: A Maine coon cat stands in front of a vase, with sunflowers draped over his back, and looks at the camera.

• • •

It didn't feel real when Monkey died last week—not just because he was only eight, but because for 8 years he had been the one to comfort me when I was feeling too terrible to be around other humans. I suffer (and I use that word intentionally) from severe depressive episodes, which come with extreme fatigue and psychomotor retardation in addition to depressed mood. Monkey not only kept me company in those times, but compelled me out of bed to feed him when I couldn't feed myself. If I'd known he had the fatal heart defect common in his breed, if I'd known that's what caused his own fatigue, I still would have picked him over the others every time. He reassured me of the worth of a chronically ill life, both mine and his.

© PAUL D. C. BONES, JESSICA SMARTT GULLION AND DANIELLE BARBER, 2022
DOI:10.1163/9789004512702_022

CHAPTER 15

Ðdeaf Adjacency

Liminal Conditions of Not Hearing

Megan Marshall

This chapter examines deafness as both a diagnosable biological condition and an embodied collection of experiences. By juxtaposing an autobiographical narrative alongside a discussion of historical, cultural, and theoretical perspectives, I provide a framework for identifying and acknowledging the range of Deaf, deaf, and hearing identities in order to demonstrate how the weight of cultural and contextual influence is more disabling than the actual audiological condition. This chapter concludes with a brief overview of Deaf Gain theory, and my connection to it, as a perspective that subverts the connotations associated with deafness by highlighting its affordances.

Although this chapter will go into more depth in regard to deafness, Deaf Culture, and the identities and descriptions they contain, it should be noted here that:

- *Capital "D" Deaf* references people who identify and participate in most/all aspects of Deaf culture, who communicate primarily via signed language. It also applies when describing contexts in terms of Deaf Gain theory.
- *Lowercase "d" deaf* describes the general state and diagnosis of deafness; those who are partially deaf (*hard-of-hearing*) to the extent they require assistive technology to participate in the "hearing" world. People who are deaf likely do NOT use signed language or participate in Deaf culture.

Troubling Disability

In the fall of 2019, I was in the midst of a lesson that introduced basic tenets of disability theory for students in my Young Adult Literature course. I framed this discussion against two texts we'd recently covered: a novel with a highly functioning autistic protagonist *Marcelo and the Real World* (Stork, 2010) and CeCe Bell's graphic novel *El Deafo* (2014) inspired by her experiences grappling with sudden deafness caused by childhood meningitis. As the class began dissecting the either/or notion of ability, I shared an excerpt from Robert McGruer's 2002 essay "Compulsory Able-Bodiedness and Queer/Disabled Existence" where he applies Judith Butler's theory of gender trouble to the idea of normative ability, proposing that

> Everyone is virtually disabled, both in the sense that able-bodied norms are "intrinsically impossible to embody" fully, and in the sense that able-bodied status is always temporary, disability being the one identity category that all people will embody if they live long enough. (p. 374)

McGruer's words prompted a strong response from many students who voiced opposition to his claim. One raised an eyebrow before saying, "I don't buy that at all. Who's to say people need to become disabled before they die? Sometimes people are fine and then they just...die." Chatter arose about scenarios involving robust men in their seventies who were killed in car accidents or who lived long lives before succumbing to quiet death while sleeping. Students wielded these hypothetical situations to neutralize the threat of disability, keeping it far away from them. This maneuver was familiar to me, as it's something I'd practiced for a long time.

Disability in Disguise

At some point in my childhood, the tiny hair cells in the chambers of my ears' cochleae began to deteriorate. There was no event to announce what was happening; I did not wake up one day, suddenly unable to hear. This lack of defining incident means there was nothing specific to point to and nothing specific to blame. Instead, I have spent years speculating. Was it firing rifles at camp without ear protection? Did I clonk my head too hard, too often? Maybe my mother picked up a virus in the place of my conception (Morocco), and it traveled through her bloodstream and into my genetic code, biding time before settling into the task of chipping away at my audiological functions.

However, being unable to pinpoint the cause of my hearing loss does not mean that I can't enjoy placing blame, because I do. I fault my ears for my horrific math skills, which have forever barred me from high-demand careers in biomedical engineering or software development. In fact, I'm certain my math scores on every college entrance exam I've taken are among the lowest of test-takers across the globe. Though one might point to other factors, such as my lack of aptitude and effort, there's an additional explanation.

As many public-school students can attest, math gets more complex once multiplying and dividing fractions enters the picture. For me, fifth grade was the point when terms like reciprocal, variable, and inverse entered the conversation, and it was a conversation led by a teacher who had his back to the class, dashing numbers upon a chalkboard. This was before projectors and smartboards were mainstream classroom tools, and it was common for most math teachers to deliver verbal instruction while actively engaging with the information they taught, turning their backs to the class while modeling math concepts on the board.

By the tail end of my elementary school career, I had already established myself as a mediocre student, but it was also true that I wanted to do well *enough*. Unfortunately, this is when I started to simultaneously notice and ignore the fact that I didn't always understand what teachers were saying. Imagine a pot of pasta being poured into a colander, with some of the strands slipping through the holes and down the drain of a sink. This was math class. For a while I tried to catch those noodles by raising my hand and asking questions or muttering "what did she say" to someone sitting near me, grateful for anyone who would let me copy their notes. But my teachers were not always receptive to my questions, because they had *just explained this 2 minutes ago, and wasn't I listening?* Whispering in class and copying from classmates was similarly discouraged, often noted on my report cards as "distracting others" and "talking too much." Eventually, it became easier to let those noodles slip down the drain, because there was enough pasta in the colander (or information jotted in my notebook) to get the gist and keep going. Until it got to the point that those long-gone noodles were actually pieces of a foundation for understanding the rising complexity of math...like algebra.

My decline as a mathematician aligns with my development as a person who could not hear as well as people assumed. The signs of my hearing loss were usually interpreted throughout my adolescence as flakiness, daydreaming, attention deficit disorder, laziness, and the classic "Megan hears what she wants to hear." None of these assessments were off the mark, because I *was* an easily distracted daydreamer, who, like many kids, sometimes chose not to listen on purpose. Therefore, when I performed poorly on informal hearing tests—such as those given by school nurses or aging pediatricians—my parents easily believed that I was not taking things seriously, goofing off, and/or looking for attention. As I entered and progressed through high school, my identity solidified as a space-cadet bookworm who floundered academically, got in frequent trouble for not paying attention to her parents or teachers, and who could always get a laugh when after sliding my glasses on before saying, "Okay, can you say that again now that I can see you?"

I have been asked how I managed to get through school without addressing the severity of "my problem." Part of this is because, for a long time, it was not clear that my level of hearing was that out of the ordinary. Growing up I wasn't the only one who got song lyrics wrong and ignored their parents, or who was baffled by the concept of dividing fractions. Also, I had long been constructing my coping mechanisms without being aware of what I was doing, relying on speech-reading skills as well as an impressive ability to interpret body language and facial cues to fill in blanks. For instance, as the sort of kid who always wanted to be in on the joke, I learned to pinpoint the moment someone was on the cusp of delivering a punch line in order to be among the first burst into laughter. While there were times when I hated putting effort into participating in group conversation in a loud cafeteria or from the backseat of the car, it was as easy to push those thoughts aside as it was to rely on the vague smile and nod combination, my go-to method for navigating a social situation impeded by background noise.

I also understood that asking questions someone had already asked was not scoring me points with certain teachers, and in those cases, it was easier to say nothing and hope for the best. Subjects where I could read for understanding (like English and history) came easily to me, and so that's where I put my efforts. I chose individually focused sports where I didn't have to listen for coaches or captains to call out plays or shout directions. Case in point: I joined the swim team after one season playing high school basketball, where my defining moment on the court was the day I careened into scoring an easy layup, forgetting that we'd switched sides after the half, interpreting the hollering of my teammates and coach as cheers of encouragement rather than entreaties to stop.

My instincts (however indefinable) led me to forge a path filled with activities that provided chances for success; I wanted to fit in, and this was how to do it. Yet my disability was hiding in plain sight, disguised as a benign personality quirk. When members of my senior class compiled the "Predictions for the Future" list, my entry read: "Megan Marshall will open Megan's Hearing Aid Shop, where she's not only the owner, she's also a client!" As my hearing issues had yet to be viewed as much more than an idiosyncrasy, what was essentially a mean-spirited jab at deafness was part of the joke; it was "funny" because I wasn't really deaf.

"You've Been Missing a Lot"

At 25, I worked in an office where part of my job required answering phones and taking detailed messages. My mistakes accumulated rapidly, and soon an observant coworker pushed me to get formally assessed. The day of my diagnosis, the audiologist administering my exam expressed amazement that I'd managed to get by with this "severe degree" of loss. "You're way down here," she said, tapping a pencil along the slope of x-marks marching toward the bottom of an audiogram grid. "You've been missing a lot," before crediting me with "stellar speech-reading skills" when she noticed me trying not to cry.

Soon, I was fitted for hearing aids that I couldn't afford[1] and hated wearing. For the first few years, those plastic lumps of misery were constant reminders of my body's failure; they squealed amplified feedback into my brain on the regular, reminding me as they hurt me of my inadequacy. They made my ears itch and ache while doing little to help me at work, as phone calls were amplified, not clarified (plus, putting a phone anywhere near them contributed to more feedback). On top of that, I was convinced that they stood out like beacons, signaling my brokenness. These discomforts to my body and vanity meant that I often left them at home.

The improvement in technology and fit coincided with my career shift to education, and I began to wear them more regularly. I had to. It was similar to my experience getting glasses for nearsightedness in middle school: I didn't know how much I was missing until I saw it with my new-to-me eyes. Just as there was no going back to squinting in order to see across a room, once the volume dial of my world got turned up to 7, my natural condition of hearing at a measly 3 was not going to suffice.

Definitions, Perceptions, and Performance

In the years since that first diagnosis, I still struggle to articulate an easy term for what my audiologist recorded as "bilateral moderately severe to profound sensorineural hearing loss." I need hearing aids in order to continue teaching, to go to movies and catch at least half of the dialogue, or to have a meaningful part in conversations that aren't one-on-one and face-to-face in a quiet environment (even so, those I'm speaking with should not have excessive facial hair, soft voices, or issues with how intensely I stare at their mouths). At night, once my ears are emptied of hearing aids, my family knows that attempting meaningful conversation with me is futile. But am I deaf if I can hear their voices or the faint sound of a door slamming, or am I deaf because of my inability to parse words out of the sounds they make? Or am I something else?

Answers to questions like mine are varied, likely because of uncertainty about the best approach for categorizing people in terms of their deaf (or hearing) status. Part of this is due to disparities regarding how and when someone loses their hearing (National Association of the Deaf, 2020). There are also other considerations: Is hearing loss relegated to one ear or is it bilateral? Is the loss symmetrical or is one ear worse than the other? How early or suddenly did it occur and how quickly was it addressed? How much linguistic ability does one have? (CDC, 2020). Even official definitions of deafness, such as this 2017 statement of the Individuals with Disabilities Education Act (IDEA) "a hearing impairment so severe that the child is impaired in processing linguistic information through hearing, with or without amplification" invites questions. What would be labeled a failure when it comes to processing information through hearing: missing ALL words, MOST words, or SOME words? If a child can process 20% of linguistic information without amplification but hears at 75% with amplification, are they more or less deaf than someone who can process 35% of words on their own, but averages only 60% with an assistive device? Definitions like this fail to acknowledge the unique variances of what it means to be deaf.

Scholars in the field of deaf studies have framed deafness in terms of lived experiences. In *Deaf in America* (1990), Carol Paddon and Tom Humphries claim that

> the lowercase deaf [refers] to the audiological condition of not
> hearing, and the uppercase Deaf [refers] to a particular group of

deaf people who share a language—American Sign Language
(ASL)—and a culture. The members...have inherited their sign
language, use it as a primary means of communication among
themselves, and hold a set of beliefs about themselves and their
connection to the larger society. We distinguish them from...
those who find themselves losing their hearing because of
illness, trauma, or age; [because] they do not have access to the
knowledge, beliefs, and practices that make up the culture of
Deaf people. (p. 2)

They also maintain that while Deaf people may be both Deaf
and deaf, the opposite is not true. Though deaf people may be
accepted as part of the Deaf community through active use of
ASL, participating in social and/or political activities, or otherwise
demonstrating an authentic investment in allying with members of
Deaf culture, their lived experiences remain significantly separate
from those who are more intrinsically Deaf (Paddon & Humphries,
1990). This is why Deaf culture is sometimes viewed as "collectivist"
(Mindess, 1999; Paddon & Humphries, 2005) and insular. Deaf
Studies scholar Thomas Holcomb (2013) emphasizes this point,
explaining "Deaf people are expected to be fiercely loyal to the Deaf
community...and spend most of their social time with Deaf friends"
(p. 24).

Ultimately, these explanations seek to show that deafness,
capitalized or not, is a dynamic condition resisting easy
categorization. Instead, one's deaf identity reflects the intersections
between a person's diagnosis and experiences, all of which are
informed by historical, cultural, and social contexts.

Ancient History and After

Historically, deafness has been regarded as a condition that renders
people socially and/or intellectually inadequate to the extent that
they lack the capacity to interact normally with others. This view
corresponds with the traditional medical model of disability, in
which one's biological and/or neurological deficiencies require
treatments, cures, or "fixes" that will correct or minimize impairments
(Grover, 2021). In relation to deafness, this has long meant the use
of hearing aids, cochlear implants, and/or targeted interventions via

social services and special education programs (McAnally, Rose, & Quigley, 2004) that have often been bolstered by the use of audist[2] approaches that label deafness and markers of deaf culture, such as signed languages, as inferior (Markotic, 2001).

This pathologizing has deep roots. Reviews of Greco-Roman literature suggest that deaf people were banished from social life, and considered "on a par with idiots" (Ferreri, 1906, p. 463). Aristotle is said to have claimed the deaf to be incapable of learning and of no use to rational society, while Plato went so far as to suggest they—along with all those who were visibly disabled—be put to death (Eleweke, 2011; Schmale & Eriksson, 1998. Centuries later, Saint Augustine is said to have described deafness more pragmatically, deeming deaf children manifestations of God's anger sent to punish parents. However, unlike Plato and Aristotle, there is evidence that Augustine was receptive to the notion that the deaf could communicate; he analyzed the significance of gestured exchanges he observed between deaf people, noting similarities between spoken language and signed interactions, which he felt indicated the potential for the deaf to "hear" God's word (Bragg, 1997).

This interest in signed vs. oral communication highlights the religious origins of formalized sign language, which was viewed as a means of bringing deaf people closer to God. In fact, although historians have pointed out that communication based on signed gestures likely extends to the beginning of mankind (Stokoe, 2001), the first public school focused on educating the deaf was founded in France by Catholic priest Charles-Michel de l'Épée in the mid-eighteenth century. He wanted to ensure the deaf were able to learn their way into heaven and developed a system of methodical signs (combining French grammar with the already-established rudimentary signed language of the deaf) to teach students to understand the word of God (Sacks, 1991).

Deaf Culture in the USA

In the early nineteenth century, Dr. Thomas Hopkins Gallaudet traveled from Connecticut to France to study with one of de l'Epee's successors, Abbe Sicard. There he met and took lessons with Laurent Clerc, a former student of Sicard's and a prominent deaf educator. Clerc accompanied Gallaudet back to the United States, and in

1817 they founded the American School for the Deaf in Hartford, Connecticut (Burch, 2002). Graduates of this school went on to form similar institutions in other states, providing deaf students with instruction in what eventually became American Sign Language (ASL). The establishment of ASL helped lead to the founding of what is now known as Gallaudet University in 1864,[3] the world's first postsecondary institution for deaf students.

For some, the proliferation of ASL was alarming. In 1884, Alexander Graham Bell issued warnings about the rise of Deaf culture, claiming that ASL encouraged the formation of a "defective race of human beings [that] would be a great calamity to the world" (Bell, 1884). Bell was no stranger to deafness: his father was a teacher for the deaf (using oralist methods); his mother was partially deaf, and his wife Mary Hubbard Bell, was profoundly so. Despite this connection to deafness (or perhaps because of it) he fought to keep deaf people from forming communities, and actively encouraged lip reading and oral communication over ASL (Bell, 1884; Wiles, 2015).

This practice, known as oralism, signaled a shift in the education of the deaf, perpetuating the idea that the best way for deaf people to integrate into mainstream society was to communicate in the same manner of the hearing. Oralists advocated speech training, teaching deaf children "to generate sounds, to mimic the mouth shapes and breathing patterns of speech" (PBS, 2007). Accounts from the 2007 PBS documentary "Through Deaf Eyes" show that the rise of oralism was widely considered to be the "ideal mainstream" approach for the education of deaf children; yet the use of ASL was not erased. Deaf schools, whether they embraced ASL or oralism, ensured that deaf people were brought together, thereby solidifying the presence of Deaf culture in the United States.

Other Than Hearing

The growth of Deaf culture is at least partially due to the very structure that scaffolds the Social Model of disability. This view posits that rather than limitations being the "fault" of the person with the disability, the failure exists with mainstream institutional and social structures that are not accessible or accommodating (Grover, 2021). In other words, the physical body doesn't disable someone, but a non-accessible society does. Within this society, deafness is able to swiftly reduce one's capital, be it educational, cultural, or economic. For although arcane views like Aristotle's have been invalidated by the formalization of worldwide signed languages and expansion of Deaf Culture, they have also been reinforced. While deaf people have the same intellectual capacity as hearing people, mainstream education is still designed to serve (and privilege) the hearing (NCD, 2018), which hampers access to the cultural and economic capital necessary for obtaining social status (Bourdieu, 1984).

Othering is structured upon a "set of dynamics, processes, and structures that engender marginality and persistent inequality across any of the full range of human differences" (Powell & Menendian, 2016). Putting this concept into conversation with the notion of performativity clarifies how degrees of deafness are interpreted, especially in terms of how society labels those who are either unable or unwilling to perform according to societal norms and expectations. In "Arguing with the Real," Butler (1993) examines "performativity as a specific modality of power as discourse" asking readers to consider how it is that those who designed and maintained societal expectations have accumulated the discursive authority to do so (p. 187). Therefore, even with assistive technology that helps one to "perform" as hearing or the benefits afforded by Deaf culture, most D/deaf people face systems, practices, and infrastructure established by the hearing *for* the hearing, reducing their power to fully reject marginalization.

Pathologizing Otherness

What many see as inborn rights does not necessarily extend to those with disabilities. In his article "Disability as Diversity" Couser (2008) calls this a "natural form of human inequality" (p. 98) that supports the paternalistic management of disabled bodies. Often, a person with disabilities must be modified with assistive (and costly) devices and/or rely on others to provide accommodations for access to participate in society. Once afforded this assistance, they become "privileged" with access to experiences, spaces, and opportunities that others generally take for granted.

Conventional wisdom posits that D/deaf people should seek medical interventions in order to correct the "body-gone-wrong" (Michalko, 2002), such as cochlear implants or hearing aids. On the surface, these interventions are seen as "gifts" that afford the experience of listening to voices of loved ones, to birdsong, to music. This gift also has a capitalistic function, in that it provides deaf people with the means of achieving mainstream educational and economic success for contributing to society (Marx, 2013), and granting the opportunity to maintain relationships with hearing people. To that end, the focus on successful integrations into mainstream spaces is what drives much of the research focused on deaf subjects' experiences in school, the workplace, and within relationships (Kamil & Lin, 2015; Vas, Akeroyd, & Hall, 2017).

My Loss, My Gain

Helping to push against the assumption that there is a normal way for a body to perform is the theory of Deaf Gain, which defines deafness as "less biological dead end...than evolutionary adaptation" (Bauman & Murray, 2014, p. xix), and a phenomenon that has long contributed to the world's biocultural diversity (Barnes, 2016). Moreover, empirical findings show the deaf brain is not just shaped by its loss in audiological capacity, but also by enhancements to visual and manual systems (Sutherland & Rogers, 2014). In other words, hearing loss is offset by additional benefits, which contribute to our sociocultural ecology.

I personalize this concept to argue there is no "natural" way to function in hearing (or Deaf) cultures except for the way(s) that I construct for myself. In other words, instead of mourning what was lost, I build on what has been gained, such as the heightened ability to "read" people's facial expressions and body language, and accept it as a gift that the world will go mute when I need it to, thereby increasing my focus and alleviating stress. This gain also means I'm engaged as a teacher, always alert for visual cues. Furthermore, my own experiences as someone who slid through the cracks has made me more perceptive to those who try to hide that they are struggling.

Certainly, participating in hearing society is exhausting, and it's easy to feel like a part-time citizen in an able-bodied realm, struggling to maintain probationary status. In new situations, my disclosures still lean self-deprecating. "My ears are terrible at hearing" seems easier than telling someone that I'm deaf, partially because I'm still conditioned to avoid appearing disabled, but also because to many, deaf = Deaf, which I'm not. In fact, the Deaf community is apt to view me as "more" disabled than Deaf people, as I lack ASL skills and require accommodation to participate in hearing society. It is a strange place to occupy, identity-wise. Yet, perpetual adjacency to both spaces has led me to accept that while I will always have to work harder to live as I want to, the boundaries of this world are flexible, and I can push against those edges to change its shape.

Discussion Questions

1. The Social Model of disability proposes that the primary disabling factor impedes one's ability to fully participate in their communities. In other words, it's the medical condition that prevents full participation in society. Are there limitations to this concept, and if so, what are they? To what extent could anyone (even "able bodied" people) view the world as disabling?

2. What are some reasons that the author's students appear to oppose the idea that "everyone will be disabled if they live long enough"? How did the chapter's discussion of mainstream beliefs and power structures provide some context for their resistance? How did the author describe her own history of resistance?

Notes

1   The American Speech-Language-Hearing Association reported in 2021 that less than half of U.S. states require that health plans cover (even partially) the costs of hearing aids, and the majority of those limit coverage to children and young adults. The cost of hearing aids ranges from $1,000 to $6,000 per ear and can be expected to last 4–7 years with proper care.

2   Audism is the belief that the ability to hear gives one privilege over those who cannot. The term was first used by Tom L. Humphries in 1975.

3   The "History and Traditions" page in Gallaudet University's website provides a timeline of institutional name changes. Though established in 1864, Gallaudet University was initially called the National College for the Deaf and Dumb, changing to the National Deaf-Mute College in 1865, to Gallaudet College in 1896, and then to Gallaudet University in 1986.

References

America-Language-Hearing Association. (2021). *State insurance mandates for hearing aids*. https://www.ashsorg/advocacy/state/issues/ha_reimbursement

Barnes, E. (2016). *The minority body: A theory of disability*. Oxford University Press.

Bauman, H.-D. L., & Murray, J. J. (Eds.). (2014). *Deaf gain: Raising the stakes for human diversity*. University of Minnesota Press.

Bell, A. G. (1884). *Upon the formation of a deaf variety of the human race*. U.S. Government Printing Office.

Bell, C. (2014). *El Deafo*. Abrams.

Bourdieu, P. (1984). *Distinction: A social critique of the judgement of taste* (R. Nice, Trans.). Harvard University Press.

Bragg, L. (1997). Visual-kinetic communication in Europe before 1600: A survey of sign lexicons and finger alphabets prior to the rise of deaf education. *Journal of Deaf Studies and Deaf Education, 2*(1), 1–25.

Burch, S. (2002). *Signs of resistance*. New York University Press.

Butler, J. (1993). Arguing with the real. In *Bodies that matter* (pp. 187–222). Routledge.

Centers for Disease Control and Prevention (CDC). (2020). *Data and statistics about hearing loss in children*. https://www.cdc.gov/ncbddd/hearingloss.data.htm

Couser, G. T. (2008). Disability as diversity: A difference with a difference. *Ilha do Desterro, 48*, 95–113.

Eleweke, C. (2011). History of deafness and hearing impairments. In A. F. Rotatori, F. E. Obiakor, & J. P. Bakken (Eds.), *History of special education* (pp. 181–212). Emerald Group Publishing Limited.

Ferreri, G. (1906). The deaf in antiquity. *American Annals of the Deaf, 51*(5), 460–473.

Grover, P. (2021). *Conceptual models of disability*. The American Academy of Physical Medicine and Rehabilitation. Retrieved April 20, 2021, from https://now.aapmr.org/conceptual-models-of-disability/

Holcomb, T. K. (2013). *Introduction to American deaf culture*. Oxford University Press.

Individuals with Disabilities Act. (2017). Sec. 300.8 C (3). https://sites.ed.gov/idea/regs/b/a/300.8/c/3

Kamil, R. J., & Lin, F. R. (2015). The effects of hearing impairment in older adults on communication partners: A systematic review. *Journal of the American Academy of Audiology, 26*(2), 155–182.

Markotic, N. (2001). Oral methods: Pathologizing the deaf speaker. *Mosaic: An Interdisciplinary Critical Journal, 34*(3), 127–140.

Marx, K. (2013). *Capital: Volumes 1 and 2: A critical analysis of capitalist production.* Wordsworth Editions.

McRuer, R. (2002). Compulsory able-bodiedness and queer/disabled existence. In R. Garland-Thomson, B. J. Brueggemann, & S. L. Snyder (Eds.), *Disability studies: Enabling the humanities* (pp. 88–99). MLA Publications.

Michalko, R. (2002). *The difference that disability makes.* Temple University Press.

Mindess, A. (1999). *Reading between the signs: Intercultural communication for sign language interpreters.* Intercultural Press.

National Association of the Deaf, Community Culture. (2020). *Frequently asked questions.* https://www.nad.org/respirces/American-sign-language/community-and-culutre-frequently-asked-questions

National Council on Disabilities. (2018). *IDEA series: The segregation of students with disabilities.* https://ncd.gov/sites/default/files/NCD_Segregation-SWD_508.pdf

Padden, C., & Humphries, P. (1990). *Deaf in America.* Harvard University Press.

Padden, C., & Humphries, P. (2005). *Inside deaf culture.* Harvard University Press.

Powell, J. A., & Menendian, S. (2016). The problem of othering: Towards inclusiveness and belonging. *Othering & Belonging, 1,* 14–39.

Public Broadcasting Service. (2007). *Through deaf eyes* [Documentary]. https://www-tc.pbs.org/weta/throughdeafeyes/about/transcript.pdf

Rose, S., McAnally, P. L., & Quigley, S. P. (2004). *Language learning practices with deaf children.* PRO-ED.

Sacks, O. (1991). *Seeing voices: A journey into the world of the deaf.* University of California Press.

Schmale, J., & Eriksson, P. (1998). *The history of deaf people.* Daufr.

Stokoe, W. C. (2001). *Language in hand: Why sign came before speech.* Gallaudet Press.

Stork, F., & Stork, F. X. (2010). *Marcela in the real world.* Scholastic, Inc.

Sutherland, H., & Rogers, K. (2014). The hidden gain: A new lens of research with d/Deaf children and adults. In H. Dirksen, L. Bauman, & J. J. Murray (Eds.), *Deaf again: Raising the stakes for human diversity* (pp. 269–282). University of Minnesota Press.

Vas, V., Akeroyd, M. A., & Hall, D. A. (2017, January–December). A data-driven synthesis of research evidence for domains of hearing loss, as reported by adults with hearing loss and their communication partners. *Trends in Hearing.*

CHAPTER 16

S-I-L-I-C-O-N-E Inject-Ear | Silicone Injections

In American Sign Language (ASL) Gloss and English

Raymond Luczak

above-lights-open-down f-l-u-o-r-e-s-c-e-n-t audiology clinic {all-around} e-e-r-i-e	The audiology clinic is fluorescent, a gray white light that breathes no shadow.
walls c-e-m-e-n-t floor l-i-n-o-l-e-u-m tall-plant corner fake	The walls are cement, the floor linoleum. Even the tall plant in the corner is fake.
audiology-person {wander- back-and-forth-by-my-side} p-o-w-d-e-r something l-i-q-u-i-d stir-stir-hard c-u-p	She moves in and out of my vision, stirring up powder and liquid in a plastic cup.
{scoop-up-mixture-from-cup slender-cylinder push-mixture-inside} audiology- person {tilt-my-head}	She spoons and forces the gelled mixture into a large baster before she tilts my head.
{strains-hard-inject-mixture- into-ear-canal} feel cold shiver-up-both-my-arms	The coolness of silicone injected deep into my ear canals shivers rivers.
me close-eyes suffer i-c-e shock	I close my eyes and absorb the thrill of hypothermia.

me-awaken {try-wriggle-ears-
opening-mouth-moving}
ears feel warm same-same
m-i-t-t-s

Awakening, I wriggle my ears
back.
My ears are now warm as mitts.

me-wait-wait s-i-l-i-c-o-n-e
ear become hard
become e-a-r-m-o-l-d future

Minutes pass as the silicone
hardens,
future clamshells of what I should
hear.

audiology person {pull-back-
ear-careful-pull-out-silicone
wipe-off} e-a-r-w-a-x

She carefully pries out each
impression,
taking away remnants of
cerumen.

silicone-impressions} two
drop-inside b-a-g name mine
those-two gone fine

As she seals each in a tiny bag
with my name,
I say goodbye to these babies.

strange {impressions-stuck-
in-ears} hear nothing perfect
clinic cold but {ears-pressed}
hear nothing home warm

Cradled inside my ears, their coos
had been
the only thing breathing in the
clinic.

Note

ASL gloss is simply using English words and ASL idioms in the ASL sign order. Just to be clear: there is no standardized ASL gloss system at all. It is impossible to convey even a fraction of all the rich nuances of an ASL sentence on paper. For instance, there are no mentions of the location for each person (or animal) referenced in the signing space, the spatial relationships between these people, the sign dialects, and so on.

CHAPTER 17

Utensils and Fire

Jessica Spears Williams

The field of Medical Sociology is broad, and the methods used by researchers in the field are many; however, most theories used in the field explain disability as some type of undue burden on society that requires disabled people to mask or hide their disability, or to expect to be treated as some type of burden to others as an unproductive member of society (Parsons, 1975). As I sit here looking through my notes that I have used as both a student and an educator, I have realized that the theories that I have most aligned with have not come from academia, but instead from the lived experiences of disabled non-academics who were trying to communicate their needs and limitations to others. These theories aided me in not only understanding my own limitations, but also in helping those around me.

Oftentimes, disabilities are invisible, which places an undue burden on us to find ways in which to explain our limitations to others. Santuzzi, Waltz, and Finklestein (2014, p. 204) define invisible illness as illnesses that have "no visible manifestation or have visible features that are not clearly connected to a disability," and in my own life I have found that to be true. I live each and every day in pain, but to the stranger my pain is not visible, and thus how can I say I am disabled? My family and friends have learned of my "pain face," and try to stop me from overdoing it, but when you don't look sick to the world around you there will always be comments about your performance that do nothing positive.

In order to help others begin to get a glimpse of the lived experience of a chronically ill person, many people have written essays, blogs, and even social media posts that use some type of metaphor to aid others in understanding. Because these are non-academic theories, they are often neglected by disability textbooks and ignored by academics who could use them to better help society, scholars, and even professionals begin to understand the lived experience of the disability community. Because the first step to helping is, after all, understanding.

© JESSICA SPEARS WILLIAMS, 2022 | DOI:10.1163/9789004512702_025

The theory that first came along to help the chronically ill community, explained through metaphor, is "The Spoon Theory." This theory, as written by Miserandino (2003) in her article, "But You Don't Look Sick," has been applied to both physical ailments and mental illnesses, and was one of the first theories that aided me in better understanding my own body. In her theory, Miserandino tells her friend that everyone wakes up with a finite number of "spoons" in the morning, and that every task requires a certain number of them. Spoons, in this case, are a metaphor for energy. With each task, the person sacrifices a spoon, and while there may be days where there are many spoons, there are often more days where disabled persons wake up with a negative spoon balance. In fact, before I found this theory, I remember sitting on my bed sobbing in defeat, because I did not have the energy (spoons) to shower, blow-dry my hair, put makeup on, and get dressed to attend my daughter's cheerleading banquet. Not to mention, had I been able to get through those tasks and attend, I would not have had the energy to attend to the other areas of my life that were being neglected: housework, graduate school assignments, dog care, and spousal support. As I carried Spoon Theory around with me and discussed it with other women in my life who had chronic health conditions, I realized that the one desire we all shared was to have more spoons, because once you add chronic illness to your lived experience there are simply never enough spoons to get through the day.

Out of Spoon Theory came a community who refer to themselves as Spoonies, who write blogs, social media posts, etc. to discuss their limitations in a way that others can understand. The disabilities/chronic illnesses that Spoon Theory helps us articulate to one another and the world is a great example of what Charmaz meant when she suggested that "serious illness challeng[es] people to integrate and coordinate the minutiae of their lives in new ways and, at times, to reinvent themselves" (2009, p. 50). I can no longer attend to life in the way that I once did, and find myself reserving spoons for the activities that bring joy to my life, as opposed to activities that do not. Within the spoonie communities, our roles as women, wives, girlfriends, mothers, graduate students, daughters, sisters, and teachers have all been affected by our illnesses, in ways that we cannot always articulate, but listening to other Spoonies share their stories has done exactly what Karp theorized and helped me "gain greater insight into my own life difficulties" (2009, p. 38), in addition to being an excellent way to aid others in understanding even a little of what it is like to have chronic illness.

Spoon Theory doesn't work for everyone though. And to address this, a whole field of theories has emerged using utensil metaphors. Fork Theory (Rose, 2018) suggests that unlike Spoon Theory, where people start their day with spoons/energy, people are often stuck with forks, both big and small, and oftentimes reach a point where they simply cannot function any longer. Everyone has a different ability or skill at handling the forks, but eventually everyone is going to be left feeling stabby. For me personally, I find that the more my chronic pain increases, the fewer spoons I wake up with, and the more stabby I am. For some people, forks could be small annoyances that feel like being stabbed with appetizer forks, and for others, forks could be the big one I use when shredding a pork butt, but ultimately everyone has a limit of what they can handle, and when combined with Spoon Theory, aids others in understanding chronic illness.

Now that we've moved halfway through our utensil drawer, let's talk about knife theory. Knife Theory (Masson, 2019) is what happens when you wake up with no spoons, and you borrow energy from the next day. While Masson (2019) uses an endearing example of the lack of spoons in the silverware drawer and having to use a knife to get his condiment out, the visual is a great example for those who need to understand what happens when there is simply not a spoon balance left. If I must grab a knife out of the drawer, I am not actually helping anyone, and someone is likely to get hurt—typically myself. If I "borrow" energy that I do not have and push myself beyond my limits, I am only hurting myself. When my energy drops, I often do things like fall and break body parts or drop objects, because with limited energy comes a smaller ability to balance my fragile body or to grip onto what I'm holding. Had I just acknowledged or even realized I was out of spoons, sat my ass down, and waited for my next spoon allotment, instead of grabbing the knife—blade first—my life would have been easier for the last 6 months. In the professional world, people would likely refer to this as burnout, but in the spoonie world we often struggle with admitting our own limitations and instead prefer metaphors in which we admit we feel stabby, even if the person we are hurting is ourselves.

As you can see from Spoon, Fork, and Knife Theories, the disability community is adept at coming up with metaphors to help the non-disabled around us visualize what our lived experience is like, but none of the utensil theories creates such a vivid picture as Johnson (2016) does in her Matchstick Theory. While her essay is written with an undercurrent of anger, I feel like it is an excellent example of what it's like when you combine the utensil theories into one. Matchstick theory suggests that instead of utensils every movement is like a matchstick, and we all know how finicky matchsticks can be. I mean, I once went through an entire box of matches trying to get a single fire lit, because some would break, and others just fizzled out. This imagery is probably more accurate in discussing the lived experience of the disabled community because matches are unpredictable. One example that Johnson used was going to the store to find out there are no accessible parking places. For me, this typically means, I'm just not going to the store, because I know that if I park elsewhere, I will not have the energy to get back home and put my groceries up—and we are only talking about 50–100 feet more distance, right? Because that's what it's like to be disabled. There are times that an extra 50 feet will be my undoing.

Perhaps my favorite part of Johnson's essay, and the reason I am including it is this quote: "These are my goddamn matches. I decide when and where to light them and how long to let them fucking burn. End of story" (2016). Because let's face it, for the chronically ill, there are people who are constantly standing there with their hands out asking for a spoon, and are often shocked when they get knifed instead. But additionally, the reality is that as a disabled person I do have to decide where I use my utensils or matchsticks. If I want to go camping, and burn the entire box, that is fine, but I am going to pay for it next week—professionally or personally—and that is what utensil theories never address. A matchstick doesn't burn without leaving behind a sign it was burnt: be it a smell, an ash, or the embers of a fire.

Ultimately, none of these theories are academic in nature, and I am positive my theory teacher would be rolling his eyes and tsking at me, but these theories are written by people in the disability community and thus come from their lived experiences. These theories aided me in communicating my own limitations to not only myself, but to my friends, family, employers, etc. These theories give voice to the ones this book is meant for and written by, and thus these are the theories I will identify with when writing about chronic illness.

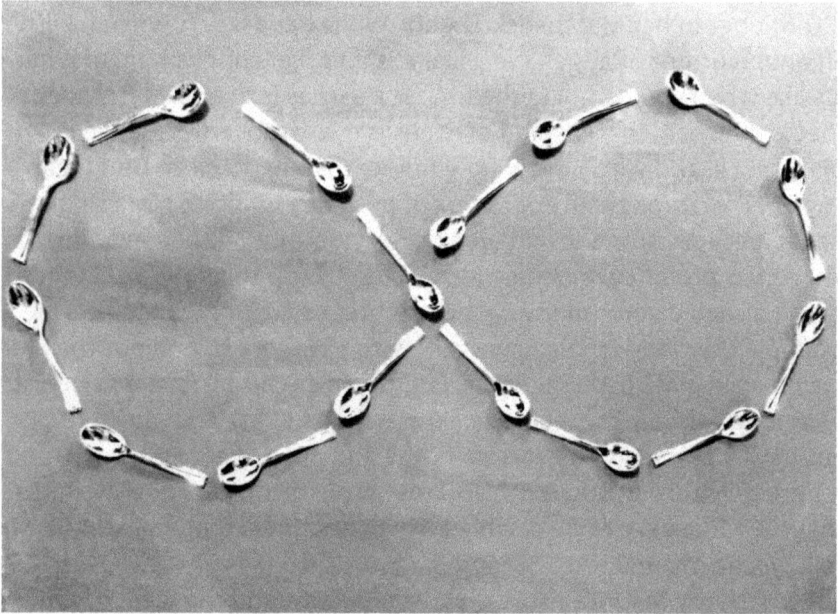

ID: Metallic spoons form an infinity symbol on a painted canvas.

Discussion Questions

1. Why would the author choose to focus on non-academic theories as opposed to academic theories? Does this focus weaken the arguments provided?
2. What makes a theory "academic"?
3. Is there room within academic fields for non-academic writers?

References

Charmaz, K. (2009). Recollecting good and bad days. In A. J. Puddephatt, W. Shaffir, & S. W. Kleinknecht (Eds.), *Ethnographies revisited: Constructing theory in the field* (pp. 48–62). Routledge.

Johnson, P. (2016). *Matchstick theory.* https://psarahjohnson.com/matchstick-theory/

Karp, D. (2009). Learning how to speak of sadness. In A. J. Puddephatt, W. Shaffir, & S. W. Kleinknecht (Eds.), *Ethnographies revisited: Constructing theory in the field* (pp. 37–47). Routledge.

Masson, T. (2019). *The Knife Hypothesis, a companion to Spoon Theory.* https://medium.com/@tilaurin/the-knife-hypothesis-a-companion-to-spoon-theory-d20764c28349

Miserandino, C. (2003). *'But you don't look sick': The stories behind the smiles.* http://cdn.totalcomputersusa.com/butyoudontlooksick.com/uploads/2010/02/BYDLS-TheSpoonTheory.pdf

Parsons, T. (1975). The sick role and the role of the physician reconsidered. *The Milbank Memorial Fund Quarterly. Health and Society, 53*(3), 257.

Rose, J. (2018). *Fork theory.* https://jenrose.com/fork-theory/

Santuzzi, A. M., Waltz, P. R., & Finkelstein, L. M. (2014). Invisible disabilities: Unique challenges for employees and organizations. *Industrial and Organizational Psychology, 7,* 204–209.

CHAPTER 18

Seeing Brains

Shakespeare, Autism, and Self-Identification

Nicholas R. Helms

> Nay, I'll ne'er believe a madman till I see his brains.
> FESTE (Shakespeare's *Twelfth Night*, 4.2.122–3)

∵

My favorite character in Shakespeare is probably Feste, a vagabond performer of a type known in early modern England as a "fool." Feste splits his time between the houses of Illyria's nobles (Olivia and Orsino) singing songs, telling jokes, speaking a bit of truth to power, and begging for tips. And in a pique of revenge, he also ties up Malvolio, Olivia's steward, locks him in a dark room, and tells everyone that Malvolio has gone mad. As if that's not enough abuse, Feste gaslights Malvolio, telling him he won't believe anything the man says until he sees "his brains."

I said Feste was my favorite character. I didn't say he was a good person!

Feste's claim that he'll "[never] believe a madman" until he "sees his brains" has always stuck with me. It's a shockingly vivid piece of metaphor that evokes sixteenth- and seventeenth-century anatomical theaters, which were medical lectures where doctors would dissect human cadavers in front of public audiences. Lianne Habinek writes in *The Subtle Knot* that the human brain was more than mere "grey matter" in the early modern period: it was considered "a black box violently to be unlocked...and a subtle knot that traps the soul—and thereby makes us human" (2018, p. 3). Feste's curiosity about the minds of madmen can only be satisfied by surgical violence, laying bare Malvolio's thoughts along with his brains, a diagnosis that would no doubt prove fatal to the patient.

But there was of course no Neurodiversity movement in early modern England, and madness was typically pathologized as a type of distracted thought that marked one out for exclusion, isolation, and public scrutiny, as Carol Thomas Neely (2004) makes clear in *Distracted Subjects*.

I see a fair bit of myself in Feste: an intellectual vagrant, analytical to a fault. But I also see myself in Malvolio: locked in a dark place, bound, and forbidden to name my own mind. What follows is a brief account of my efforts to believe myself, to see my own brains.

•••

I'm an assistant professor of literature who studies Shakespeare, character, theories of mind reading, and empathy.

I'm also autistic.

I came out as autistic on Twitter in September 2019. This was probably not news to a lot of people who followed me on Twitter. My profile listed me as neurodivergent, and I'd been liking and retweeting stuff from Autistic Twitter since at least the previous April.

As I started to talk more openly with folks in my day-to-day life about being autistic, the responses ranged from the sympathetic, to the bored, to the affirming:

me: I'm 99% sure I'm autistic.
them: Yeah, I'm 99% sure you're autistic. I think I am, too.
me: I want to talk to you about how I think I'm actually autistic.
them: We've talked about this before, I think.
me: I've been researching self-diagnosis, and I wanted to hear about your own diagnosis.
them: Have you heard the expression "I can smell my people"?

Let me say up-front that this is a self-diagnosis, or, as Michelle Swan (2018) puts it, a self-identification. I was officially diagnosed with Obsessive Compulsive Disorder (OCD) at 14, which is why I've had the #neurodivergent tag on my profile for a while now (a term coined and championed online by @uvGκassi). For various reasons, I've always sought OCD treatment with a general practitioner, which usually just means an SSRI and a pat on the head. SSRIS, selective serotonin reuptake inhibitors, are antidepressants commonly prescribed to treat the symptoms of OCD (Soomro et al., 2008). As a result, I've been lumping Autism Spectrum Disorder (ASD) symptoms under OCD for about two decades, including special interests, stimming, and social anxiety.

It doesn't help that I was educated in the Simon Baron-Cohen school of "mindblindness" autism. In my research and my teaching, I apply cognitive science to Shakespeare's plays. I've always been puzzled by tragedy and how things can go so badly so quickly for characters like Cordelia, Hero, and Ophelia. Why do Shakespeare's characters (particularly men in power) so easily (and perhaps willfully) misunderstand those around them? They insist on seeing the "brains" before believing their words.

Here's where Theories of Mind Reading entered my research: "mind reading" is the human capacity to make judgements about what another person is thinking, feeling, or planning. Theories of Mind Reading try to explain how it is that we can make such judgements about other minds, and why it is that our judgements are so often overconfident and inaccurate. Baron-Cohen's 1995 *Mindblindness: An Essay on Autism and Theory of Mind*, parses mind reading through a medical, empathy-deficit model of autism. According to the book, autistics are "mindblind," largely incapable of imagining the mental states of others due to an overall lack of empathy. And if mindreading is something that humans do all the time, the book implicitly defines autistics as inhuman.

A few things began to chip away at my preconceptions, fortunately. For starters, I became aware of the Neurodiversity movement and critiques of Baron-Cohen's work. Remi Yergeau's (2018) work in particular does an excellent job of tackling the ableism infused in Theories of Mind Reading. In addition, learning about Anthony Hopkins' Asperger diagnosis felt eerily familiar. I was making my own career of thinking slowly and carefully about reading, interpreting, and the construction of literary character, things that are essential for actors. There's also the story of Dr. James Fallon (2014), the neuroscientist who discovered he was a psychopath while researching psychopathy. MEsearch, indeed.

One of the reasons I originally started studying tragedy, character, and theories of mindreading was that I'd always felt that I was pretty bad at reading others. Lots of social awkwardness in my life! So studying literary character became a way to learn how to read people. A fellow academic pointed this out to me subtly in the fall of 2018. After I gave a presentation at the Ohio Valley Shakespeare

Conference, someone came up to me and tentatively asked if they could ask a somewhat personal question:

> "Did you choose your research because you felt like you couldn't read people well?"
> I said, "Yeah, as a matter of fact."

I didn't think more deeply about it. But in the background, my self-identification as autistic was percolating. My first book *Cognition, Mindreading, and Shakespeare's Characters* was finally published in February of 2019. For the first time in a decade, I felt I was able to slow down and take stock of my own mind, and a lot of separate realizations from my professional and personal life came crashing together. The irony here is that contemporary theories of mindreading are heavily built upon an outdated deficit model of autism. I had forged an understanding of who I am by first trekking through the sludge of ableist stereotypes in cognitive science and literary studies.

Then flash forward to April 2019's Autism Awareness Month and @mykola's 2019 tweet/thread about coming to self-identify as autistic as an adult. @mykola's thread was a list of questions, such as: "Do you need a lot of time alone? Even in a relationship or family, even when you really love the other people in your life, even (especially?) when there isn't anything particularly pressing for you to do?" These questions started a bit like diagnostic surveys such as the Autism-Spectrum Quotient Test (developed by Simon Baron-Cohen and colleagues), but instead of being a clinical list of vague statements with which one agrees or disagrees, @mykola opened up the diagnostic criteria into invitations for personal narrative. Compare the above set of questions with the first statement of the Autism-Spectrum Quotient Test: "I prefer to do things with others rather than on my own." @mykola's flurry of questions both clarifies and expands upon the diagnostic criteria, encouraging readers to revisit moments in their own life. These questions feel more reflective than they do like items on a personality quiz.

The thread hit me like a freight train. After decades of feeling isolated in my own head, I felt seen. I suddenly had a frame for reexamining and understanding social interactions in my life that hadn't made sense to me for decades.

Since then, I've been paying a lot of attention to the #ActuallyAutistic and disability studies communities—on Twitter and in the academy—as well as to the subreddit @mykola created to better explore the ideas from his thread: r/AutismTranslated, currently at 10,000 total subscribers. Autism is the missing lens for my life. It explains so much of my experience (past and present), and it has me excited for the future, for further getting to know myself. So why haven't I sought out an official diagnosis? Wouldn't medical certainty give me a better foundation for my journey of self-discovery? And wouldn't some official paperwork make it easier for me to find accommodations at work and throughout my life?

No, I don't think it would. This is a highly personal choice, of course, and it's one that's informed by Michelle Swan's (2018) "5 Reasons I am Self-Identified as Autistic." Swan points to the high costs of diagnosis (often in the thousands of dollars), the discriminatory diagnostic criteria (historically weighted against women and people of color), and the potential trauma of the diagnostic process (which is overwhelmingly based on the medical, deficits model of disability). Swan views self-identification, rather than official diagnosis, as the path of defiance: "I would rather take the acceptance of the autistic community over the bureaucratic approval of a professional any day." Choosing to self-identify is, in part, a rejection of the ways modern medicine has pathologized disability.

To Swan's excellent reasons, I'd like to add that self-identification can be a positive use of one's own privilege. I'm a white cishet man with steady employment as a tenure-track assistant professor. The accommodations I need at work—reduced face-to-face social interactions, a distraction-free office environment, public stimming, and preferring email to Zoom, to name a few—are ones that I can easily obtain by donning the role of the "eccentric" professor. This role-playing is a type of "masking," what Leah Lakshmi Piepzna-Samarasinha (2019) calls "faking neurotypicality." In an intersectional defense of Greta Thunberg's "Resting Autism Face," Piepzna-Samarasinha writes about the persistent demand that society places on autistic folks—particularly on women and nonbinary autistics—to mask, to smile and conform gesturally to social norms, rather than to simply be ourselves. My job as a professor gives me more freedom than most when it comes to where and how often I need to mask, and being "out" as autistic opens up opportunities for me to advocate for others.

Meanwhile, my disabled students are expected to provide medical paperwork up-front to the office of disability services at my institution, as well as to formally notify me of their institutionally allowable access needs through the appropriately countersigned forms. What do students do if they become disabled in the middle of a semester? What do students do when they are barred from diagnosis by cost, by the scarcity of health care, by medical racism and neglect? What do students do when they have no words for their disability while they're in school?

Disabled college students face a myriad of barriers to adult diagnosis, and therefore to having their access needs recognized by schools: self-stigma, mistrust, gender bias, and systemic racism are among the most insurmountable of these barriers. Through a 2018 survey of UK university students, Eilidh Cage et al. (2020) point to the barriers that self-stigma imposes on students who are considering seeking a mental health diagnosis. In a 2017 study of barriers to adult diagnosis of ASD, Laura Lewis identified a variety of factors that lead to delayed or forestalled diagnoses: "anxiety, cost, access to adult ASD specialists, fear of not being believed, inability to describe symptoms, mistrust of health care professionals, stigma, complexity of the health care system, and lack of perceived value of formal diagnosis" (p. 2412). Lewis identifies the chief barrier as "the fear that professionals would not listen to or believe the symptoms reported to them" (p. 2420). Dori Zener, in the article "Journey to Diagnosis for Women with Autism," analyzes the gender biases implicit in diagnostic criteria, noting, "identification of autism in women is often a long and roundabout journey involving years of struggle, appointments with multiple professionals and a fragmented understanding of their challenges leading to misdiagnoses and greater misunderstanding" (2019, p. 7). And the CDC notes that Black and Hispanic children are still less likely to be diagnosed with ASD than white children (2019).

There are systemic injustices at play for students that I can't remedy by myself. But I do have the privilege and the accompanying safety to be open about my disability in public, at work, in my classroom, and to do so without the authorization of the medical establishment. For me, to publicly self-identify as autistic is to say, "I don't need medical paperwork to justify my social and sensory access needs. Likewise, my students don't need that paperwork to justify their access needs."

This is step one in creating an accessible classroom.

It's also step one in how I can see my own brains, reconciling Feste and Malvolio within myself.

Discussion Questions

1. How are literary representations of madness and disability related to contemporary discussions of neurodiversity, disability rights, and disability justice?
2. How might contemporary disabled identities be used to analyze and empathize with people from the past, whether in fiction or in history?
3. What is the authoritative basis for medical diagnoses of disability? For self-diagnoses? What about self-identification?
4. What makes a college classroom accessible for disabled people? What makes it inaccessible?

References

@mykola. (2019, April 2). Hey, how's this for autism 'awareness' month [Tweet]. Twitter. https://twitter.com/mykola/status/1112883937272107008

Baron-Cohen, S. (1995). Mindblindness an essay on autism and theory of mind. The MIT Press.

Baron-Cohen, S., Wheelwright, S., Skinner, R., Martin, J., & Clubley, E. (2001). The Autism-spectrum Quotient (AQ): Evidence from Asperger syndrome/high-functioning autism, males and females, scientists and mathematicians. Journal of Autism and Developmental Disorders, 31(1), 5–17. https://doi.org/10.1023/a:1005653411471

Cage, E., Stock, M., Sharpington, A., Pitman, E., & Batchelor, R. (2020). Barriers to accessing support for mental health issues at university. Studies in Higher Education, 45(8), 1637–1649. https://doi.org/10.1080/03075079.20 18.1544237

Centers for Disease Control and Prevention. (2019). Spotlight on: Racial and ethnic differences in children identified with Autism Spectrum Disorder (ASD). https://www.cdc.gov/ncbddd/autism/addm-community-report/ differences-in-children.html

Fallon, J. (2014). The psychopath inside: A neuroscientist's personal journey into the dark side of the brain. Penguin Books Australia.

Habinek, L. (2018). The subtle knot: Early modern English literature and the birth of neuroscience. McGill-Queen's UP.

Lewis, L. (2017). A mixed methods study of barriers to formal diagnosis of autism spectrum disorder in adults. Journal of Autism & Developmental Disorders, 47(8), 2410–2424. https://doi.org/10.1007/s10803-017-3168-3

Neely, C. T. (2004). *Distracted subjects: Madness and gender in Shakespeare and early modern culture*. Cornell UP.

Piepzna-Samarasinha, L. L. (2019, September 25). As an autistic femme, I love Greta Thunberg's 'Resting autism face.' *Truthout*. https://truthout.org/articles/as-an-autistic-femme-i-love-greta-thunbergs-resting-autism-face/

Shakespeare, W. (n.d.). *Twelfth night* (B. Mowat, P. Werstine, M. Poston, & R. Niles, Eds.). The Folger Shakespeare. https://shakespeare.folger.edu/shakespeares-works/twelfth-night/

Soomro, G. M., Altman, D. G., Rajagopal, S., & Oakley Browne, M. (2008). Selective Serotonin Re-uptake Inhibitors (SSRIs) versus placebo for Obsessive Compulsive Disorder (OCD). *Cochrane Database of Systematic Reviews*, 1. doi:10.1002/14651858.CD001765.pub3

Swan, M. (2018, September 6). 5 reasons I am self-identified as autistic. *Hello Michelle Swan*. https://hellomichelleswan.com/5-reasons-i-am-self-identified-as-autistic/

Yergeau, R. (2018). *Authoring autism: On rhetoric and neurological queerness*. Duke University Press.

Zener, D. (2019). Journey to diagnosis for women with autism. *Advances in Autism*, 5(1), 2–13. https://doi.org/10.1108/AIA-10-2018-0041

Pike Trickleg

Lauren (aka L. W. Salinas)

ID: An orange tabby cat lays on its back and looks at the camera like it wants to play.

•••

Pike (named after Pike Trickfoot from *Critical Role*) was found as a 4-week-old kitten: starving, covered in fleas, and shot by a BB gun that snapped one of his femurs. As he got older, he was also diagnosed with hyperesthesia, which causes sensitivity to stimuli. As someone with Ehlers-Danlos syndrome, anxiety, depression, and ADHD, I see a kindred spirit in pain, anger, and determination.

© PAUL D. C. BONES, JESSICA SMARTT GULLION AND DANIELLE BARBER, 2022
DOI:10.1163/9789004512702_027

CHAPTER 19

Hot Girl Bummer

Achieving Disabled Sexual Liberation in an Ableist World

Katherine O'Connell

I remember one particular date I cancelled several hours before we were supposed to meet at the bookshop-cafe hybrid. Usually, I try to give as much notice as I can before I cancel, but I don't always have a warning before a migraine strikes or a wave of nausea overcomes me. In a way, it's become an unfortunate litmus test: how will my date react when I apologize profusely for the way my body works ("I'm so sorry, I know this is so last minute, it's just such a bad migraine, and I really do want to reschedule") and how it has inconvenienced them. You can get a good sense of a person for how they accommodate you and your pain. What they don't know, of course, is that I am in pain every minute of the day—and have been that way at least since my early twenties—and that the pain I live in would make someone without chronic pain panic. In this instance, the date texted back that he understood, and I felt my guilt about how my body works abate, just for a minute. Because then he followed up with, "You know orgasms can cure a migraine, right?" I do, in fact, know that the endorphins released during orgasm can reduce migraine pain. And I also know that he wasn't texting that out of an altruistic desire to help me manage a chronic pain condition. Rather, he was viewing my disability and disabled body through the lens of the male gaze—the idea that my body is an object that exists for heterosexual male pleasure. Even as disability is conceived as inherently unsexual, even sexually repulsive, our bodies and conditions are also often fetishized, particularly if they can be exploited for someone else's sexual gratification.

In that moment, he was not actually thinking about me and my pain (like an ice pick shattering my skull). Had he known that the migraine rendered me temporarily blind, bent over my toilet with debilitating nausea, tears streaming, he might not have been so eager. But my actual experiences in my body were not of any consequence to him, because my migraine gave him an avenue to reorient the conversation to his sexual expectations and desires

© KATHERINE O'CONNELL, 2022 | DOI:10.1163/9789004512702_028

without any consideration of mine. He could so easily take my confession of pain—something that is often rendered as shameful, that needs to be kept secret—and twist it because the dual forces of ableism and heteronormativity let him objectify my body and erase my disability at his convenience. Disabled people are trapped by the ways that ableism and heteronormativity work together to control our sexuality and reproduction. Ableism others and oppresses disabled bodies, and the sexuality of disabled people, policing our desire and how we can act on it. Heteronormativity punishes non-normative sexual acts and desires. For disabled people to be liberated sexually and writ large, we must expansively reimagine sexuality for ourselves beyond these boundaries and learn to center our bodies and desires in our sexual practice.

Desexualizing Disability

In *Carnal Acts*, Nancy Mairs (1994) writes, "The sexuality of the disabled so repulses most people that you can hardly get a doctor, let alone a member of the general population, to consider the issues it raises. Cripples simply aren't supposed to Want It, must less Do It" (p. 275). Cripples who do "Want It," as Mairs (1994) puts it, are especially not supposed to know what we want or center our desire and pleasure in any way. Rather, we are supposed to relent to whatever our potential partner wants, regardless of our own boundaries and desires. Efforts to prevent disabled people from understanding our sexuality and pleasure begins early. Disabled youth are often prevented from accessing any sex education, and therefore barred from learning the same language as others about describing their sexual identities and desires (Treacy, Taylor, & Abernathy, 2018). Additionally, children with disabilities are 3.4 times more likely to be the victims of sexual violence than their able-bodied peers (Treacy, Taylor, & Abernathy, 2018). Lack of access to sex education and the experience of high rates of sexual trauma, combined with oppressive societal views of disabled sexuality creates an atmosphere that bar disabled youth from the sexual growth and exploration their able-bodied peers engage in.

The prevailing view is that we are either unsexy and asexual (a determinism that undercuts and harms disabled people who are asexual) or hypersexual in a way that is conceived as sex-starved, wild, and/or grotesque. As Anna Mollow (2012) notes, "These contradictory constructions of disability create a double bind for people with disabilities: if disability can easily be interpreted as both sexual lack and sexual excess (sometimes simultaneously), then it seems nearly impossible for any expression of disabled sexuality to escape stigma" (p. 286). We are put in a situation we cannot win, where any expression of our sexuality is seen as aberrant and in need of control.

Additionally, because disabled bodies are typically viewed as undesirable we are not typically considered as viable sexual partners unless we can be fetishized. When my canceled date brought up the potential of orgasm to cure my migraine, he did not do so out of a radical centering of my disabled sexuality. Rather, my disability and pain became an entry point to sexualize me in the way that most benefited him. I am uninterested in my disability being the conduit for another person's sexual pleasure that does not consider me, my erotic self, and my fullness as a person. But because I am aberrant—disabled and queer—I am expected to be grateful for the smallest amount of sexual attention, particularly when it comes from cisgender men.

This forced gratitude is a trap for disabled people, it demands that we be thankful for people "overlooking" part of ourselves, and it requires that we ignore ableist attitudes that come alongside it. And if we must be grateful for any sexual attention, then it reinforces that respect for our sexuality and desire are not something we deserve inherently as people, but that it is something we are bestowed by benevolent able-bodied people. Further, when we're told we should be grateful for sexual attention, it delegitimizes our frequent experiences of sexual coercion and violence. The chorus tends to first ask, "Who would want to assault us?" And then follows that with the second blow: "Shouldn't we be elated that someone wanted us at all?" Ultimately, in this gratitude model of disabled sex we are fetishized and dehumanized, set up for trauma and victim-blaming, and our desires and erotic power are neglected.

Queering Crip Sexuality

Despite having our sexuality stifled our entire lives, disabled people have clearly defined sexualities and desires; we have, and enjoy, sex. Similar to the word *queer*, which I use throughout this piece, the word *crip* has been reclaimed by disabled people in a radical way. To crip something is to disrupt and subvert ableism, to be unapologetic about our disabilities, and to create space for disability where it previously didn't exist. It is critical to understand the parallels between queer and crip communities when it comes to our policing by society. In his articulation of disabled people as a sexual minority, similar to queer communities, Tobin Siebers explains, "Disabled people experience sexual repression, possess little or no sexual autonomy, and tolerate institutional and legal restrictions on their intimate conduct. Moreover, legal and institutional forces inhibit their ability to express their sexuality freely and to develop consensual relationships with sexual partners" (2011, p. 38).

Central to cripping sexuality is widely asserting that disability *is* sexy. But beyond that, as Robert McRuer wrote in 2011, we must also be "simultaneously hip to how its sexiness might get used, or hip to how disability has already been used in so many problematic ways by the modern state" (p. 114). This is why we must bring in a framework of disability justice and use that lens to crip sexuality and understand that sexuality is a central component of our humanity. Sins Invalid (2019), a disability performance group that depicts the humanity, beauty, and sexuality of disabled bodies, writes in their disability justice primer *Skin, Tooth, and Bone* that "DJ [Disability Justice] is a framework through which we can be more consensual in accessing sex, it's a better way to approach sex, better than an ableist combative gendered heteropatriarchal approach to sex, or a patriarchal rape culture or hook-up culture to access sex" (p. 114). Such a framework takes us away from models of sex that confine us or force us to be grateful for attention, and sets up disabled people as sexual actors in our own right. It also removes the male gaze from the equation and allows us to see our bodies as sexy and erotic outside of the confines of heterosexist and patriarchal expectations. It is a necessary entry point into reimagining our sexual selves and understanding the vastness of crip sex possibility.

To build on Mairs' (1994) assertion that cripples are not supposed to want sex, cripples are also not supposed to have sexual knowledge or identities, and we're certainly not supposed to exist outside the strict paradigm of heterosexuality. The existence of queer disabled people directly challenges the belief that we are not supposed to be sexual beings, because it means we have developed sexual identities and sexual desires beyond cultural norms, and have potentially even acted on those desires. It must also be said that the existence and self-determinism of asexual disabled people disrupts standard cultural narratives. In her essay *Last but Not Least—Embracing Asexuality*, Keisha Scott (2020) writes of her horror at the thought that her disability destined her to be asexual until she learned more about the vastness of what asexuality is. Part of cripping sexuality is the unlearning that Scott describes—that her disability didn't predetermine her asexuality, but that you can be both outside of the paradigm prescribed by our ableist society. Like all systems of oppression, ableism and heteronormativity go hand-in-hand. Ableism relies on heteronormativity to specifically suppress queer disabled desire, and to keep us safely desexualized and docile. The unruliness of disability, that our bodies and minds reject the norm, reject capitalist productivity, is too much for abled society to handle. And then queerness opens a door to sex that goes beyond the normative definition of sex as penis-in-vagina penetration. The result is limitless possibility for how we can have sex *and* define it for ourselves.

Crip sex requires redefining sex the way queer individuals and communities have done, with expansive imagination. It requires the nuanced understanding that as much as queerness and disability can lead to new models of sexual pleasure and rich erotic possibility, sex is also thorny for disabled people to navigate, particularly when pain is involved. It requires that disabled people "demand access," as Robert McRuer and Anna Mollow (2012) put it, to sexuality, desire, and pleasure. It means disabled people have to embrace the still very radical idea that our bodies deserve the same pleasure as other bodies if we want it. And this can be difficult to do because disabled people are so cut off from our own sexuality, and so often told to hate our bodies and how they work. Our ableist society treats our disabled bodies as wrong, and society is designed—literally, architecturally, and systematically—to exclude us. So for disabled people, even asserting our right to sexual desire and pleasure can take immense work. And the narratives we internalize about our lack of sexuality, our bodies, and worthlessness in this capitalist society are a lot to fight against. But as Black feminist lesbian poet Audre Lorde (2007) asserts, the erotic is power, and once we have "experienced the fullness of this depth of feeling and recognizing its power, in honor and self-respect we can require no less of ourselves" (p. 54). Sexual identity and redefinition are critical aspects of the self, and when we begin to access our sexual selves and desires, we can learn to center our needs beyond the realm of sexuality.

Duality of Crip Boundaries

Understanding boundaries and the ways that crips must simultaneously break the boundaries society sets for us while asserting new boundaries we create for ourselves, is critical to cripping sex. Disabled people are often bound by what society says we cannot do—or what society does not allow us to do—through lack of accessibility. When we assert ourselves as sexual beings, beings who can want pleasure, who can feel pleasure, and who are desirable, we are tearing down the heteropatriarchal and ableist boundaries that prevent us from existing in our whole selves. But one of our tasks when cripping sex is also creating our own boundaries: boundaries that protect us, that dismantle the gratitude model of disabled sex, and facilitate our pleasure. We must set our boundaries for ourselves, on our terms, rather than for the comfort of others, including our partners.

I have internalized the narratives that my illnesses burden my partners (and others in my life), that my inability to spontaneously have sex whenever a partner may want renders me undesirable. For me, desexualization can happen during the act of sex, when I'm unable to position a certain way because my hypermobile joints pop out or my swollen knees give; my reproductive organs feel sharp explosive pain or my tight pelvic floor muscles reject stimulation; or my skin, so sensitive that anything other than 100% cotton can feel abrasive, screams under even the lightest touch. As Sonya Huber (2017) describes it, "Sex and desire are very complicated for people whose central nervous systems scream at them. Sex is a complex and fraught dance, an intellectually draining circus to run. After I manage to have sex, I often collapse for a few days from the effort of being in my body and sorting the signals of pain and desire" (p. 31). Like many people, I set boundaries with my partners before having sex, but my boundaries often center around the things my body cannot do, the ways that past sexual trauma, fibromyalgia, rheumatoid arthritis, and endometriosis tangle together. But the critical point is that I must set my own boundaries around what my body can do during sex, and what I want to be able to do regardless of my pain.

Some partners have treated me like a porcelain doll, rejecting my assertions that yes, I can enjoy rougher sex or kink, even when it triggers a condition. As well-intended as they may be, partners inadvertently desexualize me when they refuse to acknowledge my sexual desire and agency. I call this benevolent desexualization—while the goal is not to strip me of sexual agency, but by treating me as delicate and untouchable, my body and desires are removed from sexual decision making. Part of the imaginative boundary-making disabled people do so consistently is pushing through our pain or perceived limitations to have autonomy and do what we want. This is not done out of a capitalist desire to work or produce through our pain, but because we are the experts in, and owners of, our unruly bodies, and we get to decide how we use them. One of the most frequent questions I have received when presenting on sexuality and disability is how people can get their partners to understand that yes, sometimes pain flares during sex, and yes, sometimes the person in pain wants to keep having sex anyway. Or sometimes they want to stop. And fundamentally, the answer is that no one can set our boundaries for us. No one else gets to decide when my pain is too bad for me to do anything, including having sex. Active sexual consent requires flowing communication and checking in, and it also requires trusting that disabled people, and people in pain are in charge of how we engage in the "fraught dance." Or, as Sins Invalid (2019) puts it simply in *Skin, Tooth, and Bone*, "[Disability Justice] practiced in a sexual context advocates for communication that works for everyone around sexual desire and what we do when we're sexual" (p. 118).

Crip Sexual Liberation

Ultimately, we have to expand our imaginations, creating our own boundaries outside of ableist ones, and centering our desires and pleasure are how we escape the paradigm of ableism, heteronormativity, and patriarchy. When we do this, we are not only forcing the world to recognize us as autonomous sexual beings, but as full people. Cripping sex is part of the solution for our collective liberation: to reimagine our relationship between our disabled bodies and minds, develop disability-centered avenues to enjoy our erotic selves, redefine intimacy, and further develop our experience of pleasure. When we center disability in our sexuality, we allow it to be an asset, part of the expansive possibility in queer, crip sex.

Disabled people reimagine what sex and intimacy look like every day. Long before they became popular because of the coronavirus pandemic, disabled people have been hosting virtual play parties.

Sex toys, from run-of-the-mill vibrators and dildos to aid designed virtual play, become disability aids to help us experience pleasure that may not be possible with another person. A frequent narrative in heterosexual relationships is about sex toys and whether or not they dilute the sexual experience. These typically focus on the ways that cis hetero men feel inadequate in comparison to even the weakest vibrators. Crips can skip this conversation altogether—of course, toys don't dilute sexual experiences, they facilitate them. Sex toys, liquid-absorbing blankets, props and wedges, harnesses that can be worn around the thighs or arms rather than the pelvis, and other sexual items across the spectrum make sex accessible, hot, and fun. Again, when we view sex through crip and queer lenses we can see how expansive sex is and enjoy it without ableist restrictions.

We rely on language, understanding the importance of clearly communicating physical and emotional boundaries, and to describe the hot things we want to do to each other. Redefining sex to center our disabled desires and pleasure—whether that is want for human touch, or the need for particular stimulation to offset pain, or for any other reason—can be a transformative act for us in our sex lives and outside of it. We need to see our sex lives and desires as legitimate outside of heteronormative and ableist confines that tell us we don't deserve sex and pleasure, and limit our imaginations. Critically, we must understand how nuanced queer and disabled sex can be. Holding space for our bodies and desires also means that we must recognize when we do feel impeded by our disabilities. While I find beauty, eroticism, and intimacy in laying naked with a partner when my body can't handle touch, I acknowledge that the feeling of fighting my body on what I want can be frustrating. That sometimes I would like to experience sex the way I did before certain conditions manifested. Reimagining sexual intimacy can be freeing, and we can also acknowledge the pain—physical and psychological—when our desires and our bodies' capabilities diverge. Importantly, we also need to understand that we, as disabled people, or people with chronic pain, are the ones in charge of our bodies at all times. When we remove the artificial boundaries that ableism creates that restrict our sexual pleasure, we get to set our own that put us in control. Returning to the concept of benevolent desexualization, we can appreciate our partners not wanting to hurt us, but this comes at the expense of our desire and control of our bodies. Thinking about sex through a lens of crip queerness frees us to explore and learn what we want, what we need, for pleasure and sex. It's fundamental, when we think about how we define sex for ourselves, and when we communicate with our partners, to be clear about our desires and boundaries. It's also critical for partners, especially able-bodied partners, to understand that we know what we want, how much we can take, and nobody can set those boundaries but us.

To be disabled and sexual, putting your desires and boundaries first, is to take a sledgehammer to one of the most fundamental aspects of ableism—sexual control. To combine that disabled sexuality with queerness means transforming the way we see sex both as individuals and culturally. It means that we are taking up space we are not meant to take up, that we are asserting that we know what's best for us, and that we deserve to live fully human lives with intimacy and pleasure. In a world that constantly tells us it knows better than we do about our bodies, conditions, needs, and desires, the assertion of disabled sexuality can be a path to our liberation, and to a crip sex revolution.

Discussion Questions

1. What does the author call the "gratitude model of disabled sex"? How does this appear in the piece?
2. How does the author make the connection between queer theory and "cripping" sexuality?
3. What are three ways the author argues we can move toward crip sexual liberation?

References

Huber, S. (2017). *Pain woman takes your keys and other essays from a nervous system*. University of Nebraska Press.

Lorde, A. (2007). *Sister outsider: Essays and speeches by Audre Lorde.* Crossing Press.

Mairs, N. (1994). Carnal acts. In P. Foster (Ed.), *Minding the body: Women writers on body and soul* (pp. 267–282). Anchor.

Mallow, A. (2021). Is sex disability? Queer theory and the disability drive. In R. McRuer & A. Mallow (Eds.), *Sex and disability* (pp. 285–312). Duke University Press.

McRuer, R. (2011). Disabling sex: Notes for a crip theory of sexuality. *GLQ: A Journal of Lesbian & Gay Studies, 17*(1), 107–117. doi:10.1215/10642684-2010-021

McRuer, R., & Mollow, A. (Eds.). (2012). *Sex and disability*. Duke University Press.

Siebers, T. (2011). A sexual culture for disabled people. In R. McRuer & A. Mollow (Eds.), *Sex and disability*. Duke University Press.

Sins Invalid. (2019). *Skin, tooth, and bone: The basis of movement is our people*. Primedia eLaunch LLC.

Scott, K. (2020). Last but not least—Embracing asexuality. In A. Wong (Ed.), *Disability visibility: First-person stories from the twenty-first century*. Vintage Books.

Treacy, A. C., Taylor, S. S., & Abernathy, T. V. (2018). Sexual health education for individuals with disabilities: A call to action. *American Journal of Sexuality Education, 13*(1), 65–93. doi:10.1080/15546128.2017.1399492

Abacus

Kimberly C. Merenda

ID: A very large, very hairy brown and black dog sits with his tongue out in the grass.

●●●

Abacus and I share the disability of chronic illness. Abacus deals with his chronic illness much better than I do mine. I try hard to learn from Abacus's embodied ways of knowing and being: pain can't be fought or denied and so during times of pain, rest and practice self-care; find and fully embrace pleasure when possible; a nap in the sun makes everything better.

DOI:10.1163/9789004512702_029

CHAPTER 20

Selected Poems

Jessi Aaron

Crippled Symphony

If I were you
      I'd rather be
           dead

Here comes the choo-choo train!
                Choo-choo!

You think you're
        immune

Everybody has problems
I broke
    my leg once

Wanna race?

You're so
    inspirational.

Who am I
     to complain?

I love your spunk

inspirational spunk
you're immune

Your poor mother,
lucky she
    kept you.
If I

© JESSI AARON, 2022 | DOI:10.1163/9789004512702_030

They have you
        working?
wanna
        race

Choo-choo!
Good for you.

We usually cut off
                the child's toes.
lucky
        for you
who am I

Because of your
                situation (no name)
rather be dead
everybody

What does she want
                to eat?
(no name)

inspirational /cut
mother / immune
                Choo-choo!

Are you all by yourself?
I'd rather be
        spunk
(no name)

Choices

cw: Forcible Touching

To be pitied
and nurtured:
this is my lot in life.

Little cripple too big
for her britches.

My self invaded
with your conditional love.

Your large body hovers
reaching to force my rhythm,
extinguish my comfort.
Nails across the tops of my ears,
head withdrawn.

You, irritated,
hands fast and hard against my clothes,

don't stop
when I say "no"
until I have said it three or four times
and am angry.

You cannot read the world as I do.
You say I make things difficult.

I do not try to speak to you of sensitivity
space and respect and brilliance in

touching
brushing
cleaning

You wash my pussy like the drain of a sink,
rough circles back and forth
scrubbing this object of no one's desire.

I know your argument:
If you were like me, you say,
you would do things differently.

Like me
Like me

Worth less than those who have a choice.

If you were me, you would submit, yes,
sell yourself to those who feed on pity
and superiority.
Consume their pay-by-the-hour care
in exchange for your self-control.

You would just sit back
and let them do it.

Like me, I imagine
you would not really
think of yourself

as human

anyway.

Walk

Back at MDA camp
in the pine-thickened
wilderness, I fell
tenderhearted hushed
in little-girl flutter love
with those weakling

hips and ankles,
the boys' up and
swing-it-girl walk,
tippy-toes, arch-backed
moon-faced dance,
muscles in atrophy:

dying children, but
then, alive and just so,
tucked in under

my withered birth
limbs. They were better
off than me, back then,

their gait forever
sexy and tenuous.
Gaze fixed, I inhaled
their idiosyncratic flight,
losing sight altogether
of all of the other,

lesser perfections.

Speed

My body born
without muscles in all
four limbs, this vegetable
newborn, who never kicked
a uterus or sucked
a thumb, loved the view
from the top of things.

I would sit atop the riverside grass,
cascading clover herbal sweet and cool
on freckled summer skin.
The river, down there,
white with someone else's history
tumbling secrets buried and polished
in round-rock transparency.

I would bury my feet in the sand dunes,
fluffed by Northwest winds, wild
flowers and blue spruce drinking in salted air.
The sea below, holding in everything and pulling
for more, its voice everywhere and
in my head.

And once I dared climb the little snow hill,
a warm fire-orange ski cabin
nestled into its side. I lingered
cold wet and dry at once
with motionless fingers.
White and more white below.

Then came the moment:
Throwing my weight, I would fall over
and roll—boom boom boom—
down into
river, sea, snow,
nothing but speed.

On my first day of high school
the teachers spoke very slowly,
crouched down to eye
level but not leveling
with me. A pat on the head.
Fast-talking, foam-spitting
poetry teacher, licked her lips
in measured breath.
  Take your time, dear. I don't expect
  you will write much.
They had been warned
that I was slow.

Half a lifetime later: the hills
have fallen flat
as grown-up hope.
I slide heavy into the airboat.
Scarred alligators suspicious,
sanderlings startled into flight,
great blue heron and wood stork
slow and staring in the shallows.
Murky swamp air snaps
fresh across my cheeks,
tears pinched from squinting eyes.
  Wanna go slower?

    No, I like it
    like this.
I lift my head
to hit the wind hard.
    Just give me some speed.

Discussion Questions

1. Who do the narrative voices belong to in "Crippled Symphony"? What preconceived ideas do these narrators have about disability?
2. How does the narrator of "Choices" experience the act of receiving care? Describe the power relations reflected in this context.
3. One might say that the narrative voice in "Walk" disrupts traditional discourses surrounding children with muscular dystrophy. In what ways does this portrait contrast with traditional cultural norms?
4. To what extent do the narrator's personal identity and personality align with social expectations? Describe the effects of this relationship as she comes of age.

Opal, Orbit, & Ruby

Aubree Evans

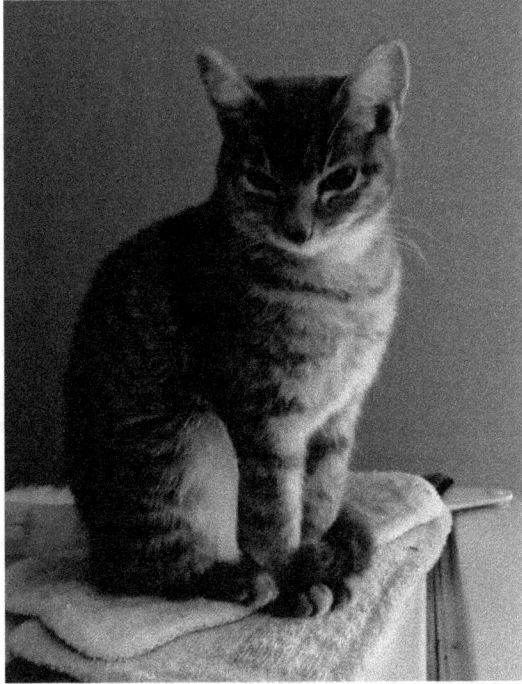

ID: A collage of three animals. A long-haired cat stretches out on an outdoor bench, a grey dog looks at the camera with its tongue out, and a dwarf cat looks sweetly at the camera.

• • •

The little grey dwarf cat is Ruby. The stretched out long-haired cat is Opal, and the dog is Orbit.

On one hand they comfort me when I am in pain, particularly Ruby and Orbit. They lay with me and comfort me when I'm on my heating pad and when I have trouble breathing. Ruby and Orbit both also have disabilities, and I feel like we can be slow together. On the other hand, my pets sometimes exacerbate my asthma and my mobility limitations when they get underfoot.

DOI:10.1163/9789004512702_031

CHAPTER 21

Maybe Do Talk to Strangers on the Internet?
An Interview with Corin Parsons

Corin Parsons (with Paul D. C. Bones)

A note on cripping the writing process: We took an iterative and collaborative approach to this chapter. When it became clear during the submissions process that I was stretched beyond my energetic means and struggling to complete the work, Paul suggested an interview as an alternative way to include my voice in the collection. After the interview was transcribed by Danielle Barber, Paul and I both edited the interview for length and clarity. I also incorporated several points that had slipped my mind during the initial conversation. I made the choice to include this note and italicize those additions in the following text in order to pay tribute to the powerful ways in which disabled people make it possible for one another to tell our stories.

Mobility Aids

Paul: One of the things I really wanted for this book was the experience of someone who uses a mobility aid and I know that you use a wheelchair. Can you talk a little bit about that, how you decided to start using it, and how you feel about it? Because I know that there's a lot of thoughts about being "wheelchair bound" or about a wheelchair being like a cage, and from what I can tell, even though I don't use one, that is very much not true.

Corin: That definitely hasn't been my experience—even though I know that those views are prevalent, if not, dominant. I started using a wheelchair because, in short, I was really struggling to function. I could (and still can) walk for short distances and stand for brief periods—but only at the cost of so many other things in my life. I knew that a lot of people with my condition, Ehlers-Danlos Syndrome (EDS), use a wheelchair at least some of the time to manage pain,

© CORIN PARSONS, 2022 | DOI:10.1163/9789004512702_032

fatigue, and other symptoms, so I Googled "When is the right time to start using a wheelchair?" and I came across some very good advice somewhere on the internet that said the right time is "whenever you start asking that question"—and I should say that this wasn't just good advice; it was also an important lesson about learning to listen to my body and respect its needs.

My wheelchair has been a game-changing tool for me, but one thing that I encountered pretty quickly was a belief in a kind of hierarchy of mobility aids. I had a therapist who tried to tell me that using a wheelchair was a "drastic" choice relative to a cane or walker. It didn't matter that neither of those options were appropriate for my needs; he just thought that I wasn't "disabled enough" to use a wheelchair (whatever that means). I'm really glad that I didn't listen to him because it wasn't a drastic choice! Well, I mean it was [laughs] insofar as it drastically improved my well-being—but it wasn't a drastic choice in the way that he meant it. So this imagined hierarchy is both harmful and inaccurate; the right mobility aid is whichever mobility aid helps you do the things that matter to you while also taking care of your body.

A related belief is that a mobility aid is a last resort—that only suffering can justify using a mobility aid and that your difficulties must be "extreme enough" to outweigh the stigma and shame of "relying" on one. This is false. Deciding to use a mobility aid can be a process of prioritizing your comfort! You are not obligated to endure increased pain and fatigue, or to miss out on valued activities and experiences. If a mobility aid would improve your quality of life, that's a good enough reason to use one! Moreover, it's completely acceptable to use a mobility aid strategically. In other words, you can use a mobility aid for something trivial now (like errands and appointments) so that you have the capacity later to do something that you value (like gardening) without it.

Another thing that I encountered is how perceptions of mobility aids differ from embodied experiences of using them. People tend to view a wheelchair, for instance, as a diminished—if not tragic— way of moving through the world. That's why there's one particular conversation that stands out in my memory: shortly after I started using my wheelchair one of my students came up to me after class and kind of leaned in conspiratorially and was like, "So, be honest with me: is it a little bit fun?" Yeah, it is! Thanks for asking that question! I'm faster than everybody. It's like biking down a hallway, which feels delightfully against the rules. And among wheelchair users there's this very specific pleasure gleaned from rolling across a really smooth and level surface such as a polished concrete floor like you might find at a hardware store. That crip joy is something that a lot of people don't understand because joy is antithetical to the constructed meanings of mobility aids.

Of course, there are some drawbacks. You have to navigate a world that's not built for how you move, and people try to make that your problem even though it's not. Also, social interactions definitely change, although not necessarily for the worse [laughs]. I mean, it's tough being disabled in general, so I don't want to make unhelpful comparisons, but I found that before I started using a wheelchair— when people didn't know that I was disabled but just knew that I couldn't do things in the "normal" or expected way—they were really cruel and impatient; however, as a wheelchair user interactions are mostly just awkward, which I don't mind. I've always been kind of weird, so as long as I don't think too hard about the underlying ableism, it's just like "Cool, now you're weird too!" [laughs].

I do think, however, that underneath that awkwardness is the fact that most nondisabled folks don't really develop disability competence because the dominant culture teaches us that it's "polite" to ignore disability, so they're incredibly uncomfortable interacting with people they perceive as disabled. They don't know what to do! Folks are eager for direction, so if you're a little bit shameless—like yours truly—it can be easier to guide them through the interaction. I found that was much harder to do when I was still disabled but not perceived as such because I wasn't using a mobility aid. I was presumed to be non-disabled and just sort of willfully non-compliant, which people took very personally rather than allowing for the possibility that I was disabled. This is one reason why compulsory able-bodiedness is so harmful. I really wish people would start instead from the assumptions that 1) some people are disabled, and 2) everyone is doing what they need to do in the way they need to do it.

Paul: Do you have any stories about super awkwardness with other people reacting to you in the wheelchair?

Corin: Oh yeah! When people don't know what to say, they'll tell you anything—from their entire life story to just wonderfully mundane details of their day. For example, I was scheduling a follow-up appointment with my doctor's administrative assistant, and just out of the blue she told me, "So there are coats on that chair over there because the hook behind the door broke and to get it fixed we have to submit a maintenance form and it's going to cost $80, so I was thinking that I could just go buy a hook and put it up, but..." And there I am like, in all earnestness, "This drama is thrilling please tell me more!" Honestly, I enjoy that. Tell me about your life [laughs]! It happens all the time. I mean, you get people doing the "regular" weird stuff that you would anticipate—like dramatically leaping out of your way, making a big production of holding open a door for you, or offering to carry you places—but the unexpected weird stuff is way better, and impromptu "story time" is the best [laughs].

Sometimes interactions are awful though. For instance, people have issues with disabled folks existing in public space. We're not supposed to take up space—which is a tall order, especially when spaces aren't constructed with us in mind and it is therefore almost impossible for us to use those spaces in the ways they were intended. People will absolutely make it their mission to police how you take up space. One time, I was at a protest, and a woman came over to tell me that I was "in the way." Um, ma'am... this is a protest. Being in the way is the whole point! It's a funny example, but it also illustrates how entitled people feel to tell you that your presence is a problem—even though non-disabled people created the problem by not anticipating the mere existence of disabled people in a given space.

And, of course, folks like to say inappropriate things to ambulatory wheelchair users. As I mentioned earlier, I can walk for short distances and stand for brief periods, but there are consequences for doing so. A wheelchair therefore helps me manage those consequences; and feel better, do more, and just generally take proper care of myself. I have heard so many horror stories from other ambulatory wheelchair users of people accusing them of "faking" and trying to get attention or sympathy. Luckily, I haven't encountered this much, and that's probably because if I am using my wheelchair, I am engaged in an activity that requires me to use it, so I'm not standing up or walking a lot. There are times, however, when I do stand up. For example, when I was teaching in person before the pandemic, I would get out of my wheelchair to write on the board or something if it was a good day. My students were always cool with it, which I appreciate. It's nice when it's not a big deal and folks are just like, "Oh okay, that's how you move through the world."

Similarly, I have a wonderful tattoo artist who was asking me how I would feel most comfortable being positioned when getting tattooed, and they framed it as, "I don't want to make any assumptions about your mobility." I think that's kind of where folks should start: don't make assumptions about what someone can or can't do based on mobility aids, and if necessary, just ask—by which I mean, ask if it's a matter of meeting access needs.

Whether or not it's acceptable to ask a person about other aspects of their disability or experience definitely depends on the individual. I am pretty open to questions in general, but I appreciate when someone asks whether they can ask me something (such as, "Can I ask a question about your wheelchair?"). It lets me know that the other person doesn't feel entitled to the information and wants to respect my boundaries. I want folks to learn about disability so— although I know that not everyone feels comfortable taking on the responsibility of teaching people about disability and exposing intimate details about themselves in the process—I personally don't mind. That said, if they do ask, they're not just going to get the answer that satisfies their curiosity; they're going to get the whole story and hopefully learn a little bit in the process.

Disability Twitter

Paul: Alright, so we met via Disability Twitter and I know that you just had your one-year anniversary. So one of the things I thought I'd ask is: What has that community meant to you and how do you see the community, what's important about the community? Can you talk about the community in general, I guess?

Corin: I knew about Disability Twitter well before I joined Disability Twitter, and I was aware of it as this incredible space of disabled knowledge production. I'm sure somebody has actually written about this and has more insightful things to say, but I do think that Disability Twitter has had an outsized impact on how we, as a community, understand ourselves and mobilize—which is one reason why it frustrates me when I hear people saying, "Well, online advocacy isn't real advocacy" or "Online friendships aren't real friendships." Even pre-pandemic, it was hard for me to go out and engage with people in person—that's just a high-cost activity for me—but I can have conversations all day with people on Twitter, and those are real, thought-provoking, life-changing conversations. They form the basis of real relationships.

I also want to push back on this artificial separation of online and offline worlds because many of these relationships that started online and were cultivated through the space of Disability Twitter are not confined to the digital realm alone. Through Disability Twitter I've met a number of disability activists who are local to me, including several other disabled folks from my university. Many of these connections, foraged online, have not only grown into cherished friendships; they've facilitated on-the-ground disability education and organizing. I'm currently working on an open access critical disability studies learning module with someone who goes to my university, but we met through Disability Twitter. Similarly, the person who started the Disabled Graduate Students Association (DGSA) at our school is also someone I met through Disability Twitter—in fact, most of our core DGSA group met on Twitter. So what I am trying to say, is that online spaces are legitimate activist spaces!

I want to note, however, that interactions don't have to move offline or result in close friendships or working relationships to be valuable. One of the most powerful things that Disability Twitter does is simply to let disabled people know we are not alone in our experiences. I'm thinking of one tweet in particular. I'm also neurodivergent in addition to having EDS, so one day I tweeted, "Growing up neurodivergent means I've been conditioned to assume that whatever brings me joy will be viewed as embarrassingly uncool or unbearably obnoxious." Anyone who has had that experience knows how isolating it feels, but this tweet racked up 28,677 likes. People read that tweet and said "I see you" or "This resonates with my experiences," and in a society in which disabled people don't get to see ourselves and our experiences reflected back to us very often, that's really powerful.

The final thing that I appreciate about Disability Twitter is that it isn't just a space for advocacy and support; it's also a space of crip joy. I don't think that most non-disabled people understand the depth of joy, humour, and creative energy in our community. Disabled people are "supposed to be"' miserable—to such an extent even that misery is materially enforced through the inadequate and punitive social programs supposedly put in place to "support" disabled people. We are terrorized emotionally and energetically by the systems that we rely on for survival. And that's why it's so important to have spaces in which we can revel, unapologetically, in our joy.

It feels good. These are great people, and I'm so glad that I can access that community and connection and joy from my couch or from my bed. Disability can be really isolating—even if you're not isolated from other people in your day-to-day life, chances are you're relatively isolated from other disabled people—so I am really grateful to Disability Twitter. It's an incredible community. I just love it [laughs].

Paul: Not to victim-blame or anything, but you did make yourself into an accidental sex symbol. For example, "Who wore it sweater" with Charis?

Corin: [laughs] Yep, I don't know. That was just...*I know I did it to myself, but I'm actually quite bashful so it's low-key mortifying— although not altogether unwelcome.*

Let me back up and tell the whole story: I was having one of those days of feeling really good in/as myself, so I took a picture, and I liked what I saw reflected in the photo—it captured how I felt in that moment—so I decided to post it to Twitter. In the photo, I am seated in my wheelchair and leaning forward with my elbows on my knees and my hands clasped with one foot on the ground and the other on the footplate. I'm wearing a cream-coloured Aran fisherman sweater, cuffed jeans, and dark green boots, and I'm looking directly into the camera. Now here's where I made a grave error in judgement: I playfully captioned it "Them: disabled people can't be sexy. Me: Ok, I won't." I had no idea what a "thirst trap" was, but apparently that's what I'd created. Almost 10,000 people liked the photo, and a lot of them left kind of spicy comments! The best part was that other folks responded or retweeted with their own photos, so it ended up being a bit of a celebration of crip embodiment.

I was really taken aback by the response—mostly in a good way— and I decided to just lean into it to see what would happen. So I started posting more photos of myself, usually wearing sweaters (which is honestly just how I dress, but people seemed to like it). Eventually, that also led to another Twitter friend Charis (whose handle is @ BeingCharisBlog), proposing a friendly competition using the hashtag #WhoWoreItSweater.

Paul: Could you describe it a little bit?

Corin: Yeah, so we dressed up in sweaters and tried to look "sexy" for the camera, usually in our wheelchairs. That's it. It wasn't really a competition, though; we wanted everyone who felt like dressing up to do so. It was meant to be a celebration of our appearances as disabled people.

It turned out to be a really liberating experience for me personally, and I tweeted about that as well. I said:

> *I don't post pictures of myself bc I am confident but bc I have every right to celebrate my crip bodymind and posting pictures is part of that process—of showing up in/as myself, beholding my bodymind, and proclaiming aloud that this bodymind is loved and lived in and good.*
>
> *I'm not confident. I am obstinate. I refuse to believe that confidence is a prerequisite to coming as you are. If you can't be confident, be audacious. Be flamboyant. Be playful. Be joyful. Be fierce. Be whatever lets you show up as your crip self.*

I also think that spirit of insisting on the right to show up in/as yourself actually played a role in me coming into my transness and coming out as trans shortly thereafter, which is another conversation for another time.

Paul: You mention both you and Charis are wheelchair users. How important is it to sort of show the sexy side of disability? Oh God, did I just say the "sexy side" of disability?

Corin: I do think it is important because it's clear that disabled folks are desexualized and infantilized in the dominant culture—although there also seems to be a countervailing hypersexualization of disabled people (and perhaps some pressure from within the community itself as well), but to be perfectly honest, I haven't untangled any of that yet. I'm sure that other people have written about it much more eloquently than I could! The bottom line for me is that disabled people are whole people, and for many folks that includes being sexual. For me, personally, I just want space in society to be boring-sexy—like a goofy dad in khakis sexy. I want to be someone's cup of tea—not necessarily everyone's cup of tea. So that's why it's really funny to me that I was momentarily a Twitter "sex symbol," but I enjoyed the experience and learned a lot about myself.

CATS!

Paul: As you know, I love your cats, particularly Finn—and I'm sorry I love your cat-husband, Bear, as well. But! So Finn is a para-kitty, is it just her two back legs?

Corin: According to the imaging that's been done, two of her vertebrae are fused at an angle. From what we know, it was probably congenital. So yeah, she's got some narrowing along her spine, it affects her hind leg mobility, and she gets around by scooting on her bottom.

Paul: And how did she come into your life?

Corin: I met her when I was doing some PhD-related volunteer work at an organization called VOKRA, the Vancouver Orphan Kitten Rescue Association. She was at VOKRA's Operations Centre because she was medically complicated. In addition to her mobility stuff, she also had recurring urinary tract infections (UTIS), gastrointestinal issues, and ringworm.

Finn was rescued at about 2 weeks old with her feral mom and her brother Henry. Finn is actually Instagram friends with Henry, so it's fun to see how he's doing these days! Anyway, Finn and Henry caught a cold and had to be separated from their mom because she was so aggressive that it was hard to medicate the kittens, and colds can be deadly to young kittens. Shortly thereafter, they also developed ringworm, which isn't a big deal—it's a fungus, like athlete's foot—but it can spread quickly, and it takes a long time to clear up. So, Finn and Henry were in quarantine at VOKRA's Operations Centre, and that's where I met her.

I was the one who gave her daily ringworm baths and cleaned her little bum (we thought that she was incontinent at the time, but it turned out that she just had a sensitive stomach and the loose stools were leading to UTIS; we've since found a diet and elimination routine that work for her, so she no longer gets daily bum baths). Anyway, because she needed a lot of one-on-one attention, I got to know her pretty well, and when it was time for her to go into foster, I was the obvious choice because I had a good handle on her care needs. Of course, I "foster failed" and ended up adopting her—which I knew that I would from the day I brought her home, but we did pretend for a while that I was just fostering her.

Paul: As a disabled person, is there any special connection because she's also disabled? Or, is that just an ableist projection? "Well of course the disabled person would see themselves in the disabled cat."

Corin: That's a great question! My academic research is actually about how categories of social difference are constructed with and through nonhuman animals, so even though my research focuses specifically on cats and gender, I am also really interested in the relationship between me, as a disabled person, and Finn, as a disabled cat. A lot of the narratives applied to disabled nonhuman animals parallel those applied to disabled humans as well, and ableism is definitely at work in our relationships with animals—especially disabled animals. Sunaura Taylor has written a wonderful book about this called *Beasts of Burden: Animal and Disability Liberation*.

I also think that me being disabled has impacted my relationship with Finn just on a personal level. When I first brought her home, the plan was to do physical therapy and get her walking, but it became pretty clear that, no, what she actually needed was a way to move around that was comfortable for her—and it wasn't walking, or even using a cat wheelchair (which we tried as well). She was showing me what worked best for her, and I needed to find ways to facilitate it. I would hope that a non-disabled adopter would have understood that too, but I think that as a disabled person, it made intrinsic sense to me to take my cues from her rather than trying to make her more "normal."

I also suspect that Finn likes that I'm disabled. I don't mean that we both have the same understanding of disability, but what I mean is that she clearly thrives in circumstances shaped by my disability. For example, I spend a lot more time at home than most folks, which is great because it allows me to better meet Finn's care needs and to give her the constant affection that she demands! I've also noticed how much she seems to enjoy my sick days because it usually means that I'm lying on the couch or in bed, so she gets to cuddle up and take a nap on me—which she adores. (You can check social media for the photographic evidence.) Also, for whatever reason, both Finn and Bear love to steal my wheelchair; it's apparently the best seat in the house!

Paul: Oh, that reminded me. Was it Finn or Bear that will tap on your wheelchair?

Corin: Oh, on the brake? Yeah! She will do that to get my attention because it makes noise. She'll just reach up and tap the brake! I would say she's a weird cat, but it's not weird; it's just how she's figured out how to get what she needs.

Paul: Which is very cat-like behavior.

Corin: [Laughs] It's true! People will always see her and be like, "Oh what a sweet little angel baby" because she's very cute and she wears a diaper; they think she's like a doll or something—but no! This cat is unnervingly self-possessed. She knows what she wants. She knows how to get it. She knows when she wants to be babied, and then other times she's all business. Actually, come to think of it, the way that people disregard her agency is quite familiar as a disabled person! But the point is: she figures out how to get her needs met. She just does it in a different way, which I think is a quintessential disability experience.

Discussion Questions

1.   How does Corin's description of his relationship with his wheelchair differ from what we often see in popular media?
2.   Why do we view mobility aids as a bad thing? Often, we hear that once we start using them, we're unlikely to stop. How does this relate to the idea that disability is something we must overcome instead of accommodate?
3.   We often view disability as a desexualizing event or characteristic. Why is it important for disabled people to be "cute," "hot," "attractive," and/or "sexy"?
4.   Corin and Paul met on Twitter. We often view online friendships as being less real than in-person ones. How is this an expression of ableism?

Finn & Bear

Corin Parsons

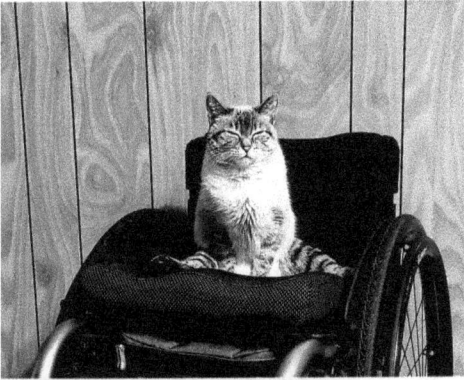

ID: (Top) A partially paralyzed lynx-point cat sits on her human's wheelchair and squints. (Bottom) A dark brown and white longhaired cat wearing a leash stands tall on a grassy lawn.

•••

Finn is a crip feline researching human behaviour while her crip human completes a PhD on cats (supervised by Bear).

DOI:10.1163/9789004512702_033

CHAPTER 22

Finding Empowerment in the Middle
Navigating Hidden Disabilities in Academia

Summer M. Jackson

A *hidden disability* is a blanket term used to describe disabilities that are not immediately observable to others. In my experience, having a hidden disability is a double-edged sword. The positives are that I do not have to disclose my disability if I chose not to, which I often do not. The ability to manage my social identity is a fundamental form of social control. However, having a hidden disability often makes me feel the need to "prove" myself when I need assistance. Because my disability is invisible, I frequently feel I am dismissed or considered a low priority. I also struggle with an internal dialogue of not being "disabled enough" to warrant accommodations or even a voice in the discussion. It took me a long time to recognize that I have a disability. This, I have learned, is very common among the hidden disabilities community (Benness, 2019; Gill, 1998). In a way, it is similar to imposter syndrome, in that I feel like a fraud who should leave discussions on disabilities to those who are visibly disabled. The more research I have done, the more I realize that these experiences and feelings are the rule, not the exception, for those with hidden disabilities.

The road to diagnoses was long and, needless to say, frustrating, which is common for those suffering from hidden disabilities. It took multiple doctor visits and tests over a two-year span to finally have a name for what I was experiencing. I have Meniere's disease, which is an inner ear disorder that results in vertigo and hearing loss (Mayo Clinic, 2020). The best way to describe this disorder is to compare it to a long night of drinking and listening to loud music; your ears are ringing, and the room is spinning, but you have not had any of the fun of a night out. Aside from the vertigo and hearing loss, my symptoms include tinnitus (or ringing in the ears), ear pressure, ear fullness, and nausea. When I have attacks or feel one about to come on, I also experience anxiety, which can amplify the Meniere's symptoms. This disorder often strikes suddenly after long periods with no attacks, which further contributes to the anxiety. Exhaustion is also

© SUMMER M. JACKSON, 2022 | DOI:10.1163/9789004512702_034

common following episodes. The first attack I ever had ended with an emergency room visit. Following the initial attack, I experienced a number of episodes before I was officially diagnosed.

Meniere's is not an apparent disability. The ability to pass as non-disabled person provides me with the power to control my identity and minimize, if I so choose, the impact of what could potentially be a stigmatizing label (Cavet, 1998; Goffman, 1963; Valeras, 2010). Meniere's, while considered a chronic condition, presents inconsistently. This type of inconsistency is referred to as *dynamic disability* (Benness, 2019). A dynamic disability is best described as being unpredictable in both presentation and severity of symptoms. I have gone months at a time where my internal and external realities synced. Yet, when those realities differ, my experience is often made to feel illegitimate. Frequently, those who experience hidden disabilities that fluctuate in presentation, suffer from self-doubt and their needs are not identified or addressed (Fitzgerald, 2000).

While the way we construct our identities tends to be fluid and are impacted by a variety of social and cultural factors, the binary structure of disability—you either are or you are not disabled—is inappropriate for people like me, who fall somewhere in the middle (Valeras, 2010). Incorporating a hidden disability into a self-concept is a continuous cycle that may take years to accept and manage effectively. Dynamically disabled people often feel unconformable with identifying as disabled, as they do not fit into one specific category all the time (Benness, 2019). For example, I struggle with asking for accommodations as I do not need them all the time. Most days, I can hike, swim, and do my regular day-to-day activities without issue. However, when I experience attacks, I feel betrayed by my body. I no longer feel in the driver's seat of my own life or safety. When people speak to me and it sounds distorted, I feel foolish asking for them to repeat themselves. The vertigo can leave me incapacitated, and whatever plans I had that day, or deadlines I needed to meet, have to be pushed back. How I look—physically—and how I feel—internally—dramatically differ. Often by that point, I feel it is too late to ask about accommodations. And if I do ask, I fear I will be viewed as a liar or a fraud. Even worse, when I do seek accommodations, and they are brushed off as a low priority, it discourages me from asking for help in the future. These are legitimate fears and many invisibly disabled individuals regularly face such challenges.

My disability has impacted my professional life in a variety of ways. I am an assistant professor at a predominately teaching university. My job requires that I stand in front of a room, full of students, for an extended period of time. When I experience attacks, I need something to hold on to in order to make sure I do not fall. It is an incredibly scary feeling to be standing in front of a classroom and the class suddenly starts to spin. A tactic I use to ensure my safety is to anchor myself to something stable, like a podium. A podium in a lecture hall seems like a typical, standard piece of equipment and yet, more often than not, I have walked in on the first day of class to find it missing. I have requested a podium be in my classrooms nearly every semester and yet, I struggle to consistently receive one. The requests were often dismissed or treated like I was asking for preferential treatment. It took significant time and effort to track down the appropriate department to request this supposed standard piece of equipment. Having to take the time to locate a podium before each class period was time that could have been better spent working with students. I was repeatedly met with what I perceived as frustration after asking multiple times about a podium, which ultimately made me feel like a nuisance. Inevitably, I would give up asking and just hope I did not have any attacks. Walking into a classroom and seeing the lack of podium was anxiety-inducing and impacted the confidence I need to do my job effectively.

I remember one day in particular I was in the middle of a lecture and was hit so unexpectedly with vertigo and ear ringing that I nearly fell over. I had turned my head toward the projector screen and remember seeing the projector flip sideways. Many who struggle with Meniere's experience drop attacks—which is when the individual suddenly falls to the ground. A thought flashed in my mind about how embarrassing it was going to be to suddenly fall over in front of my class, and how the comment section in my course evaluations was sure to be very interesting after this. Thankfully, this was one of the rare times I had a podium. I remember gripping it for dear life and after a couple minutes, the attack subsided, and I was able to continue lecturing. If I had been in one of those classrooms that did not have a podium, I am confident that the attack would have ended differently and possibly derailed the entire day of lecture.

Hidden disabilities allow for discretion in disclosure. I and others like me get to decide whether or not to draw attention to that part of ourselves. Many of those who fall somewhere in the middle of the able/disabled identity continuum can decide whether to reveal or conceal our disabilities. Revealing this part of oneself can come at the cost of experiencing shame, stigma, prejudice, and discrimination. However, having a hidden disability can also be empowering.

Since my diagnosis, I have developed a new and profound sense of awareness from my own experiences and the experiences of others who struggle with dynamic or hidden disabilities. I also understand that while people with disabilities encompass an extremely diverse group, my voice and experience is valid and important. I do not pretend to speak for an entire community, or assume I understand every experience of those who identify as disabled. Rather, I strive to listen and learn. My experiences sparked curiosity of a realm I was mostly ignorant about. Not unlike the path to my Meniere's diagnosis, the path to discovering this middle ground of the disability community took time and research. My experience and research have fostered advocacy. I have become a better advocate for myself and others like me who grapple with identifying where they belong.

My hidden disability has also made me a more empathetic and compassionate instructor. I do not feel the need to "see it to believe it." I have a greater understanding that disclosing a hidden disability is difficult and that those who struggle with invisible and dynamic disabilities have likely been made to feel they need to "prove" it in the past. Disclosure is a personal and continuous process that necessitates an internal debate of risk versus reward. Risks include, among many potential outcomes, the possibility of future discrimination. I make an effort to make my students feel heard and seen, even if their disability cannot be. Being an inclusive instructor can take many forms, but what I have found to be the most important advocacy for inclusivity is the ability to listen to my students' needs. I strive to create a welcoming learning environment. Again, I do not presume to understand all the experiences of my students with differing abilities. However, I approach the classroom with empathy, not sympathy, in the hope of creating an inclusive and productive learning environment. Such an environment requires flexibility and adaptability to meet student needs and ensure they are reaching their goals.

My disability has, in a lot of ways, pushed me to create strategies and develop techniques to ensure my students are able to have equity in the classroom. Designing inclusive solutions for the entire spectrum of needs can be extremely labor-intensive. Yet, my experiences have taught me that success does not always require huge, time-consuming adjustments. Similar to my requirements of a podium, I have found sometimes simple solutions can resolve barriers in the classroom. For example, I previously had a student who struggled with severe, debilitating migraines. This student felt comfortable enough to disclose this information to me. We discussed possible triggers, of which fluorescent lighting was one. Because of that conversation, I changed all my lecture slides to dark writing with light backgrounds to make sure the words were easily readable on the screen. I also made the words larger on the screen, so she did not have to strain to read them. I then started every class period by turning off the majority of the overhead lights. I would keep the blinds open for natural light so students could still see. It got to the point where I would walk into the classroom and students would have already turned off the lights and opened the blinds. It was a simple, yet effective change in the classroom that worked for everyone.

I would like to think I would be as understanding of an instructor without my disability, but the truth is, I do not know if that would be the case. The experiences I have had living with a hidden, dynamic disability has made me more aware of the importance of making students feel legitimized. I also recognize that disclosure is often reserved for friends, family, and partners and thus, when students do disclose, it is of the utmost importance to honor that disclosure. Students may not be fully aware that what they are disclosing is a hidden disability (Cavet, 1998). The student who suffered migraines did not identify as disabled, rather, she saw herself as just someone who suffered from terrible headaches that made sitting in a classroom difficult. She may never identify as disabled or be able to properly articulate her needs in her future workplace. In part, she may never seek help or basic accommodations because she does not know what invisible, dynamic disabilities are. Those who fall into such categories reveal a fluctuating group of people who struggle with the proper way to construct their identity. The binary identity structure of being disabled or not is inadequate for those who are somewhere in the middle (Valeras, 2010). A better understanding of the nature of disability and the lived experiences of those who identify as such is important for successful work and educational environments. We tend to view disability as either/or, all the time or not at all. However, like with other forms of identity, this does not account for the breadth and depth of disability identity. Hidden disabilities are fluid and nuanced. They are complex and not always apparent to the observer. My hidden disability has empowered me to become a more inclusive and compassionate instructor and a better advocate for myself and others who silently grapple with where they belong.

Discussion Questions

1. What are "hidden" disabilities? The author describes having a hidden disability as a "double-edged sword." What are the implications of having an invisible versus a visible disability?
2. What might be some of the challenges experienced by those with hidden disabilities? How do they differ from having a visible disability?

References

Benness, B. (2019, December 8). My disability is dynamic: Maybe the media has led you to believe that all disabilities are visible and static. Disabilities caused by chronic illnesses can be anything but. *Age of Awareness.* https://medium.com/age-of-awareness/my-disability-is-dynamic-bc2a619fcc1

Cavet, J. (1998). *People don't understand: Children, young people, and their families living with hidden disabilities.* Joseph Rowntree Foundation.

Fitzgerald, M. (2000). "You look so well": The multiple facets of hidden disabilities. *Society for Disability Studies Quarterly, 20,* 254–258.

Gill, C. J. (1998). What are the problems of having a "hidden disability"? *Post-Polio News, 1.*

Goffman, I. (1963). *Stigma.* Prentice-Hall.

Mayo Clinic. (2020, November 14). *Meniere's disease.* https://www.mayoclinic.org/diseases-conditions/menieres-disease/symptoms-causes/syc-20374910

Valeras, A. B. (2010). We don't have a box: Understanding hidden disability identity utilizing narrative research methodology. *Disability Studies Quarterly, 30,* 3–4.

Rocko (More Formally Known as Rocko Taco)

Summer M. Jackson

ID: A brown pit-mix with pointy ears snuggles with its owner.

• • •

Rocko is a rescue dog and retired blood donor dog. He was adopted from a veterinarian clinic where his blood saved the lives of other dogs that needed transfusions. On days I experience vertigo and ear ringing, he stays with me and helps with both physical stability and easing my anxiety.

CHAPTER 23

Taking Center Stage in the Face of Shame and Scars

Jasmine (Jaz) Gray

Mainstream media is ultimately a stage. Over the past thirty-one years of my life, I have been on a journey learning how to claim my stages. From birth with a rare craniofacial disability to my baptism, from a would-be actress in front of the camera, to a health communication scholar and a network television subject, I have had to contend for full participation in a range of spaces—some affirming and supportive, and others that seem to justify my exclusion at every turn. As a subject in a docuseries on commercial television, I became the main character in a dramatized version of my own story without control over my narrative, profit from my participation, or an ownership stake in the intellectual property produced by the efforts of me and my family. All of this while leading up to and following my 44th surgery, a 12-hour procedure to replace half of the disfigured jawbone I have used my entire life to speak with a section of the fibula in my right leg.

Media participation has become a central concern in what disability media scholar Elizabeth Ellcessor calls the "politics of disability representation" (2017, p. 2). The media representation of disability centers a concern for the presence of disabled characters in mainstream entertainment narratives. Media participation demands particular attention to the lack of opportunities for disabled people to ultimately acquire equal access to resources needed to produce media independent of, and particularly within, the mainstream media industry. Such access can directly influence our capacity to overcome stigmatization and acquire the cultural, social, and material capital needed to become fully liberated. By telling the story of these different stages I have occupied in my life, centered around my recent experience as a main subject in a reality TV show, I hope to flesh out the stakes of an important debate within the disability justice community.

Logline: What happens when a would-be child actress with a craniofacial condition turned entertainment-industry professional turned health communication academic is transformed into an accidental disability-rights activist through a baptism by fire?

Light

Setting: Graduate Student Housing in Chapel Hill, North Carolina
Time: Spring, 2019

The half of my face that is not paralyzed turned upward into a smile as the two blondes, one with a few grays and the other with a ponytail, spoke to me through the screen of my laptop; they thought I was "awe-inspiring." At thirty years old, a graduate student at UNC Chapel Hill, I had finally learned my love language—words of affirmation. A television producer telling me that I inspire amazement felt very close to love. I thought it was divine intervention. What were the chances that a production company from London would come across an article I'd published in a nonprofit newsletter, just as I had finally grown vulnerable enough to voice out loud my journey to emotional healing from medical trauma and body shame? What were the odds that they would be casting the final subject in a network docuseries called *Medical Marvel* right as I prepared to fly home for my father to drive us from Memphis, Tennessee, to Little Rock, Arkansas, for my 44th medical procedure?

After two media degrees with one on the way, I was far from naïve about the television industry. I knew everything that glitters is not gold. However, the prospect of this particular role seemed dazzling. The producers of this major reality television series, focused on people with craniofacial conditions before and after a major procedure, nodded encouragingly from the other side of my computer screen. They had recruited six others to be a part of the docuseries, four white men, one white woman, and now me; we would each have an hour-long episode dedicated to our individual story. They said that I could rest assured that the crew would be small, warm, and friendly, and that the footage would be "beautifully shot." Their aspirations sounded honorable: documenting the physical, practical, and emotional changes that medical treatment can bring a person.

Now is the perfect time, they suggested, to record a "kind of mini casting tape." As I tried to make the mental switch from what had been essentially an off-the-record, casual Skype conversation to what would now be an on-camera, recorded interview, Codie and Molly explained that they would ask me some pre-planned questions and then cut together clips to send to the series director and network liaison. These entertainment executives would have the final say about my participation. They asked me to scoot closer to the camera. A little closer still, and then could I also turn my swollen right cheek toward them? As I did, I could see a little red light flashing.

Water

Setting: Parkway Village Church of Christ in Memphis, Tennessee
Time: Fall, 1998

This particular Sunday morning, November of 1998, autumn in Memphis is fading fast, and winter is on the horizon. Inside a red brick building with a hunter green roof and white church steeple, behind the burgundy curtain of a baptistry, the water is lukewarm. I place my bare toes on the first step. Before I can move any further, my momma's strong hands calmly gather my hair and tie it down with a white turban wrapped tightly. The white cotton gown I wear hangs off my shoulders and long over a chest that isn't quite there yet, and then billows at my knees. In the water, I can see Daddy coming. He stops halfway. The water reaches his belly area and ripples in waves toward me.

Over the 45 surgeries I go on to have after this day, my dad will use his last vacation day, or even go without pay, to be at every single one and to be my primary caretaker for weeks afterward. From dressing open wounds on my face, emptying oozing drains from my neck, and washing out saliva suction machines to concocting the best homemade Ensure smoothies a foodie could ask for three times a day—he will see and do it all. He smiles at me now. And I float. Down into the blue-gray painted pool. As the curtain creaks open revealing the auditorium, I put my hands over my mouth and nose in anticipation. When I arise from the water, through clogged ears, I can still hear the cheering faintly.

I felt different coming up out of that water. Relieved but something more. My baptism was not the biggest stage I would ever be on, but it was the most important. I had willingly allowed the Most High co-authorship of my story and decision-making authority over my life. I knew exactly how Christ had died. How, at thirty-something years young, he had willingly decided to suffer—to carry his own cross, to be spit on, beat up, to have his garments sold off for profit piece by piece, to have stakes, burnt orange with rust, driven through his hands and feet—so that I could have life that would never truly end and a connection to a purpose beyond myself. And yet, even then, after this kind of rebirth, even for Jesus himself, the call on my life—to persevere in the midst of the suffering and stigmatization I was about to endure—would prove more than I could bear without family and faith to help me fight for the future I saw for myself.

In the months following this day, I would be underdiagnosed with a port wine stain and misdiagnosed with a hemangioma before being correctly diagnosed with diffuse arteriovenous malformations throughout the right side of my cheek, jawbone, mandible, tongue, and lip—arteries connect to veins without capillaries invading healthy tissues and organs (Kelly, 2015). My aim from early in life was to represent myself with authenticity and the courage of my convictions. As my health deteriorated, I would build upon this spiritual practice by honoring each opportunity to show up as my full self—to live, learn, work creatively, and persevere with a disabling, chronic condition. People like me, with visible differences and invisible illnesses, who want desperately to simply be treated fairly within the entertainment industry, we do not always have the physical and emotional bandwidth to weather the doubly disabling combination of industry exploitation *and* illness. However, in the words of vulnerability researcher Brené Brown, "You either walk inside your story and own it or you stand outside your story and hustle for your worthiness" (Brown, 2018).

Fire

Setting: Holiday Inn ballroom in Memphis, Tennessee
Time: Summer, 1999

The summer before sixth grade, I feel like I am really hitting my stride. I am working my way up on the local arts "scene" as they said in the biz. After booking a few plays at community theaters and my first modeling gig, I convinced my mom to take me to an audition for a children's modeling agency, excitedly proclaiming, "It could be my big break, Momma!" Yet, as I sit in a gold banquet chair with a crown back and gray foam cushions in the ballroom of the Holiday Inn, I am willing myself not to burst into tears, or into flames, as I stare bewildered at the stage. So-called talent agents, behind a long table with the white tablecloth and half empty water glasses, gaze smugly at the line of kids in front of them whose images they have deemed capable of making money representing various products. And I noticed something—they are all beautiful, various ages and ethnicities, the epitome of diversity and inclusion except everyone's face is perfectly symmetrical, everyone's body is complete.

By this time, I have endured two surgeries by a local plastic surgeon who told my parents he could definitely decrease the size of my growing bottom lip with no problem. He had no experience treating vascular conditions. And he had failed. And my lip had grown back twice the size it was before. And there is now a keloid down the center, a pink and protruding scar. I am hurt because the lady in the black slacks with the clipboard had smiled in my face, had given me encouraging nods as I strutted my stuff on the makeshift catwalk, yet she had not called my name. I can feel something rising up in me—an epiphany. "Girl, duh," I think to myself. "They not going to choose you with this big lip and stupid scar." I look intently across the ballroom until I make eye contact with my mom standing in the entrance, looking right at me. She knew. And I knew that she knew that I knew. Things would never be the same.

This was my first inkling that the arc of the moral universe in the entertainment industry bent toward exploitation. Twenty years later, I would receive further sociopolitical education through the cognitive dissonance of taking doctoral classes on media production and community empowerment while experiencing increasing powerlessness during my participation in the filming of a version of my story for TV. Communication researcher Vicki Mayer (2011) explains that the combination of creative arts and commerce illuminates a key tension between the two for those who hold power within these roles, particularly in nonfiction TV programming. The aim is simple—mandated from network executives and advertisers through production companies and to these creative professionals interacting with us as subjects—exhume as much as possible (or "get what we need") from the subjects toward producing the content while keeping expenditures as low as possible. For the identities, like mine, at the center of this entertainment content, these actions can lead to a lack of agency that must be counteracted. As a TV show subject having what would become a traumatic procedure with a long recovery, a lack of critical awareness tied one arm tightly behind my back while a lack of physical and emotional health tied the other squarely across my heart. I felt unable to fight.

Fears

Setting: Childhood home in Memphis, Tennessee
Time: Spring, 2019

The filming for *Medical Marvels* was punishing. It took place as I prepared for and recuperated from my 12-hour jaw replacement surgery. By the end of the process, my family and I had filmed off and on with the production team over a total of 7 months. During the shoots, certain days are marked for interviews at our family home in Memphis. I am asked to shoot and then reshoot a master interview 2 hours long. Each time, I am asked to be vulnerable, to share and then reshare my memories of the traumas I have overcome so far. The second time, the emotional intensity drains me in a way it does not the first time. My parents and younger sister are also interviewed in our living room for several hours and asked to relive moments of their journeys with my illness. My dad bursts into tears when he is asked to describe how he felt having to change out my wound packing after a surgery complication left me with a hole where my cheek should have been. I have the urge to stop the filming, to tell my Daddy not to cry. I start to cry myself, so I get up and leave the room. By June, when I'm asked by my mother's sorority to speak to a group of high schoolers, Momma will tell me afterward that I held back and did not tell my full story. I agree, although I don't yet understand why I gave them the abbreviated version.

An "iatrogenic" disease is one that is caused by medical treatment itself. The film crew, I began to realize, was not merely recording pain and suffering; they were themselves inflicting it. During the filming process, I did not yet have the critical knowledge to understand what can happen when people with disabilities and illnesses—and I would contribute our family members as well—are subjected to what

Arthur Frank calls "multiple tellings" of our stories in a rhetorically appropriate manner in order to appease the interest of a listening audience (2013, p. 71). My family and I were being "written on from the outside" as we listened to our own speech; although we were doing lots of talking, prompted by the crew, we had essentially lost our voices (Frank, 2013, p. 71).

In what I originally think is collaboration with the crew, I become a de facto coordinating producer, a role I have held on independent projects but have never been credited for on a commercial production. I arranged a scene at an upscale African-inspired lifestyle boutique to shoot my sister and me on a "spontaneous" (read: staged) shopping trip to "catch up from college." I arrange another shoot at a quaint, quiet massage parlor called Spa Therapies, where I receive soothing treatment under the banner of "self-care." I also arranged an in-depth interview with my surgeon Dr. Suen in Little Rock, which I listened to from outside the closed door of an empty office turned makeshift set, complete with a backdrop and lights.

The crew arranges to film me walking around downtown Memphis. Although I've only been downtown a handful of times in the past 10 years—"the trolleys and people make for great shots," says the director who is also the cameraman. He and the producer strap a Go-Pro on my chest and ask me to walk back and forth down a long stretch of sidewalk in the middle of crowds of people. They say they need to get footage from my perspective of how people react to my presence, to my face. By the end of the day's shoot, my legs are hurting, and they still have not gotten the perfect sequence they have been working me all afternoon to capture. I have not yet had the bone in my right leg removed, but the tissue from my left leg has been used to reconstruct my chin. It's left a long, pink scar, a dead weight on my thigh, and sharp shooting pains when I'm on my feet too long. I have to keep reminding the production team—both on the ground and in London—of this pain throughout the production process. Still, the team is so desperate to get this particular shot that they try to put it back on the schedule for another shoot months later. By then, I've started to push back, finally.

Soon, my family and I would lose the façade of collaboration we had with the production team; the false notion that we had equal decision-making control over what parts of our lives would be shot and included in "my" TV episode. I realize that, even if I insist on the crew filming a particular scene that I deem crucial to my journey with disability, they could very well appease me but then leave the footage on the cutting room floor. Nonetheless, I keep trying to participate in the staging of my story.

During all of this, my mom jokes that I need a producer credit. I tell my mom that I have actually done the production work, and the least they can do is give me a coordinator credit for my professional production resume. We decide I should ask. I approach the producer outside in the driveway as the director is setting his camera up to film the introductory montage scene with my family. He agrees that I've done the work but argues that the production will push back. "Why?" I ask, my eyes narrowed and brows furrowed. "Well," he says with that half smile that is becoming less cute each time he whips it out, "Because the viewers may think the show is staged if you get a credit." My throat goes dry. The viewers watching my trials while eating dinner from the comfort of their living room are more important than crediting me for my work. I smile back before responding as calmly as I can, "I doubt the viewers will notice my name is in the credits, but I will know." He says, "Of course," and promises he will ask. Perhaps he did: but I never did hear anything back from London.

In *Justice and the Politics of Difference*, Iris Marion Young and Danielle S. Allen conceptualize exploitation as the ways in which "the labor and energy of one group benefits another" (2011, p. 50). By the end of the fall of 2019, my family and I were officially overworked and drained of energy. At this point, I understood all this work was to serve a company creating a product I had little actual control over. My family, friends, and doctor were all trying their best to accommodate me. But I had not truly enjoyed shooting "my story" since the first day of filming.

Power

Setting: Home, Memphis, Tennessee
Time: Fall, 2019

Sitting up in my bed, texting back and forth about additional days that the production team wants to film, my fingers get those shakes that have become familiar yet remain exasperating. Peering over the white wooden banister of our family's living room, I could see my mother downstairs getting ready for work. I decided to confide in her about what's been happening with me—the anxiety and stress over all this work, all this back and forth on top of school and in the midst of trying to heal. I no longer had the energy to lie to myself by saying, "Well, at least my story will get out there." Yet, I had not been allowed to view any of the footage, make any editing suggestions, or even know what footage they planned to include. At least, awareness would be gained for those with craniofacial conditions. Yes, but at our own expense, figuratively and literally. At least, I was being paid. Except I was not. There is no "at least" anymore. It was just no longer worth it for me unless something were to change.

When I told my mother how I felt, I think she heard the guilt in my tone. She reminded me that this network and production company have sent a two-person crew back and forth to Chapel Hill, Memphis, Little Rock, and Nashville several times now—from London. That's thousands of dollars spent, plus them being paid for their hard work. "These people are employees," she said. "We are not." She reminds me that, on top of the medical bills for my last few surgeries, we were still paying for a $10K dental procedure not covered by insurance. Meanwhile, the production crew was excited to film my next dental appointment for "interesting" footage. She asked me how much I was being compensated for me, my family, friends, and doctors "doing all this stuff." I admit that I was not, and we are not, getting paid. I told her I got $1,000 to cover what they called "loss of earnings." I told her there is a law in the UK that apparently prohibits television productions from compensating people who participate in medical documentary content even for shows making a commercial profit. She suggested we both review my contract.

As I read through the contract again, the same words have new meaning. I had agreed that I would not sue them if I did not like the "exploitation" of my portrayal for commercial use. I had agreed to release them from all liability and obligations for "emotional distress/pain and suffering" that arose from my participation. I had agreed that I would not, at any time, assert that any representation of identity violated any of my rights. I had agreed that I may "discover facts or incur or suffer claims" that I did not suspect when I signed the agreement that may have affected my decision to participate in the show. "Ya think?!" I say under my breath. I assumed any and all risk. I think, "How in the world could I have allowed this to happen?" The contract seemed to be a standard form.

A question flew into my mind: how had the fine print of this contract spoken so precisely to my actual experience—"emotional distress/pain and suffering"? My exhausted mind started to clear like a fog lifting. And there was light: they *knew* that the filming would be distressing, draining, debilitating. *Every person with a disability or health condition who had participated in producing commercial content and pushed back, their stories were in this fine print.* And now mine was too. Momma looks at me, a sigh in her eyes. "A lawyer should have looked this over," she says. "I don't think it would have mattered," I think but refuse to say out loud. Back in May, delighted by the prospect of telling my story of disability, I did not have the context to anticipate what the words in my contract would truly mean. But the executives did, they knew.

In writing about powerlessness, empowerment, and health, Professor Nina Wallerstein explains that empowerment and powerlessness are two sides of a coin that, when tossed up in the midst of our lives, can have significant health consequences. While powerlessness breeds sickness and disease, empowerment is a "health-enhancing strategy" (1992, p. 192). Wallerstein asserts, "Empowerment becomes the avenue for people to challenge their internalized powerlessness while also developing real opportunities to gain control in their lives and transform their various settings." Through literal blood, sweat, and tears, my experiences over the past 7 months had shown me a visceral truth. While there are available stages for disabled, disfigured, and different bodies in creative commerce, we will need more than our dreams and our drive to finally and definitively take our places on them.

Nothing about us without us. Nothing—not the image of our likeness, not the inspiration of our stories, nothing—without relinquishing control, without investing resources, and without imparting critical understanding (Zimmerman, 2012). For far too long, people with disabilities and chronic illnesses have been kept as mere charitable beneficiaries (at best) to a behemoth of a media industry that has a historic track record of exploiting our stories while withholding the support we need for entrance into spaces we should have been in all along and an equitable seat at the table. In 1810, the "freak show" that toured Sarah Baartman, a now infamous Black woman trapped in an atypically shaped body that other people thought inspiring, interesting, and entertaining, claimed that Sarah had gone willingly onto stages and into cages for them—she had, after all, signed a contract (Holmes, 2007).

Through agreeing to share my lived experiences, I exposed my personal darkness to public light willingly—I, too, signed a contract. But Sarah died at 26, overworked, diseased, and alone. By God's grace, that is not my story. Throughout my life, I have been tested by trials and refined like gold. And in the middle of each fiery furnace, under submission to immense heat, I have gained clarity. And what is left of me now, as impurities melt away, glows. I take my bruises, blue and purple on this brown skin, as lessons learned, put them up for public display, and live to tell my side. In between redressing the lingering wounds on my chin and on my heart, I have found healing through voicing a transparent, empowering version of my story through this writing. And in the process, I believe I have spoken truth to power.

Discussion Questions

1. What is the difference between media representation and media participation? What role could each play in redefining disability?
2. What is exploitation? Explore the relationship between exploitation and illness and/or disability.
3. How can powerlessness and empowerment impact health?
4. What does the phrase, "Nothing about us without us" mean? Explore some examples from the chapter as well as any from your personal experiences.

References

Brown, B. (2018). *In you must go: Harnessing the force by owning our stories.* https://brenebrown.com/blog/2018/05/04/in-you-must-go-harnessing the-force-by-owning-our-stories/

Ellcessor, E. (2017). Kickstarting community disability, access, and participation in my gimpy life. In E. Ellcessor & B. Kirkpatrick (Eds.), *Disability media studies.* NYU Press. https://doi.org/10.18574/nyu/9781479867820.001.0001

Frank, A. W. (2013). *The wounded storyteller: Body, illness, and ethics* (2nd ed.). University of Chicago Press.

Holmes, R. (2007). *African queen: The real life of the Hottentot Venus*. Random House.

Kelly. (2015, August 12). *Gray's anomaly: A source of empowerment*. https://news.uams.edu/2015/08/12/grays-anomaly-a-source-of-empowerment-2/

Mayer, V. (2011). *Below the line: Producers and production studies in the new television economy*. Duke University Press.

Wallerstein, N. (1992). Powerlessness, empowerment, and health: Implications for health promotion programs. *American Journal of Health Promotion, 6*(3), 197–205. https://doi.org/10.4278/0890-1171-6.3.197

Young, I. M. (2011). *Justice and the politics of difference*. Princeton University Press.

Zimmerman, M. (2012). Empowerment theory: Psychological, organizational, and community levels of analysis. In J. Rappaport & E. Seidman (Eds.), *Handbook of community psychology* (pp. 43–63). Springer.

Aisling & Truthe

Jennifer Stahl

ID: A Maine Coon (left) and a Cavalier King Charles (right) both stare at the camera. The cat looks annoyed, the dog looks sad.

• • •

We got Truthe when she was 6 months old in 2014, and I was just beginning to have a downhill experience with my health. Aisling came home with us in mid-2015. Both kept me company while my boys were in school. I have celiac disease and recurrent iron deficiency anemia, as well as several comorbid conditions. I am often unable to get out and about due to feeling poorly. I was also diagnosed after getting the girls with C-PTSD. My girls alert me when I have dizzy spells due to low blood pressure or comfort when I have recurrent migraines and severe endometriosis pain. I don't know what I would do without them.

CHAPTER 24

Assistive Tech, Assertive Tech

Cole Sorensen

cw: Self-Injury

I had never been able to communicate my thoughts until I stopped trying so hard to speak them. I can speak, technically. It's just that my mouth and my brain have the habit of disagreeing on what exactly it is that I want to say or when I want to say it. My brain has a lot it wants to say, and it spends hours rehearsing it, going through it again and again. But my mouth doesn't listen. It takes shortcuts. It falls into a rut of only saying the things it knows how to say, things it's practiced over and over. It's enough to carry on a conversation, usually, but I spend the entire time fighting with my body and listening, helpless, as words come out of my mouth that I don't really mean. As a kid, for a few years, I was almost completely nonspeaking. That's when my parents first heard the word *autism* applied to me, though they never really wanted to believe it. They just stuck me in therapy for a few years until I was talking and figured that would be that. It wasn't. Limited speech, in certain situations, doesn't really get you that far in life as it turns out.

There are certain things my mouth knows how to say really well, things like, "That's okay," or "Sure, that works." Agreeing to something takes a lot fewer words than disagreeing does. Disagreeing often needs a reason, or an apology, or the offer of a compromise. Even though my brain might know how to do that, it takes a little while, and by that time my mouth has already jumped in with, "Alright." I end up agreeing to things I don't want to do, with no way to change it. That's gotten me into a lot of bad situations. I can respond to questions and speak when spoken to, but initiating conversation is a lot harder. I compare it to the concept of inertia. An object in motion stays in motion, but an object at rest stays at rest, unless acted on by an outside force. When a conversation is in motion, I can join in and keep it in motion without too much effort, but getting it going in the first place takes more force than I'm capable of. It turns out that you're pretty limited in what you can say if you can only join in on a conversation where someone else has decided the topic, and only really respond when you're asked a question (and not always accurately at that).

So, to say that social interactions were generally frustrating to me was a bit of an understatement. I had so much I wanted to say, and now and then I was able to get it out, but much of the time I wasn't. I might sit there, silently willing my conversation partner to ask me just the right question in just the right way that, if I was lucky, might trigger my speech for long enough to let me get my thoughts out. But if that question didn't come, I'd just get more and more frustrated at them for not reading my mind, for not picking up my hints in how I behaved, until eventually I just exploded with anger. Or I'd verbally agree to something I really didn't want to do and then get upset when it happened, seemingly out of nowhere. It all got blamed on my autism. The adults in my life decided that's just the kind of person I was, that I'd always "overreact to nothing," that it couldn't be helped. I've been a lifelong head-banger, hand-biter, forehead-hitter, and all anyone ever seemed to think of was managing that behavior, never what caused it to begin with. Eventually, communication issues caused me to start avoiding any kind of interaction with others. That got blamed on my autism too. They taught me that suffering and isolation were what my disability meant, and I believed them. I thought that there was something broken about me.

My entire life, the people around me have often refused to treat me as competent, as a full human being with the capacity to make my own decisions. Although it frustrated me, for years and years I considered them justified in that. If I didn't have a way to make it clear that I understood, I thought, I couldn't expect that kind of dignity from anyone. It was easier to just sit back and let others take over, make decisions for me, dissociate through conversations, and do what I was told. I could occasionally summon the words to push back against decisions I disagreed with, though not reliably enough to really assert myself as a person with thoughts and opinions in the eyes of most. I was nearly prevented from moving out from my parents' house when they judged me "incapable" of living on my own. My significant other's mom tried to stop them from seeing me, accused them of "taking advantage of me," suggested I was unable to consent to a relationship or sex. I was almost denied access to gender-affirming surgery simply because I couldn't find my words fast enough to answer the surgeon's questions and he didn't believe that I could understand the decision I was making. In each of these instances, all I could do was fumble after words, hope that I could string enough together to convince them of my right to autonomy and my capacity to understand.

Even in autistic spaces I felt like an outsider a lot of the time. I had been active in autistic communities for many years, but I still didn't understand why I avoided interacting with people, even those I cared about, and the main emotion I seemed to feel toward others was frustration. That wasn't something I saw many others in my community talking about, and so I convinced myself that my issues regarding communication and relationships with others must just be my own fault. I wanted to connect with others more than anything, but even talking to other autistic people was frustrating and difficult. I felt lonely, isolated, and inadequate. I told myself that I just wasn't trying hard enough, that I didn't care about others, that I was self-centered and selfish.

It wasn't until I was in college that someone suggested I try an alternative and augmentative communication (AAC) app on my phone because I had mentioned that, in times of high stress, I had a hard time speaking at all. *Alternative and augmentative communication* is a name for any strategy that helps people communicate in a way besides speaking. I started using the app with limited success. I found quickly that, even though I'm able to type, it's not a very effective way of communicating for me. Trying to type out my thoughts takes almost just as much energy as speech does, and more often than not, I just end up sitting there with a blank screen in front of me, stuck. Buttons worked better, I found. I was able to program this app with some message buttons I could use when I was upset, messages like, "It's too loud," or "Can you get me some water?" I started to add buttons with single words programmed in too, to let myself compose my own sentences, but the amount of scrolling and searching it took to locate the words for even a basic sentence left it feeling like far more effort than it was worth. I used the app occasionally, in those few times when speech wouldn't come at all, but otherwise didn't bother.

That all changed when someone in one of my disability groups on social media posted a picture of their new AAC layout. They used a symbol-based app, where each button had both a written word and an icon representing that word on it. I had initially thought *Well, I can read just fine, I don't need symbol-based AAC*. But this layout stuck with me. They had shared a picture of their home page, an 8 row by 14 column grid of buttons, with a keyboard in the center. Around that was an assortment of core words, common words that make up a large percentage of day-to-day speech like "I," "is," "for," or "the." Each of the core words also had a symbol to go with it. I was drawn to it, enough that I brought my laptop over to show my partner. With the screenshot pulled up on the screen, I pointed to the buttons to spell out a message: "LOOK AT THIS C-O-O-L B-O-A-R-D I SEE (saw) ON-L-I-N-E," I wrote. I had intended it to be just a demonstration, but I continued, "I can't believe how easy it is to say something with this." For the rest of the afternoon, I kept using it to communicate. And I could actually, really, communicate. I could say anything and everything that came into my head. I could comment on the movie we were watching, comfort my partner when they were sad, talk about my plans for the following day. I didn't have to wait for a prompt to speak, I could just communicate whenever I wanted to. It felt unbelievably freeing.

Nothing had changed in my ability to speak, but suddenly, my brain knew that there was an easier option. The realization that I could communicate in a different way instead meant that it started getting harder and harder to force speech. Over the course of a week, I went from using AAC for maybe an hour or two a week, to using it for a solid 75% of my communication. In the following few months, that grew to about 95%. At first, I was thrilled. I had a way to communicate! I could communicate so much better, so much easier, so much more fully. It was incredible. I was sharing so much more of what was on my mind, I was actually enjoying conversations, I was talking about the things I wanted to talk about. That joy and excitement lasted for a week, maybe two. After that, the grieving set in. As much as I was thrilled to have a method of communication that finally worked for me, I was scared too. I didn't know what it meant for me, my future, my relationships with others. It was big, unknown, and terrifying. I worked with students at the time, both K-12 students and university students. I didn't know how they'd react to the change. No matter how much more fully I can communicate using AAC, the fact is, it's slower. I need others to be patient with me, allow me time to communicate. I didn't know if others would be willing to do that for me. It felt hard to ask. Asking for accommodations from others, especially something that fundamentally changes every interaction you have with a person, is incredibly vulnerable. I was scared that others would view this communication as "lesser," as an inconvenience, as a burden. I grieved that I was leaving speech behind, but only because of all the things I feared I would lose because of it. Gradually, though, I started to see the ways that AAC had such a positive impact on my relationships overall, and a positive impact on my happiness too. It was a big change, and that was terrifying, but it was a good change.

For several months, I used nothing but that screenshot of somebody else's app. I had no access to a printer, but someone I knew had an old tablet. It was way too old to run any apps but I was able to save the screenshot onto that device and point to the symbols or letters I wanted to slowly spell out my message. I didn't have funds to purchase a newer tablet that could run apps, nor could I afford an app, which often costs hundreds of dollars. Eventually, after a few months of searching, I found a speech-language pathologist (SLP) who felt comfortable working with me. Many SLPs tend to only use AAC for people who are completely nonspeaking, which I was not. The first time I met with this SLP and she gave me a loaner device to try out, though, it was incredible. I took to the device immediately. She had barely finished showing me the app before I started communicating with it, somewhat tediously at first, without knowing where all the buttons were, but gradually growing more and more fluent. I could joke with her, talk to her about my wants and needs and preferences, reliably communicate all the things that were on my mind. She let me take it home and keep using it for a few weeks. I poured hours into the customization, filling it with vocabulary and editing the organization to what worked best for me.

The letterboard had offered me a taste of freedom in my communication, but this was so much more. For those first few weeks, I just talked. I talked about everything and nothing at all, just talking to hear the words come out of my device, words that I chose, words that I meant and wanted to say. And then the day came to return the borrowed device and I sobbed. I felt like I was losing a piece of myself that I had been missing for so long, that I had gotten access to for just a moment and then was taken away again. I was an absolute mess. I'm someone who doesn't often cry in front of others, but I cried in front of my SLP that day having to return the device. That was 6 months ago, and I've spent those 6 months in a cycle of loaner devices, returning them, grieving, and eventually getting a new loaner device, while we wait for funding from insurance for a device of my own that, for all we know, might never come. Insurance may decide that I have "too much functional speech" to even qualify for a device. All I can do is wait and hope.

I first realized how much more AAC let me self-advocate only a few weeks into using it. I had injured my leg and ended up in the emergency room. I was still using my letterboard then and brought my partner along to verbalize for me. The triage nurse was explaining the situation of my communication to another staff person, when I suddenly caught her calling me "she" instead of "he." It's a common enough occurrence—I'm a small, effeminate, trans-masculine person, and people misgender me often. Normally when it would happen, I would always notice, but the conversation would move on too fast for me to react. This time was different though. The instant I heard it, my hand went into motion and my finger landed on the symbol for "he." My partner verbalized it, the nurse apologized, and the conversation moved on. It was a single word, but I was amazed at myself. I had never been able to do that before; I had never been able to react that quickly and correct someone in the middle of a conversation like that. To get my mouth to cooperate would have taken ten times as long, and by the time I got it working, I would have been worried it was too late and just never said anything. The simple action of sliding my finger across the board, on the other hand, was something I could actually manage. I've been able to start directing my own support workers too, going from having my case manager assign support workers through an agency and letting her handle the majority of the communication with them, to actually interviewing and hiring my own support workers directly and completely taking agency over my support. I feel more confident just going out and running errands, or otherwise being out and about, because I know that I have a reliable way to communicate if I need help, even if I get upset or overwhelmed.

I can express myself so much more eloquently with AAC, and yet the way that people treat me has gotten more and more condescending. My AAC device makes me visibly and obviously disabled. I was pretty clearly autistic before, granted: rocking back-and-forth, flapping my hands, wandering off in the middle of a conversation. But my AAC device makes it undeniable. Every person who interacts with me is forced to confront my disabled identity, and, a lot of the time, it makes them uncomfortable. They don't know what to make of me. Sitting in my apartment lobby one day, for instance, I was approached by a delivery man who apparently used to live in my building, many years ago. He asked me how much rent was nowadays. It was a casual enough interaction. I pulled my device out and typed in a joking response: "Too much!" But as soon as he heard my device, his demeanor changed. "Oh, God bless you!"

he said in a sickly-sweet tone. "Oh, that's just fantastic. Good for you, sweetheart, bless your heart. Have a Merry Christmas, I love you!" What started out as a trivial bit of small talk had changed into something dehumanizing, left me feeling humiliated and more than a little uncomfortable. I have never been much for small talk; I tend to wish that strangers would just leave me alone most of the time. Since I switched to using a communication device, though, I've found myself actually missing it. Sometimes I wish I could have that casual interaction with strangers again, just to have that small acknowledgement that they see me as human, as a peer. I felt isolated before I had my communication device, but some of that isolation remains now, just from a different source. The isolation comes from stigma now, from the assumptions others make about my capacity to understand.

I've found community too, though. Discovering AAC has led me to find a community of other AAC users, people like me who understand the ways in which my brain works, who understand the areas where I struggle and the experiences I've faced. It's nice to know people like me, for the first time in my life. I'm getting better at asserting myself against some of the more blatant ableism I face, and when I can't, at

ID: A tablet with an AAC app sits on a wooden table. It has a full keyboard and buttons with small images to identify words.

least I'm able to recognize it and vent about it later to people who can relate. I have an entire folder on my device dedicated to phrases like "Speak to me like an adult," "Talk to me, not my support worker," and "Don't patronize me." Using those phrases takes a lot of practice, and I've spent quite a bit of time committing the movements for accessing those buttons to muscle memory in hopes that it will help me use them when the time comes that they're needed. My body still sometimes needs some support in communicating all the things my brain wants to say, but AAC means that for the first time, it's actually possible. That's something I never imagined I'd have.

Discussion Questions

1. How does Cole's story illustrate the ability of technology to accommodate, rather than overcome, disability?
2. Google "accessibility tech." What kinds of options are out there, and what impairments do they accommodate?
3. Cole writes about being spoken over, spoken for, and treated like a child. This is a common experience for disabled adults. Why do you think we associate disability with being a child?

CHAPTER 25

Modern Day Changelings
On Being an Autistic Parent of an Autistic Child

Alison Kelly

cw: Infanticide, Death of a Child

I'm an autistic mom with an autistic son, and one of the things we love to do together is paint. I came up with it to make Christmas presents for the family. I have my art and I obviously want to share that love with Elliott. Usually when it comes down to it, to do a few pieces together, where I'll start one and I'll let him finish it, or he'll start one and then I'll finish it. So, it's more of an assembly line, I would say. One of us starts it and one of us finishes it. I'll do a drawing and let him color it, or I'll let him scribble on some paper and I try to make sense of it or make some compositional decisions or design decisions with it. It's a fun project that we get to work together. He loves to paint so much. He has gotten so good as well. His work has gotten so impressive, especially for a 7-year-old boy. I'm very proud.

It's a strange place for me to be as a mother with autism to a kid with autism. That is—it's almost like a duality. There are two distinct communities in the autism world that—I don't want to say that they hate each other, but they're opposing forces. There're autism moms and then there's people like me, adults with autism. And then of course there's the kids with autism, but they never actually get to speak for themselves because the moms won't shut up.

I just feel that in the community, as an adult with autism, it feels like autism moms are more interested in "Look at me I'm an autism mom, look at how hard I work for my kid, look at all these things that I do," and I don't know if maybe it's a coping mechanism or because they don't really understand what it's like to have autism. I can't really criticize anyone's coping mechanism—just because I don't always have the most appropriate ones—but I feel like it's a way to cope and I don't know. It just feels like "look at me" as opposed to "look at my kid." Right?

Maybe that's okay; maybe the internet appreciates what a great autism mom you are, but I just find it exhausting. Honestly, a lot of times, I feel like it's a ploy to hock whatever "special needs" shirt or reusable bag with a cute catchy phrase, or (yes, this is real) autism-themed makeup line. Maybe if I got paid to be an autism mom, I'd do it too. I can't say for sure, but I doubt it.

It's centering on their experiences instead of the kid. I think that there's a place for that as a parent. I really honestly do. You know I've had behavioral problems and things that I've had to cope with both as a parent and as an adult...my behavior problems versus my son's. I want to say problems because sometimes it's destructive. There are things that are dangerous, you know? Dangerous situations that either of us can find ourselves in due to the fact that we have autism. That's what I mean when I say problem. Just clarifying because that can also be a trigger word. Sometimes my son will see space, and run into it. Often, it's not safe, and that's dangerous, and that's a leading killer for our kids. That is a problem.

It's a unique experience to be both a mom with autism with a kid with autism because I do have disgust with the autism mom community to a certain extent. A lot of them don't believe in vaccinations or call autism a vax injury. That tells me that I'm an injury and my kid is an injury, and this entire experience is a mistake. We are not a mistake. You know it's like trashing what their kids do and saying, "Look at me, look at how hard my life is, give me attention." It's more of like "Look, my kid has autism," as opposed to, "Yeah, this is how we live."

I know moms love their kids, and I feel like it's coming from a place of love, coming from a place of care, but it's also coming from a place of ignorance as they haven't taken the time to learn from our community. They've developed their own community of autism moms and I believe the support should be there, and that is okay. I agree that, as a mother, we do need help. I mean some of the shit that comes up is crazy and terrifying and it is nice to know that there are other people out there going through it. But not to the extent that it's damaging or exploitative. And that's the problem. That's where I feel like there are problems. You see news articles of parents and caregivers killing their kids with autism because of some of these damn support groups saying sometimes they wish they'd never been born. Historically, I would have been a changeling, my son would've been a changeling, and we would have been murdered because we didn't talk. Or murdered because we ran away, or murdered because we didn't look someone in the eye. I mean that's just a progression of it, but it's still pretty damaging to say things like "I just wish I had a different life; I wish I had these things differently," and I know it's a vent. I feel like there needs to be a safe space for venting, but I also feel like there's got to be a distinction between what's safe and what is damaging, for the community as a whole. That's the biggest disconnect that I see just having to live in both worlds.

I don't want to say that I have a problem with the autism mom community as a whole, but I also just feel like, for starters, there should be more support for adults with autism because there is no community for us. They say, "Different not less." It should say, "Different not less until you're 18." There's no support for adults with autism. There are things that you can do through the city, such as a special needs dance—which that word bothers me. I have a few people in my life that have worked in special education and, you know, to see the ability and not the disability and all of these things—it's just offensive, right? See the disability and accept us for who and what we are; our world is perfect and hideous just like yours.

Yes, we do require certain accommodations. In my life I need certain accommodations. I have special things built into my home and life that we need. I really don't go on vacation unless they have those accommodations there. Obviously, we need a little bit more universal design than a typical family. The words *special needs*—and this is how I feel about the phrase—the words aren't semantically bad. It's just like any word where you break it down to what it is, and yes, my son has special needs. I have special needs. These are things that I need that are distinct from other people. So, it's not the essence of the word that is offensive—it's that it's been boiled down to infantilizing our disabilities. It's a title to attach to us, to attach a stigma that automatically makes you piteous. We don't like fucking pity. I don't want your pity. I just want you to put a better lock on the door so my kid doesn't accidentally kill himself.

Because I know, I've been there, I've seen it and all you're doing is trying to relate to me. It's just like saying "Oh, you don't look autistic" or "Oh well, everybody's a little autistic." All of these things are not true. It's just another stigma that these words are attached *to* us, not *from* us. We didn't ask for these words. We didn't ask for these terms. We were given to them by people outside of our community. We were given these words, and these terms, and these tags, if you will, and they're not what we chose. Just like formal language a person with autism versus someone who is autistic and both words are appropriate depending on the setting, depending on who you ask. So, it's a term, it's semantics. And it's stupid to talk about a term so much and you boil it down to harmless, but it's the meaning behind it. Where we didn't choose it. We didn't ask for it. It immediately puts something on us that may not be the truth.

Paul: So, what labels or terms would you personally prefer for yourself or for Elliott?

Ali: Ali and Elliott.

Note

This was originally conducted as an interview, but the interviewer was removed post-transcription to allow Ali's voice to be presented unfiltered.

Discussion Questions

1. Alison talks about her experiences as an autistic person, and as a mother of an autistic son. How does she balance these roles?
2. Parents of disabled children obviously have a role to play when it comes to disability. Is there a limit to how much a parent can understand disability? How important is it for parents to center the experiences of their disabled children instead of themselves?
3. What programs and resources are there to support disabled adults?

Untitled Artwork
(Elliott Roeber and Alison Kelly)

Elliott and Alison love collaborating on artwork. Their process is ongoing and ever-changing; sometimes Elliott starts a piece and Alison finishes the piece and vice versa. Alison drew the first image, and Elliott painted it. Elliot drew and painted the second image.

ID: A painted image of a panda.

ID: An abstract painting of dark lines and bright colors.

CHAPTER 26

Stone, Water, Land, Spine

Elizabeth Glass

cw: Suicide

If I could get to Rock Bridge, I would splash in the water beneath it, touch its sandstone, and lie on its damp, mossy top. I'd sit above it at Creation Falls, watch the flowing water. I would think about how I want my ashes scattered there one day. On the first trip, my partner Guy went with me. In 1994, we stood beneath the waterfall laughing and dancing, then floated in the pool below. But time has eroded the creek bed backward and there isn't room to stand beneath the falls anymore. As the lip of the sandstone creek bed has flowed downstream, particle after particle of sand being broken apart by the rippling water, the ceiling over the cave-like rock shelter is disappearing too. It was a cozy spot there, being behind the waterfall. Guy and I sat there, gently touching each other's arms, talking about our futures, each wondering if we'd be together or apart, while the water splashed in the pool by our feet. Before we hiked the trail out, we climbed onto Rock Bridge again. The warm breeze on my damp skin made me feel like I was floating above the water, above the falls, above the bridge with us on it, until Guy took my hand and smiled. When we put our boots back on, bits of the Gorge went home with us as sand on our feet.

I used to hike frequently. I volunteered at Arches National Park in Moab, Utah, for a week in 2006. I hauled heavy rocks, set concrete for walkways, and pulled cheatgrass all day, then hit the trail. I covered every marked trail—and some unmarked ones the rangers pointed out—as well as others around Moab. It's hard hiking on the desert's loose sand. Kentucky's packed dirt is much easier to walk on. It doesn't shift underfoot, and allows my boot to get purchased before taking the next step. I could hike a mile of trail in half an hour on dirt, but it took twice that long on sand. I was never fast, but I was steady, and could hike the hills and loops of the 14-mile Millennium Trail at Bernheim Forest outside Louisville easily in a day.

© ELIZABETH GLASS, 2022 | DOI:10.1163/9789004512702_040

My parents didn't take me hiking or camping as a kid. I spent all day outside during summers, but it wasn't until we moved, and there were woods behind our house, that I loved forested land. My mom jokes that I went into the woods then, and she never got me out, at least until recently. For 3 years around the time I went to Moab, I volunteered at the Red River Gorge in Eastern Kentucky a weekend every month. I worked on trails: fixing, hauling, lopping, building. I did a lot. I *could* do a lot. The day's work was followed by an evening of music, talking, gazing at stars, and drinking with friends at the volunteer-only campground—a place I was proud to have a claim to.

I had a laminectomy operation on my back 5 years ago. That was my first step toward becoming capital D, Disabled. I've embraced the word now. I've accepted that I'm a disabled person. But it's not been easy—to be disabled or to accept it.

It took me months to use a cane even though I needed one. It took even longer to use a power cart in the grocery store. Longer still to use a walker as I sometimes do now. I'm a big woman, a very big one, and being in a power shopping cart makes me feel vulnerable, like I'll be pointed at and thought of as just lazy rather than that I need it. I've seen the memes. People aren't nice to fat folks or to anyone under 70 in an electric cart. They don't know my leg goes to sleep when I stand or walk too long, or that missing part of my vertebra from my laminectomy causes my sciatic nerve to be pinched, and I fall when that foot quits working. I was shopping last week and the checkout clerk wouldn't help me put my groceries into the electric cart. Instead, my cloth bags fell out, groceries spilled and rolled away. Shoppers helped while the clerk stared at me, waiting for me to pay. The woman behind me pulled out her phone, laughing, taking pictures.

Most people don't make eye contact with someone in an electric cart. They avert their eyes from somebody with a cane or walker too. Last year I had 10 minutes to cross campus between classes and one of my students told me if I weren't so big I wouldn't have been late at times. I tried to shrug it off, but it stung like a swarm of yellow jackets. I'd only begun to accept my disability then. It's easier now, but it's another damn wasp bite every time a friend tells me to work out so I can walk faster. How many people have said, "*Why do you use a cane?*" and "*A walker now, is it?*" not in a curious way, but a condemning one? I wish it *was* as easy as losing weight to get the use of my leg back. But it's not. I don't know if it will ever be fixed. It will take another surgery if it can be, and if it didn't go well, I could be paralyzed completely. That scares me far more than staying disabled in this way.

•••

In the autumn of 2007, Guy was feeling down. Beyond down, depressed, like he was in the seventh circle of hell. His spirits rallied when I was around. He talked of suicide often, and when he didn't say anything about it, he told me he was still thinking of it. He was depressed and suicidal for at least 10 years—and I recognized its potential, if not its inevitability, because no matter the medications and therapy he tried, he stayed that low. So I stopped going out of town. The days I had time to get outdoors were the days he was home too, so I didn't do much of that either. Going to movies, out to eat, cooking dinner, watching videos, piling up with the dogs in bed, and talking with Guy was great, and it didn't hurt my foot (that tendonitis had developed in) as badly. I was able to keep his spirits up while we were together. We got closer. He was no longer jealous like he was when I went out of town because he realized there was no one else. I didn't know he thought there was someone until I stopped going, when he finally said he thought there had been. He didn't have cause to worry, but his depression made him feel unworthy of love, as it had the whole 13 years we were together. I know that my having cheated on him early in our relationship also contributed to his worry.

Whenever I said, "I love you," he'd ask, "Why?"

"Because you're wonderful."

"How?"

"You're nice and smart and love the dogs."

"That's not enough to make you love me."

"Why do you love me?" I asked.

"Because you take care of me. Because you love the dogs."

"That's the same stuff I love you for," I said.

"That's not a good enough reason to love someone."

"But you love me for them."

"That's different."

It was little use. He couldn't be convinced.

When people learn that Guy's death was indeed inevitable, that he ended his own life in 2008, they feel pity. We had grown closer than we'd ever been in the 2 years before he died, though, and I don't regret our 13 years together. We were happy together; he just wasn't happy apart. He tried to be. He saw his psychiatrist, took his medicine. Having no health insurance meant our low-paying jobs didn't allow for all medication choices to be tried. I said we'd figure it out, for him to try anything, but he wouldn't.

He said I'd be better off without him. It wasn't until Robin Williams died that I read enough articles about suicide to realize that Guy genuinely believed that, truly thought I'd be better free from him. I ache for him still, 8 years later, but have gotten to where he can make me laugh out loud again. I remember things we did or he said and laugh hard, sitting by myself, seeming a fool to anyone who sees me. I've done this most often at home, but also have done it alone in my car, at the coffee shop I frequent, when I'm with friends, and even when shopping.

•••

Hiking was my freedom, where I lost myself, where I found myself, where I was myself. During the time I wasn't hiking, I longed for the woods, for my feet on dirt, treading worn paths. I missed the feel of trekking poles in my hands, the independence of hiking by myself. The empowerment of being a woman, fearless, alone in the woods, with love back home.

"You know how I said my leg keeps going numb when I walk?"

"Yeah. What are you going to do about it?" Mom asked. We waited in the neurosurgeon's office eight days after my laminectomy.

The doctor walked in then. After looking at my incision, he said, "Well, I'll see you again in six weeks."

"Wait!" I said. He hurried out the door. "My leg is numb. It goes numb and then I can't really stand with it."

"You'll work on it in physical therapy." He turned back around.

"Will it get better?"

I didn't think he was going to answer, but "You'll see in PT" came just as the door shut.

I think Mom was more upset by his non-answer than I was.

By the next appointment it had gotten worse. I couldn't make it down the block without my leg going numb whereas it was several blocks at my last appointment.

"My leg's still going numb." He didn't respond. "It's worse." He was still quiet. "Will it get better?"

He wouldn't look me in the eye. "It will or it won't," he said, looking at his chart. "Time is the only way to know."

"How long? A month? A year? What do we do then?"

"We revisit things."

I left in tears. I was glad I was there alone because it was hard news to get. I knew it meant I would never get the feeling back in my leg. It has continued to get worse, which scares me. The walker I've begun using at times really makes a big difference, just like the cane did a year ago. I have a drop-foot—my foot falls when I raise my leg. It makes for easy tripping, and the cane stopped many falls; the walker has stopped them all. I can move my leg, and my foot goes with it, so I can still walk, but I can't move that foot independently.

It was my pain management doctor, not my neurosurgeon, who finally said I had nerve damage. When I had back surgery, I had to get a herniated disc fixed because it caused constant pain that felt like a fork poking into my spine and twisting, always twisting. I have similar pain now from the laminectomy, which was recommended when the herniated part of the nearby disc was being removed. The bone needed to come out at that spot, my neurosurgeon said, because my nerve was being pinched by a bunch of fancy medical words beginning with S that were making me have back pain and tingling in my foot that doesn't work well now. The surgery was scheduled 10 days after I got the test results, and I didn't even think to ask my other doctors about the laminectomy. They'd all already said to get the surgery to fix the herniated disc, but since this was recommended later, I didn't talk to them again. After the surgery, my pain management doc said he wished I'd asked him because he would have told me not to have that bone removed. There's the very real chance it could be just as bad—or worse—now if I hadn't had it, though. It's impossible to know.

· · ·

Guy and I went hiking in 2007, after my tendonitis was gone. We had hiked together before, but it had been a while. It was Fourth of July weekend, at Red River Gorge, my treasured space, my spiritual home. We hiked Rock Bridge loop, something we did every time we had been throughout the years, that first trail we hiked together. It was the first trail I ever went on there, way back in 1988, the one that has stayed my favorite for nearly thirty years. But there were too many people in the forest, I was out of shape from months of inactivity, and my asthma was bad since rhododendrons were blooming. (That magnificent flower on my favorite plant makes me wheeze like a busted accordion.) The deer flies bit, and bit, and bit. We were miserable. It was the last time we hiked together, the last time I hiked until almost 2 years later, after Guy died.

In my laminectomy, the parts of the vertebrae removed were above and below my sciatic nerve on my left side. The space where my nerve runs there was extremely narrow, and I was growing bone on bone, which made that space even worse. I do this well—have tiny spinal spaces and grow bone there. After the laminectomy, the bone pinches my nerve worse. I didn't have constant symptoms before surgery. Now my left foot is always partially numb. When I cut my toenails, I slice the skin around them because I can't feel the clipper snip it. Then I go around with tissues on my toes.

Whenever I stand very long—about 12 minutes—my leg gives. My cane has prevented many full-out falls and let me hobble with it and my good leg to a chair to sit, and now my walker lets me stand even longer. The cane gives me a false third leg. I haven't hit the ground many times because things—usually a chair or my car—have been there to catch me. Occasionally nothing is close enough, and I fall hard when my numb foot and leg won't hold me after I take a step, which is why I began using a walker. Embarrassingly, I now can't get up from the floor because my foot won't bend to get under me and help lift me. I have to crawl to something sturdy and pull myself up using my arms. One of my worst fears is falling where there isn't anything to do this with.

Though I don't usually fall completely, I regularly crash into things when my leg and foot stop working. When I'm shopping, I can tell when it's coming, so I quickly pay and leave, whether I have everything or not. I've landed heavily against my car from having waited too long, scarcely able to open the door and tumble inside. Sometimes I have no warning, though, and I take a step that doesn't hold. I stand shorter times than I'd have to because I don't want it to happen again. I've grabbed rolling chairs and pulled them to me, barely able to sit in them before landing on the ground. In the classrooms where I teach, there are rolling chairs everywhere, which I'm grateful for since it has happened twice while teaching. The nerve is pinched the worst when I stand, and sitting takes some pressure off and gives me back the use of my leg. Lying down takes more pressure off still.

• • •

I've never been graceful. I fell too often while hiking. That was the reason I used trekking poles. They were my early version of today's cane. Hiking in Minnesota in Superior National Forest in 2007, I was told I didn't need them. But we were hiking a burned area: topsoil had been eaten by flames, and rocks jutted up everywhere. My twitchy ankles couldn't hold. I went down on my face and head, blacked out, broke my nose, my glasses, and cut my face, knees, and hands. People were behind me so I hurried to get up and keep going—never a good idea for a klutz. A few people tried to tend to me, but I shook them off like a dog shaking water from its back. I stood still a moment, then kept hiking. I dropped to the back of the group. Salt from tears, not from pain but embarrassment, burned the cuts on my face. I needed medical attention and felt helpless; I was 800 miles from home with no car and completely reliant on others. I'd ruin someone else's hike to this special place we'd gone to see. When I got to the midpoint, I wanted to stop there and wait for everyone's return, but some folks wouldn't leave me even though they'd pass back by and I could join them for the trek out. Instead of causing them to miss what we'd traveled from all over the country to see, I hiked on. I got to the top long after others, but I made it.

   On the hike back out, fear grabbed me in that space. I couldn't breathe and black encircled my vision. It was awkward, rocky—pointed rocks twisted together and jutted at angles that would be beautiful if I didn't have to cross them. I looked left and right, but there was nowhere easier to pass. I began down into the rocky gully. Just as I was confident I could do it, my toe caught a rock and I hit the ground on my face and head, again. I had already agreed to go to the hospital—the medical center, really, since there wasn't a hospital within a hundred miles—once we'd hiked out, but now I was more humiliated. I learned I had broken my nose, something that now causes my glasses to sit crookedly on my face and causes problems with my sleep apnea masks. My eyes were both black, my body hurt, I had a concussion, and my nose wouldn't quit bleeding. The second fall wasn't as bad as the first one, but the rest of the trip, I was ashamed any time anyone mentioned my injuries or my face-flops against the rocks.

•••

One Thanksgiving weekend at my grandmother's farmhouse a few years before Guy died, we sat in a room full of my cousins and sisters, and I told him I was going to the bathroom. Another cousin had set up hot wax hand and feet dips in the kitchen, so I did that before going back to Guy in the den. When I returned thirty minutes later, he said, "Did ya' POOP?" My cousins burst out laughing. I was embarrassed then, but it makes me giggle now. That's still something we say—my cousins, sisters, and I—when someone disappears for a long time.

He had a nonsensical song he sang when it was time to let the dogs out. He'd holler out in his happiest voice, "Buh-bum-bum-buh-buh-bum-buh-bum-buh" in different notes. He had another for when it was time for them to eat, "Come on babies, le-e-t's eat, come on babies le-e-t's eat!" The tune of both were similar, though not identical to the second time, "Coming 'round the mountain when she comes" is sung in the chorus of "Oh! Susanna." One day we shopped for stereos, and when he pretended to test the sound, he spun the knob and sang the going out song, "Buh-bum-bum ..." louder and louder. We laughed hard together—holding onto each other so we didn't fall, doubled over with silly laughter—and I can get to giggling so hard tears come out of my eyes remembering this. He was sweet and silly, and I wish he were still alive, still here and around, for himself, for us, for me.

•••

On a trip to New Mexico in late 2008, 9 months after Guy died, a friend and I hiked all over Albuquerque and Santa Fe. He introduced me to geocaching—using a GPS with coordinates and clues to find a small container with space that held paper we recorded our geocaching nicknames on. I was Rhinodoodle, Rhino from the nickname Guy gave me, doodle from our dog Kookie Doodle and that Guy and I put Doodle after a lot of things after we named Kookie. My friend was Myotis, the Latin name for bats, because he loved them. Though he'd been geocaching for years, once he got us to the right area, I usually found the cache.

Before we went, I made plans for where we'd hike: Sandia Peak, Petroglyph National Monument, Bandelier National Monument, along the Rio Grande. And we went to them all. We hiked and climbed and geocached our way around the area, and I was back at home in the wilderness. I loved the feel of the mixed sand and dirt under my feet as we trekked along granite, volcanic rock, and sandstone. Each place where it felt so different; each type of rock and what covered it felt strange and new underfoot. I loved paying attention to that—to the feel of it under my feet; to how it was to trek over it. Hiking on it felt like hiking on pebbles lightweight enough to float. It had an airy texture. It was a very different feel than the packed dirt on limestone back home, which seemed soft and hard at the same time—not as hard as concrete, but more like linoleum covered with dirt that moved just a bit. The sand and dirt blend over a brown sandstone and limestone at Red River Gorge felt just right; it grabbed my feet and gave traction like hiking on a hard rubber anti-fatigue mat. The deep sand and red sandstone in Moab, Utah, were hard to walk on, like wearing hiking boots at the beach. The loam over mixed shale and sandstone in San Francisco and Sausalito where I spent 2 weeks hiking a couple years before Guy died felt soft, even better than the sandstone and dirt at Red River Gorge because the loam had a gentleness, like hiking on rock covered with an old comforter. It was tricky, though, because sometimes the soft loam would give and I'd lose my footing, nearly falling. That's why I preferred the Gorge's sandstone.

I was empowered when I was alone with the earth underneath me. I spent time at the ocean, by rivers, in the desert, in hills different from any in Kentucky. I enjoyed sitting and watching nature—the differences in the animals, plants, even bugs—from one place to another. I became part of the place when I sat quietly, no one around, and I listened, breathed deeply, felt the land beneath me not only under my boots, but also my hands, my body. Each place even had a different taste in the air—sandy grit that reached my mouth in Utah, or salty freshness in California. Each became where I belonged, a home during that time and space.

Discussion Questions

1. In what ways is disability exemplified in "Stone, Water, Land, Spine"?
2. How does the author seem to feel about her disability?
3. In what ways does the author celebrate her disability?
4. What does the author miss from her life before she was disabled?

Maximus Aurelius Gullion, Guardian of the Realm, Slayer of Demons, Friend to Unicorn and Dragon, Defender of Squeaky Toys & Spartacus the Mighty

Jessica Smartt Gullion

ID: A furry-eared Papillon (left) stares into the distance. A black chihuahua (right) stares into the camera, with one back leg raised.

• • •

I have two dogs and a cat. Maximus Aurelius Gullion, Guardian of the Realm, Slayer of Demons, Friend to Unicorn and Dragon, Defender of Squeaky Toys is a Papillion. Spartacus the Mighty is a chihuahua. They both hate the woman who delivers our mail and bark at her every day. Puff is a fluffy black special needs cat. She has Feline Immunodeficiency Virus (also known as cat AIDS). Sometimes we watch *Rent* together; it's her favorite film.

The dogs know when I am not feeling well and will come and snuggle me. The cat doesn't care.

© PAUL D. C. BONES, JESSICA SMARTT GULLION AND DANIELLE BARBER, 2022
DOI:10.1163/9789004512702_041

CHAPTER 27

Cancer Isn't Like a Movie, But If It Was It'd Be a Horror Flick

Terri Juneau Eklund

I kept thinking about how you are writing a book on defining disability, and how, or what that even looks like to me.

Everyday someone sees me and they hold the door. At first, I thought it was just a gentlemanly gesture but then everyone started doing it. Then the more I sort of started sinking into cancer (that's what it feels like—quicksand) the more I feel like I'm no longer in control of anything—my doctors will talk to Chris about my meds, my food, my surgeries…it's like I'm invisible now.

I want to shout, "I'm right here," but at the same time I'm too tired. It's not just about invisible disabilities sometimes. It's about becoming invisible with a disability too.

Like when that professor showed that silent film when we had a blind student—she didn't matter. He forgot she was even there (with her dog).

It gets into your head too.

I don't recognize my body, my face, my hands. It's not just that it's taken away my breasts or my reproductive organs…it took away Terri. I don't feel like a woman. I don't feel like anything to be honest. It disables you in all ways—financially, emotionally, psychologically, and physically—and what you are left with is just the aftermath of a storm you couldn't outrun.

Can you imagine B (I misspell her name so I refuse to call her anything other than B now) without all the things that make her female? Would you still love her? Of course. But it's not the same after this. Chris was my husband and now I feel like he's my caregiver.

There isn't a minute that I don't think he deserves someone better, someone he doesn't have to take care of, etc.

The disability is visible but what it does to you is invisible, as far as that goes.

That's worse.

They keep saying depression is a side effect of cancer and that's not right and that's not wrong.

The surgeries I can take.

Little pieces of me are taken each time.

It's the knowing that I'm slowly fading into that quicksand, that is truly the saddest part.

I'm not funny anymore. I don't laugh or snort like I used to. I don't do anything I used to. I guess I'm just saying I'm not really here in a way anymore.

I feel like that's all been cut out too. It used to be you heard someone had cancer and then they died. No one tells you that it's a slow death that robs you of all of yourself.

In the end you don't die because you weren't there anymore anyway.

I watch the people in chemo. Each week they die a bit more, laugh a lot less, and wither.

They become just faceless beings, and then there's an extra chair, and no one says anything. I hope someone writes about cancer in your book.

I hope they include all of it.

I hope they write about what it's like when people find out and you start getting treated differently.

I hope they write about what it's like to be isolated in this disease, how it feels to no longer be Terri with cancer but instead cancer with Terri.

I really fucking hope they write about it raw.

> Dedicated to her late husband Christian, who pushed her to write it even when she did not see the point. She also dedicates this to her two beautiful and strong daughters Lulu and Alice.
> I hope I made you proud.

Discussion Questions

1. We talk about the physical entity of cancer, but not all of the shrapnel that permeates a normal daily life. What about how cancer affects a person's sexual being?
2. How does cancer affect how people feel about gender, embodiment, and relationships with others?

Bacon & Pancake

Terri Juneau Eklund

ID: A black and white (Bacon) and brown and white (Pancake) Guinea pig snuggle and look at the camera.

•••

Sometimes when my breathing is bad or I'm having a panic attack I reach for Bacon. She likes to sit on my chest and she will purr when my breathing becomes steady. That purr lets me know it's all over and will be okay.

DOI:10.1163/9789004512702_043

CHAPTER 28

"It's Meant to Be a Hazing Process"
Deciphering Ableism Surrounding Academic Accommodations

Corey Reutlinger

December 9, 2019—a day I remember vividly. I paced the mish-mashed-colored, linoleum-tile floor of the ivory hallway. I picked at my scraggly fingernails. My heart drummed: *tic-tic-tic*. My eyes and cheeks burned under the migraine-inducing fluorescent lights. I waited for the verdict. Did I pass the oral defense for my PhD comprehensive exams? Of course, I crushed my talk! Still, anxiety shocked me to my core.

The classroom door opened, and my advisor asked me to enter. That day "Dr. D" wore her smoke-colored hair down over her dark, brown eyes, so I could not tell from her expression if I had passed. I sat across from my poker-faced committee members. The uncertainty of my fate in the academy was quickly shredded to pieces by the word "Congratulations!" My heartbeat softened and my breathing returned to a slow one-two-three inhale and exhale. *Tic-tic-tic*.

"I know that the belief is that these exams are meant to be a hazing process..." began one of my committee members, thinking what he was about to say would be interpreted as praise for my intense labor, but I could smell the sickening odor of a disability microaggression unfurling in his talk (Keller & Galgay, 2010). Luckily, I was not the only one to recognize the stench of the subtle snub, and my advisor retorted quickly.

"We wouldn't give you the exams unless we knew you were ready. Hazing would be to give the exams when you weren't ready." Her calculated words rolled from her tongue. They matched her glare; the combination was enough to silence the well-meaning committee member.

She was right. *Pennalism,* or hazing, was a ritualistic practice ancient Greeks started to torment or induct unprepared students into a new social space or process (Klinger, 2017). This was especially salient for bodies the Greeks deemed as deformed, blemished, monstrous, inferior, and abnormal. The rise of Judeo-Christianity in Western Europe only aggravated and transformed pennalism. *Almsgiving*, or the act of giving money or food to poor, disabled, and chronically ill people, replaced pennalism as a social practice for spiritual absolution in the rising church-states of the seventeenth and eighteenth centuries (Parry, 2013). When this began to fail, noblemen, clergy members, and private philanthropists instead constructed systems of education and public assistance for the recruitment and retention of religious followers. The hope was to encourage disabled people to "overcome hardship," get a meaningful education, and fend for themselves without relying on charity for survival.

It is these historical ties to social control that give educational policies long-lasting consequences of oppression for those who "don't fit in." They uphold an ideology of cure that aims (and fails) to correct abnormality (Clare, 2017). Hazing was one mechanism used to teach how to tolerate abuse. Engaging in (or minimizing) hazing means creating trauma. Test-taking was a way to indoctrinate my student body-and-mind, or *bodymind*, to discriminatory logics and compliance with questionable institutional practices in higher education (Price, 2015).

I thanked my committee, but my celebration left me with a short, bittersweet taste of temporary freedom from the "hazing." I felt my anxiety quickly return; I thought about my next major project. Testing anxiety manifests in subtle, negative ways due to rigorous examination procedures, including chronic abuse through panic attacks and tics (MacFarlane, 1994). The side of my neck tightened when I thought about forthcoming papers to write. I popped my shoulder from the stress, a practice I started in grade school. I learned this routine to survive. I would learn a new (and worse) routine in March 2020. The whole world would.

Introduction

I write this chapter to explore the embodied implications of underlying cultural assumptions that reinforce oppressive policies and procedures in education. Of course, when navigating a complicated bodymind like mine, storying these harsh realities is not easy. How can I use my madness and rage toward academic inaccessibility as a methodology (Gale, 2018)? I approach this chapter with a *critical evocative autoethnography*, or the intentional storytelling of the academy's toxicity by gazing into my emotions and life experiences as a guide (de la Garza, 2004; Méndez, 2013). Yet, the disabled, wounded, ill, and/or weird bodymind does not always follow a chronological or complete progression when storying (Ellis et al., 2011; Frank, 1995). Thus, this autoethnography traces fragmented and (at times) unresolved traumas to historic hazing and institutionalization practices meant not only to sustain ableism, but also heterosexism. What follows is an homage to the ambiguity of disability (and queerness): a non-story that investigates the tangled, discontinuous, nonconscious wounds of education that have wrecked my (our) love for learning (Bochner & Ellis, 2016). The many flashbacks and fast-forwards I write here exhibit what it's like to have a bodymind that the academy has left behind.[1]

September 1997: 'Coming out' as Deaf

"Corey, can you come with me?"

I shook my head at the speech pathologist, refusing to leave my seat. She was a short, stout woman who wore black-framed glasses to contrast her ghostly white hair. No, not really, I thought. It was almost time for recess, and I did not want to miss reenacting the latest *Sailor Moon* episode with my other first-grade friends.

Mrs. Egenberger gestured to follow her. Reluctantly, I trailed, feeling nauseous. Even when I was 7, my intuition could detect oppression. The Kathy Najimy doppelgänger led me to a walk-in janitor's closet filled with bleach, one-ply toilet paper, and a rusted-up mop. She sat across a narrow, wooden table and whispered that I could only hear 60% to 70% out of each ear as if this fact should be kept secret. My inattentiveness and unresponsiveness in kindergarten alerted the school to test for a disability. She then stated, "You have a speech impediment"—a stutter, to be exact. I felt confusion and shame: who was this person to tell me who I am based on observing my behaviors? Why did she imply something was "wrong" with me?

My elementary school years were devoted 'to fix' my Rs and Ws. Weekly, I resented meeting with Mrs. Egenberger. I pouted during each speech pathology session. "Rabbit," "run," "woof," "wood," I'd enunciate, repeating the same basic words for roughly 4 years while my peers played. I was relieved to "come out" of the janitor's closet when I finally received my first set of rainbow tie-dyed hearing aids in the third grade. They made the sessions bearable. Not in the classroom though. My non-disabled classmates either stared or avoided eye contact. I felt self-conscious. My disability and sexuality were a freakery (Garland-Thomson, 1997). Rather, I felt like a spectacle—an anomaly—on public display to be questioned by those unwilling to understand my weirdness as a reflection of their homophobic voyeurism and ableist curiosity. Traveling circuses and freak shows during the early nineteenth century became places where audiences paid to gawk at bodily deformities for entertainment and inquire whether "strange" identities were divine curses or gifts (Parry, 2013). The classroom was the modern-day circus: I often received, "You're so inspirational!" as a compliment for "overcoming" my deafness.

But well-intended, seemingly harmless compliments like these can often trigger feelings of discomfort for anyone who experienced developmental trauma or stigmatization going through K-12 education (Fine & Asch, 1988; Torino et al., 2019). We learn from an early age what is not socially acceptable or culturally normal protocol when interacting. We contribute to the immortalization of stigma by deciding what is "wrong" with the bodymind and what needs "fixing." The classroom even becomes a space for using disability microaggressions to bully those acting abnormally or out of line (Dávila, 2015).

Raise your hand. Pay attention. Don't leave your seat. No doodling. No eating in class. No late assignments. Don't be tardy. Attend every day. Participate in activities. I heard these rules all throughout K-12. It did not matter if I were well-behaved or obedient. I was labeled by my performativity as a dork, geek, nerd, dumb, teacher's pet, lame, crazy, and other pejoratives (Bell, 2011). I even lowered my vocal pitch during speed-reading tests to not "sound gay." This is when I started to feel pressure to masquerade as "straight" and "average" to meet unrealistic expectations. These rules meant to manage classroom behavior were tools for hazing.

I only met Mrs. Egenberger one other time after elementary school, in the seventh grade. It was to return a suitcase containing two small pager-like devices after a citywide spelling bee. One was meant to be worn by a teacher, who would clip a small microphone to their shirt. The other was meant to be worn on my belt buckle. I would plug in a wireless t-coil audio loop to drape around my neck underneath my hearing aids. I handed her the personal FM audio trainer. I used it to reduce classroom noise, but it felt like I was always contractually chained to someone who never understood my experience. It trained me to dismiss bodily red flags. Sometimes I didn't want to use the trainer; I wanted others to speak louder and slower. I internalized the hazing ritual of putting on the device. I internalized ableism (Kumari-Campbell, 2008). The exchange lasted briefly. I smiled politely and waved goodbye. I gritted my teeth and exhaled heavily, popping my neck and shoulder as I returned to class. *Tic-tic-tic.*

Introduction: Revised

Academia has taught me to revise my thinking, doing, and writing. This section considers how disability storying challenges mainstream education. I explore how entangling disability with sexuality can vex, cripple, and reconfigure our perspectives around what we constitute as hazing in the classroom and how to resist it.

   This intersectional tracing of oppression *invites* unearthing fragmented emotional, psychological, and cultural traumas that result from long-term exposure to problematic educational practices. These traumas are not only connected to academic test-taking procedures, but also are exacerbated by emerging remote teaching/learning formats. Hazing shifts through new technological platforms.

   The COVID-19 pandemic troubles what it means to be disabled, or to self-diagnose a disability—escalating an accessibility crisis in education never seen before (Barbarin, 2020; Pulrang, 2020)....

October 2020: Zoom University

It was Tuesday. Perhaps Thursday? Sometime around Halloween. Brain fog from my exams exactly one year ago had numbed my sense of time. Each day felt as soul-sucking as the last. I started my Zoom class, admitting students from the waiting room. I smiled and darted my eyes across several black screens with names. Maybe a picture here and there. I type my pronouns next to my name in Zoom; this has not been easy to set up.

   "How are you feeling?" I asked. Silence. No one wanted to share their frustrations or be a harbinger of the forthcoming mental health crisis and skyrocketing death tolls.

I know Zoom means accessibility for disabled people, parents and caregivers, international students, and anyone without financial support. Still, the videoconferencing platform acts like a modern-day *panopticon*, a space to use surveillance technology to violate privacy and punish noncompliance (Sewell, 1998). A colleague once told me to require cameras on to increase Zoom participation, saying, "It's not optional in my class. Turn on the camera or don't bother to come! I start once I see everyone's smiling faces." I frowned.

I private-messaged a few students to play the hitmen for *Mafia*. As the game progressed, everyone became impatient. I strained to hear the townspeople's discussions. I no longer used hearing aids; however, wearing headphones or reading Zoom's closed captioning was pointless. What did they say? I must've missed something. Drat, there's still thirty minutes to fill!

Emotional fatigue set in. We are expected to maintain high levels of "productivity" in the academy during a public health crisis without governmental aid. As a graduate teaching associate with a disability, I'm expected to be a therapist, a housekeeper, and a teacher—all while living off a $18,000-a-year stipend. I must justify to the university in an accommodation request why teaching in-person during a pandemic is bad. I must prove my crip life (see Carter et al., 2017).

My thoughts swirled while watching the class converse. I glance at my partner cleaning his house. Focus on the screens! It's Thursday. My breathing hastened. He is being nice today. No criticisms. ~~Turn off my video. Cry.~~ Time to talk! My stutter returns. Smile! *Tic-tic-tic.*

Our bodyminds are not meant to juggle many types of anxiety simultaneously. We problem-solve best in layers. The 2020 pandemic overhauled this drastically. My university claims, "We're #1 in innovation," yet cuts out semester breaks and finals week. It prides itself on following "hard" deadlines and 16-week semesters. Sadly, educational policies like these have undergone few revisions since the disability rights movement of the 1970s, despite how classrooms reflect deep-seated, systemic ableism (Lovett & Nelson, 2017). The one-size-fits-all mentality continues to presume disabled students can keep up with their non-disabled peers even during mass COVID-19 outbreaks (Hehir, 2004; Townsend, 2006).

My computer dings, snapping back my focus. A new email from the provost. *Loneliness has increased since the start of the pandemic... many students self-report difficulty...consider developing deliberate*

extracurricular programming such as in-person social experiences...
incentivize student participation...as you design activities, share ideas,
and promote success.... Universities do not understand. Penalizing
absences, participation grades, grading discussions, timed tests,
academic integrity clauses—the policies of our childhoods may
keep students from "falling behind academically," but they are costly
(Goldstein, 2020). They produce chronic stress, fatigue, anxiety,
restlessness, and exhaustion in our bodyminds (Ahmed, 2014).
This has only worsened inside the remote Zoom classroom, all to
"maintain the college experience."

October 2019: The Exam

I sat in (yet another) lamp-lit closet, staring blankly at a computer
screen. A few feet beyond the computer was a mirror I could use to
see the dark bags under my eyes from studying excessive loads of
reading material. The department tried to make the comprehensive
exam room, in their words, "relaxing." They even included a little
sound machine on the wall next to the computer. "It should calm
your nerves." The steady thump-thump...thump-thump of the
Heartbeat selection was painstakingly maddening and pleasurable.
The cadence soothed my tics.

My phone clock displayed 8:00 a.m. It was time to start my
comprehensive exams. I typed my first words. Nothing happened.
I pushed the K and J keys again. The cursor in the Word document
blinked at me. I felt confused. Was I overlooking an obvious detail
because of my fatigue? No. They gave me a non-functioning
computer. The clock was ticking down.

My heart banged against my ribcage. I wheezed. The closet
shrank around me. Electricity jolted through my body; my head
pounded. I climbed the stairs multiple times over 2 hours, jabbering
with administrative staff about what to do. I did not know I was
experiencing an all-too-common panic attack. I had to keep moving.
Pacing. I knew they would sort out this problem. Back and forth. I
could not stay still. Otherwise, my body would stiffen up, my vision
would darken, and my fingers would twitch. No. I didn't want that to
happen. I kept moving.

I repeat this in my nightmares. I wish the COVID-19 pandemic had
changed the way the department formatted these exams. It did

not. Like all academic test-taking procedures, the comprehensive exam process functions as an ableist hazing ritual that reinforces principles of neurotypicality. The model of late-night studying, rote memorization of names and dates, and regurgitation of terms and formulas onto a blank page in a limited time frame excludes knowledge-creation of bodyminds that differ across cognitive, affective, and physical dimensions. Capitalistic values of excellence such as "rigor," "merit," and "quality" embed college exams, projects, presentations, and homework assignments, but these ethics often exclude and prevent anyone who is not white, middle-class, heteronormative, or able-bodied from succeeding in the academy (Waitoller et al., 2019).

Sure, the administrative staff replaced my computer and extended my testing time. But I was in shambles like someone who had been dragged up from the depths of the ocean. These were anything but "reasonable accommodations," especially after almost experiencing a full-fledged panic attack (Lovett & Nelson, 2017). What I really needed was a rest day and a rescheduling. This was a microaggressive act in disguise—an injustice. To know what disabled students need on a daily basis requires more than simply providing accommodations. It is more than revamping testing procedures that continue to haze disabled students. It begs a radical shift in paradigm that conceptualizes what a *neurodiverse* student needs: abolishment of examinations.

May 2010: Beginning Neurodiversity

My bodymind is neurodivergent. I am not only hard of hearing and queer. No. I am also non-pathological by way of my emotionality and sociability. Call anxiety a "mental illness," but that is simply internalized ableism speaking. I call it a "body storm." So many students do not realize they need specific accommodations to survive the inaccessibility of the U.S. education system. *Neurodiversity* is when there is variation in neurocognitive functioning. Its history has been detached from the disability rights movement and so has its narrative as a juxtaposition to neurotypicality (Hughes, 2016). It does not mean to detract from autism or the educational policies that work for and against autism (Simpson et al., 2011). No. Being neurodivergent embraces autism *and* other states of the bodymind such as sexuality, gender identity, complex PTSD, ADD/ADHD, OCD, dyslexia, anxiety, depression, insomnia, Tourette's, schizophrenia, bipolarity and so many other disabilities (Dunn & Schwallie Farmer, 2020; Yergeau, 2018). It extends to include the politics of inaccessible spaces, classrooms, buildings, and work environments (Ahmed, 2014). It welcomes chronic debilities and partial bodily capacities such as immunocompromisation that comes from HIV/AIDS or COVID-19 and its post-viral acquired conditions (McRuer, 2006; Puar, 2017). I self-diagnose as non-autistic(?) and neuroqueer[2] (Yergeau, 2018). I enfold my anxiety, C-PTSD, deafness, queerness, poverty, spirituality, and so much more into the maddening messiness of my bodymind. I do not need a cure nor "fixing." I need accommodations that do not retrigger my already traumatized body from years of hazing (Clare, 2017). I need an education system that centers an *Ethic of Accommodation*: The COVID-19 classroom and any forthcoming academic landscape should evoke inclusivity, resiliency, affability, advocacy, and a politic of transformation for all bodyminds (Moreman, 2019).

I remember when I first felt neurodiverse. Years earlier, during my college sophomore year, I experienced a violation around accessibility. It was during the final-exam period for a 400-level Reader's Theatre course. A grade-school teacher had once told me to challenge myself by enrolling in advanced classes. I accelerated in gifted education for math when younger. My reading and speaking skills, however, needed fine-tuning. Heterosexism limited me while being labeled "gifted" for a disability pressured me to perform. I battled imposter syndrome thinking frequently: *I don't belong here. I am not good at this. I will fail my tests. I am not creative. My parents will be disappointed.*

I floundered to earn an A grade for Reader's Theatre. The final assignment was to compile a script with drama, prose, and poetry. I even wrote an original poem for the oral interpretation performance portion of the final. I felt proud of my work. Yet, when I received feedback, the professor commented, "I think you plagiarized this." I received a zero.

I felt mortified and disgusted. How could he? I put my vulnerability and integrity on display. It made the difference between a "perfect" A or a "just average" B. Getting a B grade would destroy me. I raced to visit my professor afterward. Petrified, I stumbled into his book-cluttered office and slid into the seat across his desk. He eventually peeled his eyes away from his computer screen to acknowledge my presence. I dropped a set of books in front of him, saying, "Look!

These are my resources! See the highlights?" I held pages open in front of him and handwritten drafts of my poetry. My fingers shook with my first ever electric *tic-tic-tics*. I stuttered, unable to speak between sharp wheezing. My first panic attack. My professor looked at me and said nonchalantly, "I believe you. Calm down."

Proving originality becomes hazing. Grades stem from pedagogy that enflames, agitates, and evaluates the trauma we have buried to protect ourselves (Anti-Ableist Composition, 2020). Grading invites teachers to socially control student bodyminds. The U.S. education system perpetuates this through the myth of the perfectionistic, "straight A" student, preventing healing. I eventually learned to be comfortable writing poetry again—enough to publish original works like *Deaf Song* and *Method to My Madness* to express frustrations around disability discrimination I've experienced in the academy. Still, it is the teachers who (un)intentionally stifle neurodiverse expressions that invite the most violence into the classroom.

Introduction: Reborn

This chapter is anxious. It uses critical evocative autoethnography. It

incinerates disability's medicalization and rebirths from ashes

NEURODIVERSITY.

It cuts through & complicates disabled bodyminds in academia.

My queerness,

my disability,

my experience with heterosexism,

muddles my relation to ableism

in non-pathological ~~and invisible(?)~~ ways.

This chapter narrates ~~(poeticizes)~~ how best to

craft accessibility for neurodiverse students.

It suggests

theoretical & pedagogical

...possibilities...

So, I ask:

What does it mean to provide individuated and unique classroom

accommodations for debility/capacity (Puar, 2017), emotionality

(Ahmed, 2014), or neurological queerness (Yergeau, 2018) during the era

of COVID-19?

December 2020: 'Cripping' the Classroom

I jolted awake at 2:24 a.m. It's almost winter break. Between sobs, I scrambled to recall the fragments of my nightmares before vanishing from memory. My body stuck to my sweat-soaked bed sheets. I breathed in. Out. Again, but slower, my mind racing. I had a subconscious anxiety attack, one haunting my dreams. I lay awake unable to shut off my brain. Flashbacks of my comprehensive exams, forgetting to wear a mask in public, and abusive ex-relationships flooded my thinking. Two hours passed before I crawled out of bed to teach my Zoom class. I have repeated this process of waking up at odd hours over many nights, weeks, and months.

Exploring the cultural roots of educational trauma encourages healing. It offers more nuanced conversations about constructing classrooms built around what Robert McRuer (2006) calls *crip time*, where bodyminds think and perform in their own way and at their own pace. Instead of bending ourselves to meet the clock and environment, the classroom should change to meet the many aural, verbal, visual, kinesthetic, logical, social, or solitary ways we construct knowledge. It is about building "an awareness that disabled people might need more time to accomplish something or to arrive somewhere" (Kafer, 2013, p. 26). Cynthia Lewiecki-Wilson (2003) has written extensively about how to craft such a classroom space and how to provide individualized and unique accommodations for students. An Ethic of Accommodation does not simply mean equity and inclusivity for differing bodyminds (Moreman, 2019). It means to foster a *disability justice*: humanizing bodyminds across various identity markers, dismantling harmful educational policies, changing inaccessible structures, and reshaping ideologies grounded in capitalistic "productivity" and "merit" (Berne, 2015). Neurodiversity, conceptually, demands liberating students of institutional hazing rituals and traumatic pedagogy.

Disrupting educational hazing implores practicing anti-ableism. This looks like "cripping" classroom practices and teaching to meet our unruly bodies (Erevelles, 2000). We should normalize flexible attendance, ungraded participation, "soft" deadlines, and extended testing time (Schultz, 2009)—especially for the (post) COVID-19 classroom. Students and teachers should want more collaborative group exams, photovoice assignments, or the inclusion of poetry and artwork (Pink, 2012). Doing this revolutionizes education. It situates us to end historical hazing rituals and institutionalization practices that have sustained oppression in education and in ourselves. This means anti-ableism is about forgiving our bodyminds for un/misdiagnosed disabilities. I'm still exploring mine. I'm still learning to accept myself.

Discussion Questions

1. What parts of this chapter resonate with your academic experiences? Explain.
2. Besides those listed in the chapter, what are some other examples of ableist classroom policies or procedures?
3. What are some tangible ways to practice anti-ableism in the classroom?

Acknowledgment

I thank Rikki Tremblay, Kelsey Abele, and Haley Lucero for their personal assistance in preparing this manuscript.

Notes

1   This non-story format follows Yergeau's (2016) *autie-ethnography* methodology, an autoethnographic approach that explores the autistic bodymind's connection to inaccessibility culture.
2   A person can be both non-autistic and neurodivergent. Neuroqueer meshes neurodiversity with queerness to oppose the privileging of a particular way of thinking and communicating in society. I'm uncertain whether I am autistic.

References

Ahmed, S. (2014). *The cultural politics of emotion* (2nd ed.). Edinburgh University Press.

Anti-Ableist Composition [@AntiAbleistComp]. (2020, December 2). *Grades are at the center of traumatic pedagogy. Grades enflame trauma experiences while making value judgements about the very trauma* [Tweet]. Twitter. https://twitter.com/AntiAbleistComp/status/1334180122820112384

Barbarin, I. [@imani_barbarin]. (2020, June 30). *If you would like another devastating prediction from the disability community: We are about to hit an accessibility crisis never before* [Tweet]. Twitter. https://twitter.com/Imani_Barbarin/status/1278126213723291650

Bell, C. M. (Ed.). (2011). *Blackness and disability*. Michigan State University Press.

Berne, P. (2015). *Disability justice—a working draft*. Sins Invalid. https://www.sinsinvalid.org/blog/disability-justice-a-working-draft-by-patty-berne

Bochner, A. P., & Ellis, C. (2016). *Evocative autoethnography: Writing lives and telling stories*. Routledge.

Carter, A. M., Catania, R. T., Schmitt, S., & Swenson, A. (2017). Bodyminds like ours: An autoethnographic analysis of graduate school, disability, and the politics of disclosure. In S. L. Kerschbaum, L. T. Eisenman, & J. M. Jones (Eds.), *Negotiating disability: Disclosure and higher education* (pp. 95–114). University of Michigan Press.

Clare, E. (2017). *Brilliant imperfection: Grappling with cure*. Duke University Press.

Dávila, B. (2015). Critical race theory, disability microaggressions, and Latina/o student experiences in special education. *Race Ethnicity and Education, 18*(4), 443–468. https://doi.org/10.1080/13613324.2014.885422

de la Garza, S. A. (2004). *María speaks: Journeys into the mysteries of the mother in my life as a Chicana*. Peter Lang.

Dunn, M., & Schwallie Farmer, C. (2020, October 18). *Neurodiversity: An organizational asset*. American Diversity Report. https://americandiversityreport.com/neurodiversity-an-organizational-asset-by-maureen-dunne-cathy-schwallie-farmer/

Ellis, C., Adams, T. E., & Bochner, A. P. (2011). Autoethnography: An overview. *Historical Social Research/Historische Sozialforschung, 36*(4), 273–290. https://www.jstor.org/stable/23032294

Erevelles, N. (2000). Educating unruly bodies: Critical pedagogy, disability studies, and the politics of schooling. *Educational Theory, 50*(1), 25–47. https://doi.org/10.1111/j.1741-5446.2000.00025.x

Fine, M., & Asch, A. (1988). Disability beyond stigma: Social interaction, discrimination, and activism. *Journal of Social Issues, 44*(1), 3–21. https://doi.org/10.1111/j.1540-4560.1988.tb02045.x

Frank, A. W. (1995). *The wounded storyteller*. University of Chicago Press.

Gale, K. (2018). *Madness as methodology: Bringing concepts to life in contemporary theorising and inquiry*. Routledge.

Garland-Thomson, R. (1997). *Extraordinary bodies: Figuring physical disability in American culture and literature*. Columbia University Press.

Goldstein, D. (2020, June 5). Research shows students falling months behind during virus disruptions. *The New York Times*. https://www.nytimes.com/2020/06/05/us/coronavirus-education-lost-learning.html

Hehir, T. (2004). Eliminating ableism in education. *Harvard Educational Review, 72*(1), 1–32.

Hughes, J. M. F. (2016, June). *Increasing neurodiversity in disability and social justice advocacy groups*. Autistic Self Advocacy Network. https://autisticadvocacy.org/wp-content/uploads/2016/06/whitepaper-Increasing-Neurodiversity-in-Disability-and-Social-Justice-Advocacy-Groups.pdf

Kafer, A. (2013). *Feminist, queer, crip*. Indiana University Press.

Keller, R. M., & Galgay, C. E. (2010). Microaggressive experiences of people with disabilities. In D. W. Sue (Ed.), *Microaggressions and marginality: Manifestation, dynamics, and impact* (pp. 241–267). John Wiley & Sons.

Klinger, G. (2017, March 9). *Hazing: Its beginning and evolution throughout history*. A Medium Corporation. https://medium.com/@gavinklinger57/hazing-its-beginning-and-evolution-throughout-history-fee3cd68ca06

Kumari-Campbell, F. A. (2008). Exploring internalized ableism using critical race theory. *Disability & Society, 23*(2), 151–162. https://doi.org/10.1080/09687590701841190

Lewiecki-Wilson, C. (2003). Rethinking rhetoric through mental disabilities. *Rhetoric Review, 22*(2), 156–167. http://jstor.org/stable/3093036

Lovett, B. J., & Nelson, J. M. (2017). Test anxiety and the Americans with disabilities act. *Journal of Disability Policy Studies, 28*(2), 99–108. https://doi.org/10.1177/1044207317710699

MacFarlane, A. (1994). Subtle forms of abuse and their long-term effects. *Disability & Society, 9*(1), 85–89. https://doi.org/10.1080/09687599466780071

McRuer, R. (2006). *Crip theory: Cultural signs of queerness and disability.* New York University Press.

Méndez, M. (2013). Autoethnography as a research method: Advantages, limitations and criticisms. *Colombian Applied Linguistics Journal, 15*(2), 279–287. https://doi.org/10.14483/udistrital.jour.calj.2013.2.a09

Moreman, S. T. (2019). Accommodating desires of disability: A multi-modal methodological approach to Terry Galloway and the Mickee Faust Club. *QED: A Journal in GLBTQ Worldmaking, 6*(3), 149–162. https://jstor.org/stable/10.14321/qed.6.3.0149

Parry, M. (2013). *From monsters to patients: A history of disability.* (Publication No. 3560144) [Doctoral dissertation, Arizona State University]. ProQuest Dissertations and Theses Global.

Pink, S. (2012). *Advances in visual methodology.* Sage Publication, Ltd.

Price, M. (2015). The bodymind problem and the possibilities of pain. *Hypatia, 30*(1), 268–284.

Puar, J. K. (2017). *The right to main: Debility, capacity, disability.* Duke University Press.

Pulrang, A. (2020, June 30). We need to stop patrolling the borders of disability. *Forbes.* https://www.forbes.com/sites/andrewpulrang/2020/06/30/we-need-to-stop-patrolling-the-borders-of-disability/#74eb66562ae1

Schultz, K. (2009). *Rethinking classroom participation: Listening to silent voices.* Teachers College, Columbia University.

Sewell, G. (1998). The discipline of teams: The control of team-based industrial work through electronic and peer surveillance. *Administrative Science Quarterly, 43*(2), 397–428.

Simpson, R. L., Mundschenk, N. A., & Heflin, L. J. (2011). Issues, policies, and recommendations for improving the education of learners with autism spectrum disorders. *Journal of Disability Policy Studies, 22*(1), 3–17. https://doi.org/10.1177/1044207310394850

Torino, G. C., Rivera, D. P., Capodilupo, C. M., Nadal, K. L., & Sue, D. W. (Eds.). (2019). *Microaggression theory: Influence and implications.* John Wiley & Sons.

Townsend, N. L. (2006). Framing a ceiling as a floor: The changing definition of learning disabilities and the conflicting trends in legislation affecting learning disabled students. *Creighton Law Review, 40*(2), 229–270. http://hdl.handle.net/10504/40582

Waitoller, F. R., Nguyen, N., & Super, G. (2019). The irony of rigor: 'No-excuses' charter schools at the intersections of race and disability. *International Journal of Qualitative Studies in Education, 32*(3), 282–298. https://doi.org/10.1080/09518398.2019.1576939

Yergeau, R. (2016). Occupying autism: Rhetoric, involuntarity, and the meaning of autistic lives. In P. Block, D. Kasnitz, A. Nishida, & N. Pollard (Eds.), *Occupying disability: Critical approaches to community, justice, and decolonizing disability* (pp. 83–95). Springer. https://doi.org/10.1007/978-94-017-9984-3_6

Yergeau, R. (2018). *Authoring autism: On rhetoric and neurological queerness.* Duke University Press.

Captain Jack Harkness & Pippa Millicent Tiny Panther

Tara Elliot

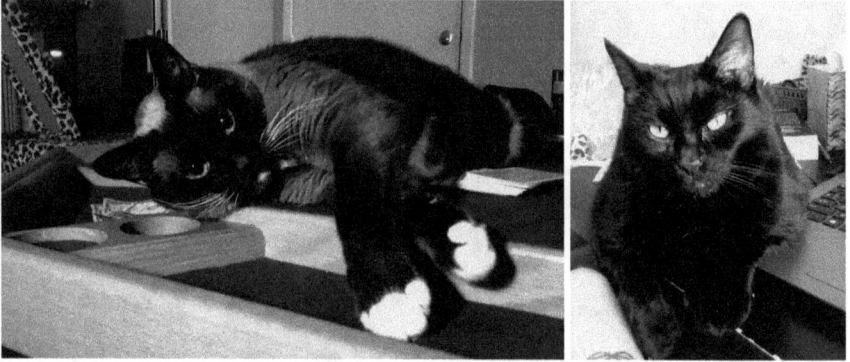

ID: (Left) A snowshoe cat lies on his side on top of a poker table, showing his white-tipped paws. (Right) A black cat smirks as she overtakes her mother's workspace.

...

Captain Jack Harkness is an 11-year-old Snowshoe. He has a strange gait due to a condition called luxating patella. Captain is generally hiding in portals to unknown lands all day, but spends each night and morning sleeping beside me with his head on my pillow.

Pippa Millicent Tiny Panther is a 10-year-old Black Polydactyl cat. Pippa has a partially paralyzed leg after surviving a spinal stroke last year. She spends most of her day sleeping at my side or on top of me making murder biscuits.

Together with their alternating shifts, they help keep me feeling loved and secure. I have PTSD, generalized anxiety, and widespread chronic pain from four car accidents. I stopped driving and was hit by a car while walking in 2011. Captain was very young when that accident occurred and never left my side. I am also a 14-month COVID Long Hauler, which has brought on more challenges and new diagnoses than one would ever imagine. I don't know what I would have done without these two next to me during this past year's struggles.

© PAUL D. C. BONES, JESSICA SMARTT GULLION AND DANIELLE BARBER, 2022
DOI:10.1163/9789004512702_045

CHAPTER 29

Night of the Living Ableds
Disability, Representation, and Horror Film

Paul D. C. Bones

If disability were to have a genre, it would be horror. Don't believe me? Let's try an exercise. I want you to think of three horror films that *don't* include disability. And remember, disability includes mental illness, physical difference,[1] and chronic illness. *Friday the 13th* (1980)? Disability—A mentally ill woman kills to avenge her dead/undead child with facial difference. *Candyman* (1992)? Disability—a supernatural Black victim of a racial hate crime kills people with his hook hand. *Us* (2019)? Disability—a blind white photographer man enlists the help of his friends to transfer his consciousness into the body of a Black photographer. *Hellraiser* (1987)? Disability—a group of physically different extradimensional beings have such sights to show you. We could do this all day. And that is because disability isn't just another horror trope, it is *the* cornerstone of how we express and understand fear.

But why? There are many things to be afraid of that don't include disability. Such as clowns. Or murder hornets. Or clown murder hornets. There are two basic reasons why disability equals fear in our minds. First, the horror canon is largely built upon prior successes, so because Norman Bates (*Psycho*, 1960) went a little mad sometimes, insanity is the go-to for why a "regular" person would commit murder. Insanity is a hidden disability, which means anyone could be insane, lose control, and stab us in the shower. Likewise, audiences reacted to the physical difference of Jason (*Friday the 13th*, 1980), so it's not enough for a slasher to be just powerful and evil, he [and I use "he" intentionally because they are almost always male] needs to have a physical appearance that disgusts us. Consequently, what we're really reacting to are old ideas that have been accepted as fact, even though there's very little about the world of 1960 (or even 1980) that uniformly applies today. Second, the *social* understanding of disability is scary. We are taught to fear insanity and shun those who look different than we do. Disability is a convenient tool for

© PAUL D. C. BONES, 2022 | DOI:10.1163/9789004512702_046

filmmakers since we have so much personal, cultural, and social baggage when it comes to the concept. So how does a disabled horror lover like myself reconcile the harm of the disability equals fear dynamic? Well, I overthink it. What follows is a brief exploration into the takeaway messages horror sends to non-disabled viewers, along with the state of representation in the genre.

Follow the Rules—Horror as a Source of Socialization

Horror occupies a unique place in American culture. It is fundamentally an expression of hopes and fears while also serving as a mechanism of social control (Weber, 1981). This last point, the implicit social control of horror, is important because not all learning is overt and intended. Socialization, or the process of internalizing norms, values, and behaviors, can occur in much more subtle ways.

Originating in Marxist education studies, the term *hidden curriculum* refers to the idea that we are often subjected to socialization and social control even when we are not aware that learning is taking place (Giroux & Penna, 1979; Anyon, 1980; Wren, 1999; Kentli, 2009). In the classroom, researchers often cite how the ultimate goals of primary education involve not learning numbers and letters, but conditioning students to sit quietly, ask permission to go to the bathroom, and obey the authority at the front of the room (Kentli, 2009). I contend that a similar process operates whenever we consume visual media.

Even when dealing with the extreme or the absurd, as is often the case with horror, the overall logic of the universe still needs to make sense, which is why horror so often relies on stereotypes to create quick backstories for expendable characters. As viewers, we tend to accept ideas and realities that fit within our own preconceived notions of what is "true" in the world, and reject what stands out as false (Schweinitz, 2010; Sherman & Frost, 2000). This is why we accept the idea that the creepy janitor has knife hands and attacks children (because of stereotypes about janitors being poor, child molesters, and deranged), but utterly reject the idea of Jason in space[2] (he clearly belongs in a camp, not in space, poorly reenacting *Alien*). Consequently, consuming horror is very much an act of reaffirming the status quo and reinforcing stereotypes.

The Horror of Disability

Madness or "insanity" is arguably the most common representation of disability in horror. From Hitchcock to Italian *giallo*, the hypersexual 70s horror to the slashers of the 80s, the pointless sequels of the 90s to so-called "elevated horror" of today, the easiest way to explain the motivations of a killer is mental illness. The overreliance on this trope can be explained as the result of several forces. First, we have essentially defined murder as an indicator of insanity, as we view it as an inhuman act that does not make rational sense. While there may be some truth to the idea of murder as madness, the fact is most people with mental disabilities and mental illness are not violent. In fact, mental illness has a stronger link to victimization than offending (Rueve & Welton, 2008; Walsh et al., 2003; Fazel & Grann, 2006). The concept of madness obscures the capriciousness of human existence and the fact that we are most at danger from ourselves, intimates, and acquaintances. Second, survey data show a higher rate of mental illness in prisons than in the general population (Rueve & Welton, 2008), which, for some, confirms the idea that mental illness is dangerous. However, it is difficult to directly compare rates between an institutionalized population where everyone has access to mental health testing (and may be forced to undergo testing, diagnosis, and treatment) to the general public, where health care is largely a matter of social class. Not to mention the fact that most prisoners are not in prison for violent crimes (OJJDP, 2020). Finally, we have been conditioned to fear mental illness in all its forms because of the uncertainty associated with it (Varshney et al., 2016). The mere suggestion that an escaped mental patient murdered seven teens with a corded drill makes intuitive sense, given what we have all learned about "crazy people." In fact, it's arguably one of the only reasons why a (presumably) sane audience would accept someone deciding to commit such an atrocious act. Seven times. Consequently, mental illness becomes the catch-all explanation for all manner of real-world violence, even absent any evidence that the offender has a mental illness. For example, every mass shooting, especially school shootings, is framed as the actions of a mentally ill person. This is true even when the perpetrator has a clear plan and rationale because we cannot cognitively uncouple the act of murder from mental illness. The overreliance on insanity as the cause of violence means that horror perpetuates this fear of mental illness, as each driller killer reinforces that link between mental health and danger.

Physical difference, especially of the face or limbs, is also very common in horror films. Within criminology, and the pre-scientific sources of knowledge we used to explain crime, there has been an urge to view evil as something we see. This is why many pre-modern societies interpreted physical differences as external signs of consorting with some kind of malevolent force (Retief & Letšosa, 2018), and early biological positivists (phrenology, somatotyping, atavism, etc.) looked for physical signs that a person was likely to commit a crime (Williams & McShane; 2010). This is clearly demonstrated in horror, especially in the slashers of the 1980s. For example, both Freddy Kruger (*Nightmare on Elm Street*, 1984) and Jason Voorhees (*Friday the 13th*, 1980) are portrayed as physically different, with their depravity manifesting as a visible stigma (Goffman, 1963; Turner & Stagg, 2006). This serves to set them apart from "normal" men, and reifies the idea that deviants are readily recognizable, when that is anything but the truth. The harm caused by these depictions for physically different disabled persons is apparent, as we already live in a society that prioritizes a "normal" standard of beauty, adding a moral component to physical difference just seems cruel.

Representation Splatters, errr Matters

The best way to address the problematic use and exploitation of disability is to put more disabled people in the room and confront it head on. Though neither had disabled actors, there are two classic scenes involving wheelchairs that stand out in my mind. The first is from *Nightmare on Elm Street 3: Dream Warriors* (1987). A personal favorite of mine, the film is all about disability since a) it's set in a mental health care facility, and b) it has a character who uses a wheelchair. It's also unique because the victims have more agency than usual, as they harness the power of dreams to take the fight to Freddy.[3] Being the dream master though, he counters this. Will Stanton, who is a wheelchair user in the physical world, can walk in the dreamscape, because of course an abled creative would think this would be the primary dream of any wheelchair user. Knowing this, Freddy attacks him with his greatest fear: his wheelchair. Or a version of his wheelchair donned with spikes, knives, and shackles. This scene clearly had no input from a wheelchair user. But it does reflect how ableism treats mobility aids—the worst thing in the world.

A second, much more positive wheelchair scene comes from *Friday the 13th Part II* (1981). Though not played by a wheelchair user in real life, Mark uses one throughout the film. What's unique about this character is that he's fully formed. He's included at the beach, he's presented as a leader, and he is seen as a sex object. I cannot stress how rare this is. Yes, there are some questionable aspects to his character—Vickie asks him to tell his story of how he acquired his disability and if his penis works—but these are contextualized as her really wanting to get to know him. Biblically. In fact, he is about to hook up with her when Jason cockblocks him, giving us the unintentionally hilarious scene of a dummy in a wheelchair careening down a flight of stairs. As a non-wheelchair user, I am not the best person to appraise this scene, but there's a real personhood and lack of stigma embodied by this character. He's a character who happens to be in a wheelchair, up until his death.

Both of those examples included non-disabled actors in wheelchairs. A more recent example that uses an authentic disabled actor would be *Run* (2020). In this film, Kiera Allen plays a young woman who has a variety of disabilities, including paralysis of her legs. Her disability is the center of the film, as (spoiler) she realizes her chronic illnesses are the result of her mother poisoning her (due to Munchausen by proxy syndrome—another disability). While the acting is excellent, which may be due to the fact that Kiera is a wheelchair user, and the character of Chloe is a case of fully formed representation on the screen, this authenticity does not extend to the script, or make for a non-problematic film. The wheelchair is used as a form of social control as Diane seeks to keep her daughter dependent on her. It's also a narrative tool that keeps Chloe from escaping her torturous mother instead of providing access and mobility. It also plays into an "overcoming disability" narrative, as Chloe is finally able to stop her mother by regaining control of her legs. Casting disabled actors is a crucial part of reducing the ableism in horror, but without authenticity behind the camera (and in the writers' room), it can only do so much.

Run is not the only recent movie to overtly embrace disability as a plotline. Films such as *A Quiet Place* (2018—Deaf), *Don't Breathe* (2016—blind), *Come Play* (2020—non-speaking autism), *Hush* (2016—Deaf), and *Birdbox* (2018—blind) have taken disability from an unspoken trope to the central plotline in various ways, with differing levels of accuracy. For example, *Hush* and *Don't Breathe* both depict sensory disabilities in a home invasion. The former uses it as a narrative tool to increase the suspense as our heroine must fight off an invader without being able to hear him. Conversely, it is the blind homeowner who stalks invaders with his heightened senses in *Don't Breathe*. Neither of these roles were played by disabled actors, and it certainly seems like the latter was crafted more from disability myth than reality.

The switch to overt presentations of disability seems like a step in the right direction, but may actually be more problematic than traditional covert depictions. First, these films rarely cast disabled actors. Non-speaking autistics and wheelchairs users are often disqualified from non-disabled roles, and studios/creators will spend hours studying disability to achieve "authenticity," but disabled actors are rarely seen as "able" to play authentic roles in film. So even when a role is well researched, in 2021 there's no reason not to hire a wheelchair user to play a wheelchair user. I mean, the wheelchair is already on the set. Second, when disability is made the central plot of a horror film, it tends to fetishize it. *Bird Box* ends when our protagonist and her children (creatively named "Boy" and "Girl") are saved by arriving at a school for the blind, which protects them from the sight demons. Likewise, *A Quiet Place* ends when Reagan discovers her hearing aid can kill the monsters. You see, "the disabled" were really advantaged all along!

Sometimes including disability just makes a movie confusing. *Come Play* was a rather bland technophobia horror film, with non-speaking autism randomly thrown in. While non-disabled actor Azhy Robertson is excellent in his portrayal of non-speaking Oliver, and the film does touch on things like stimming, the addition of autism to the plot is just bizarre. If anything, autism is positioned as a reason for us to pity both Oliver and his mom, but it rarely affects the plot in any meaningful way. The result is that audiences are asked to fear the extradimensional Larry, who sees Oliver as a kindred spirit. He even directly mentions that Oliver's mom wants to "cure" his autism, and wishes for a "normal" child, whereas Larry accepts Oliver for who he is. That's...not a horror story. Likewise, films such as *Run* and *Hush* ask audiences to sympathize with a disabled character because they are disabled, and their disability is seen as a barrier to survival. This puts the disability at the center of the story, because the assumption becomes that a non-wheelchair user could get away from their abusive mom or a non-deaf woman could more easily escape a home invasion. This isn't even a new trope, as Alfred Hitchcock's (1954) *Rear Window* had this same plot point, but from the perspective of a temporary wheelchair user.

Just Go to Therapy, Norman

So how do I reconcile the real harm horror can cause disabled people with my love of the genre? I crip code it. If one accepts that horror is all about our fear of disability—being or becoming disabled in particular—then it opens a new way to view horror. If what we are seeing are non-disabled views of disability, then as a disabled person, I understand that what's on display is ableism. In other words, ableism has been the big bad all along! The idea that Candyman, who is a supernatural killer that can travel through mirrors, has to have a hook hand to be scary becomes extremely laughable when you realize someone (Clive Barker, of all people) felt that he needed to be Captain Hook to be scary. It also makes depictions of insanity reflect the abled fear of institutionalization. I can take the completely facetious position of respecting Jason as my disabled peer, since he's proven himself so adept with a sleeping bag, knitting needle, and party horn. Or, speaking as someone with mental illnesses, they can remind me what could happen if I run out of medication and the anxiety that accompanies my fear of being denied a refill of a prescription. I mean, it's still in the absurd world of horror, and I'm not going to go after someone with a drill if I miss a few doses, but still, that's one way I can relate to it. Fears are supposed to be exaggerated, and lacking access to mental health care is definitely scary.

Similarly, a crip reading of horror allows the viewer to dig deeper into the genre, by looking at things like the social connections between mental illness and what triggers mental health episodes. What caused Norman Bates to go mad and kill? Well, incest and abuse. What about Jason Voorhees and his mom? Jason was bullied for the way he looked, and then he drowned. Mama Pam had a nervous breakdown because she lost her boy, and then he rose from the dead to avenge her. Both of these examples really speak to the need for increased access to mental health care. After all, if we can recognize that losing a kid can cause you to have a homicidal breakdown, then shouldn't we be able to understand that affordable mental health care could prevent slasher behavior? As nice as it would be to have better, less stigmatizing disabled representation in horror, it's easier for me to compromise by leaning into seeing how these ableist depictions can be subverted, at least for my enjoyment. Or maybe this gives me license to use my own disabilities in nefarious ways. Now that's a thought…

Discussion Questions

1. This piece focused on disability in horror. How is disability presented in other genres?
2. Media of all types relies on stereotypes for storytelling. What are the most effective ways for creators to break away from harmful depictions of minorities?
3. The popularity of slasher films rose alongside exposés of inhuman treatment in care facilities for disabled and mentally ill individuals, alongside the closing of many inpatient centers. How do we reconcile the sympathy for disabled victims of abuse with the fear of mental illness and disability in general?

Notes

1   *Physical difference* is the preferred term for deformity, disfigurement, and other terms used to describe conditions that significantly affect one's physical appearance.
2   Okay, if we're being honest, everything about this movie is terrible. From the bad acting/dialogue to the 90s cable porn aesthetic to the CGI. But lots of watchable movies have all of that. It's the bizarre, poorly copied plot of *Alien* that really stands out in this movie, and suspends disbelief for viewers. Even the trope of horny, scantily clad twenty-somethings hooking up, which is a major cornerstone of the genre, seems extremely out of place on a spaceship.
3   This sounded way, way cooler when I was a kid.

References

Anyon, J. (1980). Social class and the hidden curriculum of work. *Journal of Education, 162*(1), 67–92.
Fazel, S., & Grann, M. (2006). The population impact of severe mental illness on violent crime. *American Journal of Psychiatry, 163*(8), 1397–1403.

Giroux, H. A., & Penna, A. N. (1979). Social education in the classroom: The dynamics of the hidden curriculum. *Theory & Research in Social Education, 7*(1), 21–42.

Goffman, E. (1963). *Stigma: Notes on the management of spoiled identity.* Prentice Hall Press.

Kentli, F. D. (2009). Comparison of hidden curriculum theories. *European Journal of Educational Studies, 1*(2), 83–88.

Office of Juvenile Justice & Delinquency Prevention. (2020). *Arrests by offense, age, and race, 2019.* OJJDP Statistical Briefing Book. Retrieved March 9, 2021, from https://www.ojjdp.gov/ojstatbb/crime/ucr.asp?table_in=2&selYrs=2019&rdoGroups=1&rdoData=c

Retief, M., & Letšosa, R. (2018). Models of disability: A brief overview. *HTS Teologiese Studies/Theological Studies, 74*(1).

Rueve, M. E., & Welton, R. S. (2008). Violence and mental illness. *Psychiatry* (Edgmont), *5*(5), 34.

Schweinitz, J. (2010). Stereotypes and the narratological analysis of film characters. In J. Eder, F. Jannidis, & R. Schneider (Eds.), *Characters in fictional worlds: Understanding imaginary beings in literature, film, and other media* (Vol. 3, pp. 276–289). de Gruyter. doi.org/10.1515/9783110232424

Sherman, J. W., & Frost, L. A. (2000). On the encoding of stereotype-relevant information under cognitive load. *Personality and Social Psychology Bulletin, 26*(1), 26–34.

Turner, D. M., & Stagg, K. (2006). *Social histories of disability and deformity: Bodies, images, and experiences.* Routledge.

Varshney, M., Mahapatra, A., Krishnan, V., Gupta, R., & Deb, K. S. (2016). Violence and mental illness: What is the true story? *Journal of Epidemiology and Community Health, 70*(3), 223–225.

Walsh, E., Moran, P., Scott, C., McKenzie, K., Burns, T. O. M., Creed, F., & Fahy, T. (2003). Prevalence of violent victimisation in severe mental illness. *The British Journal of Psychiatry, 183*(3), 233–238.

Weber, E. (1981). Fairies and hard facts: The reality of folktales. *Journal of the History of Ideas, 42*(1), 93–113.

Williams III, F. P., & McShane, M. D. (2010). *Criminology theory: Selected classic readings.* Routledge.

Wren, D. J. (1999). School culture: Exploring the hidden curriculum. *Adolescence, 34*(135), 593–596.

Mildred Sausage, Allan Hamsteak, & Inara Bacon

Paul D. C. Bones

ID: A collage of three cats. Mildred Sausage is a black cat with white fur on her chest. She is looking up with her lip curled. Allan Hamsteak is a black cat looking curiously while lying on his side. Inara Bacon is a Birman/ragdoll mix squinting at the camera.

• • •

As someone who is often homebound and forced to lay down because of back pain, my cats are always willing to help comfort me with kitty cuddles. This same kitten therapy is also useful for anxiety and depression. I love my fur babies and don't know what I'd do without them.

CHAPTER 30

A Bright Green

After Lou Ferrigno, a Deaf Bodybuilder Who Played the Incredible Hulk (1977–1982)

Raymond Luczak

With not a single sound,
shadows fall in the lab.
Would he be caught and stabbed?
Would his secret be found?

He's perfected his smile,
trying so hard to hide
the loneliness inside.
But sometimes his guile,

too long suppressed, can tear
apart his white lab coat.
His rage needs time to gloat
and toss anyone near.

How I'd longed to turn green
each time those boys turned mean.

CHAPTER 31

Manifesto

The Committee for the Sick and Useless

The Committee for the Sick and Useless is a group of variously disabled people focused on mutual aid and acceptance. We propose a way of interacting with disability that moves beyond individuals and identity. Rather, we are choosing to look at disability as just one trait among millions that makes a person less valuable and less valued in our current society.

Health and usefulness are defined by their relationship to labour. An individual doesn't become sick when they have a virus; rather they become sick when they are unable to do the work expected of them, whether that work is employment, education, or caring for the home.

Those of us whose illness or disability interferes with our ability to work form an interest group with an immense number of seemingly abled people whose culture, beliefs, age, personality, sexuality, language, immigration status, or other inclination makes them less useful to our current society.

Our submission is an artistic work, "The Manifesto of The Committee for the Sick and Useless" which we are open to presenting in a number of ways: as a written creative work, as a poster or pamphlet in the style of other manifestos, or other suggestions by the editors. The following is a first draft of the manifesto (please note that the list of objectives is already complete):

The Committee for the Sick and Useless are a group of concerned citizens of Earth, united by a common goal. We believe it is the innate and inalienable right of all people to:
1. Do Nothing
2. Help No One
3. Feel Awful

And above all else
4. Be Useless

In this age of increasing productivity and accomplishment, humanity has begun to sacrifice our most sacred right simply to exist on this Earth, asking much and contributing nothing. The right to exist is the foundation of all human rights and duties; it cannot be made conditional, lest all rights be made conditional.

We, The Committee, do not consider ourselves at odds with health, joy, and usefulness. Rather we are united with all good and joyful people in our fight against the demand for productivity. Our enemies are those who demand that the land produce wealth, that the workers produce profit, that the sick produce medical certificates, that children grow up, and the elderly make themselves scarce.

In this admittedly revolutionary goal, we have many allies. These include, but are not limited to: queers, cripples, drug users, the unemployed, the mentally ill, the anti-colonial, the incomprehensible, the celibate, the ugly, mutes, mystics, pessimists, cats, children, teenagers, the elderly, speakers of suppressed languages, and people without a driving license.

Our objectives are as followed:

1.   [TBD]